The Indonesian Kitchen

The Indonesian Kitchen
Recipes and Stories

SRI OWEN

photographs by
GUS FILGATE

Interlink Books

An imprint of Interlink Publishing Group, Inc.
Northampton, Massachusetts

To the memory of Alan Davidson

First published in 2009 by
Interlink Books
an imprint of Interlink Publishing Group, Inc.
46 Crosby Street, Northampton, MA 01060
www.interlinkbooks.com

Design and layout © Pavilion, 2009
Text © Sri Owen, 2009
Food photography © Gus Filgate, 2009
Location photography © see acknowledgements on page 287

Commissioning editor: Kate Oldfield
Senior editor: Emily Preece-Morrison
Designer: Louise Leffler at Sticks Design
Jacket design: Juliana Spear
Photographer: Gus Filgate
Home economist: Jane Suthering
Prop stylist: Wei Tang
Copy editor: Siobhan O'Connor
Proofreader: Alyson Silverwood
Indexer: Roger Owen
Americanization: Lynne Saner
Food consultant: Hiltrud Schulz
Production: Rebekah Cheyne

ISBN 978-1-56656-739-8

10 9 8 7 6 5 4 3 2 1

Reproduction by Rival Colour, London
Printed and bound by Leefung SNP, China

A NOTE ON PORTION SIZES
In many recipes in this book, there is a note about how many people the given quantities can serve. This should be taken as a rough guide only. In other recipes, especially those for snacks, satays and condiments, it is not possible to say even approximately how many people can be served from the suggested quantities. The outcome will depend on how the food is presented: whether as an appetizer, a main course, a condiment, snack, or finger food. As a general rule, Indonesian meals are brought to the table on large platters for guests to help themselves, though there is no reason why portions should not be plated, western-style, in the kitchen.

To request our complete 40-page full-color catalog, please call us toll free at **1-800-238-LINK**, visit our website at **www.interlinkbooks.com** or write to **Interlink Publishing**, 46 Crosby Street, Northampton, MA 01060 email: info@interlinkbooks.com

CONTENTS

INTRODUCTION

This book has been taking shape in my mind for many years. I have long dreamed of writing about the food and cooking of the Indonesian islands that I am familiar with, and setting it against the story of my life and experience. More recently, I have also wanted to write about my relationship with the food and wine of Italy, and my experience of cooking in the country where I made my first European landfall.

The book, therefore, includes recipes for almost all the "classic" dishes of Java and Sumatra, with others from Bali, Sulawesi, and Kalimantan; there is even one from Irian Jaya, a province that I confess I have not yet visited. I have included, as in most of my books, a glossary, a little fuller and more detailed here, as required by the ever-widening interests and background knowledge of my readers, many of whom are now much more widely traveled than I am. And of course I have taken note, and advantage, of the changes in European food habits: the availability of exotic ingredients, the willingness to seek new flavors, and the ease with which knowledge and enthusiasm are disseminated on the Internet.

Sending a book out into the world, one naturally wishes it success and long life, as one would one's own child. I have two particular hopes for this book. The first is that it may be translated into other languages, so that it can join, and I hope stimulate, the accelerating current of interest in Southeast Asian food around the world. Even more importantly, I hope it will encourage its readers to cook Indonesian food for themselves, to go to Indonesia and to get to know Indonesians, and their multifarious cultures for food is surely a gateway to cultural enjoyment and understanding. I have always loved to cook, for myself, my family, my friends, and my customers (in the years when I had my shop). Cooking is a creative act; a cultural statement as significant as writing or reading books. I hope that my readers enjoy this book, but it will fulfill its real ambition only when they take it into the kitchen.

Chapter One: 1939–1952
Early Days

I remember the exact moment when I began to pay attention to food and notice what I was eating. I was almost four years old. We were having a party for my sister's second birthday. It was a small, quite disorganized party: half a dozen small children running around on the grass in front of the schoolhouse, nibbling boiled soy beans in their shells (edamame). When I eat these now, as an expensive starter in a London restaurant, they do not bring childhood memories flooding back, but they do make me think of my food history, its highs and lows, and the strange way it has blended with all my life experiences. Moments in the past become associated with tastes and textures. Patterns emerge: an early life spent mostly in small towns in Sumatra and Java, settled and peaceful at first, then disrupted by war. My life story and my development as a cook are interwoven, in those early years especially, with the story of my country.

In the 1930s, Indonesia was still overwhelmingly rural, a land mostly of peasant farmers trying to grow enough food to feed themselves. There were fishermen, too, and many people were employed on the big tea, coffee, and sugar plantations, owned by foreigners, most of them Dutch, as we were all subjects of the Queen of the Netherlands; however, every village family still had their own small piece of land where they grew vegetables and kept chickens, and every house was likely to be shaded by a coconut palm or a papaya or breadfruit tree. Indonesia's population then was perhaps a third of what it is today. Good land was already getting scarce, the forests were being cut back year by year to make space for new settlements, but as long as the rains came at the right time and in the expected quantity there was always enough to eat, and to eat well whenever a festival came around, which was often.

In seventy years, life for all Indonesians has been transformed several times over, and I am not sure which astonishes me more: the number of things that have changed or the stubbornness with which old ways and attitudes survive. More than half of the population now live in cities, of which Jakarta, the capital, is by far the biggest and the most dynamic — and the toughest if you're poor. Yet people keep flooding in, and Indonesia is now the world's fourth most populous nation. Aging rice farmers see their children go to college, get city jobs, and never come back, except once a year at Lebaran, the Muslim New Year. The grandchildren eat at McDonald's and spend their free time in front of TV or on the Internet. Yet the food markets remain as lively as ever, in cities as

well as small towns. Street vendors flourish, and the *selamatan*, the communal or family gathering that celebrates or memorializes any significant event, still brings neighborhoods together. From a professional point of view, one of the biggest surprises to me has been that Indonesians are publishing cookbooks about Indonesian food, traditional and new. They never did that in the old days.

I was born in 1935, in a small hill town in West Sumatra called Padang Panjang. This is in the land of the Minangkabau, my father's people, who have a reputation as chess players and politicians, and for quick-wittedness generally. They are well known to anthropologists because, although devoutly Muslim, they are matrilineal: our *adat*, or customary law, states that land belongs to the community, but the right to enjoy a particular property passes from mother to daughter. The management of it, however, is usually in the hands of a male member of the family, who has the title of *datuk*. My father's mother had, in effect, a lifetime lease on several acres of prime *sawah* (irrigated rice fields), as well as good land for growing vegetables, a coffee garden, and many fruit trees. Her husband had disgraced himself, before I was born, by taking a second wife without getting the first's permission; my grandmother had banished him and his partner to a distant town. The family council agreed that my grandmother was a competent farm manager and should continue to farm the property herself. In due course, the land would pass to one of her nieces, and my father, her eldest son, would become *datuk*. This, however, was not to be.

At sixteen, my father was sent off to Bandung, in West Java, to attend the Dutch teacher training college. He completed the course three years later. At college he fell in love with a fellow student, a Sundanese girl, therefore also from West Java. Very shortly after they graduated, they married. My mother's family were *priyayi*, people of the professional class who did well under Dutch rule; my Sundanese grandfather was a civil engineer with a high government post. My father then whisked his bride off to Padang Panjang, where, I think, she did not find life altogether easy at first. Luckily, however, she got on well from the start with her mother-in-law, who remained a valuable ally. She and my father were also respected for the school that they founded and ran for more than ten years, with great success. It was called the Mahameru Institute, and the authorities thought so well of it that any child who completed its course successfully

Page 8: The roof of a traditional Minangkabau house with cloud-wrapped Singgalang behind, West Sumatra.
Above left: Transplanting rice.
Above right: The village of Sungai Landir in a valley near Lake Maninjau.

was automatically given a place at the Dutch junior high school. I find this a little ironic now, considering that both of my parents were passionate nationalists and saw education as the best way to hasten the birth of the independent republic of which they dreamed.

I was the second child of the marriage. The first, a boy, lived only a few months, and the succession of pregnancies and miscarriages that my mother endured for almost twenty years was in part, I'm sure, the result of their desire for a son. Eventually I found myself the eldest of six sisters, a responsible position in a society where older children are expected to bring up younger siblings.

My childhood, to the age of seven, was comfortable and happy. My favorite haunt was my grandmother's kitchen, and the first recipes in this book are memories of that time. Although we were relatively wealthy and of high status (which counted for more than wealth), and even though we had a large house with a number of poorer relatives to do the household chores (for no Minang would dishonor himself or another by paying, or being paid, for domestic service), the kitchen would today be called primitive. There was no gas, electricity, or running water. It was separate from the house to reduce the risk of fire and, as far as possible, preparation and cooking were done in the open air, where we could enjoy the cooling breeze. There were some metal pans – I remember especially a great steel wok – but a lot of cooking was done in round-bottomed earthenware pots, supported on small piles of bricks over wood fires or glowing charcoal. From this unassuming, airy kitchen a stream of superbly flavored and cooked dishes went out, some to the European-style dining room where my parents ate at table, off china plates, using European cutlery, and conversing in Dutch, but most to the big room next to the kitchen where a dozen or twenty family members, business callers and workers from the fields sat cross-legged on a mat on a low platform, helping themselves to the dishes that were set before them, and eating with their fingers from plates lined with banana leaf. After eating, they discussed the events and news of the day in broad Minang, a language closely related to the present-day national language, Bahasa

Below: Old Minang houses and a *warung* – the village corner shop.

Indonesia, but a good deal pithier. I was always pleased to be invited to join my parents and sit up and learn table manners, but there was no doubt as to which room I secretly preferred.

Another joy I remember from those days was walking with my grandmother when she made her regular tour of her fields and woods, always carrying a large basket into which would go all the herbs and leaves she gathered to flavor her cooking. I went with her to market, watching her buy the few necessities she could not produce on her land: salt, tea, sugar, dried fish. She told me many stories, veering, I believe, between fact and fiction, but always with moral conclusions; she described the earthquake that had destroyed the family's *rumah gadang*, their traditional Minangkabau house with its series of upswept gable ends, years before I was born. I thought she must be very, very old; I realize now she was in her mid fifties. She gave me my earliest lessons, not just in cooking, but in the love of good food and lively talk. Her most precious advice I take with me always: "Nobody can look after you better than you yourself."

When I was six, my grandmother also took me with her to the newly harvested rice fields to take part in the open-air feast that fulfilled so many functions, practical and symbolic. It rewarded all the neighbors who had helped to cut, thresh and bring in the rice, for everything had to be done by hand. It "paid off" her debts of hospitality to people who had invited members of our family to their celebrations. For poorer families, not only was it a treat that provided nourishment for those who came to the feast, but it fed those left at home as well: more food was provided than the guests could possibly eat, and everyone was expected to take away a share of the unserved dishes for those who were unable to work in the harvest. This was not charity, but a reward for what the grandparents had done, and what the children would one day do, to carry on the life of the community. In a more prosaic way, the feast was a contest among the neighborhood wives, each determined to show off her cooking skills and, if possible, those of her marriageable daughters.

I shall say a little more about harvest festivals in chapter 6, and show how they were also occasions when young men and girls could start their courting. But some readers may think that the feast in the rice fields had something in common with what the Dutch call a *rijsttafel*, and perhaps I should say something about the "rice table" here. I have often criticized tourist hotels and restaurants in Indonesia today, and in the Netherlands, for assuming that a *rijsttafel* is just a fixed-price *menu de dégustation* at which an endless succession of dishes can be served, each barely distinguishable from the last and all cooked many hours before. I once found, in a five-star hotel in Bali, a poster promoting its *rijsttafel* with a large picture of a young white couple at a restaurant table, apparently being served the whole *rijsttafel* all at once, on dishes brought by a well-drilled chorus line of nubile Balinese maidens, dressed as for a temple festival. It is only fair to point out that the *rijsttafel* has a long and interesting history, which has recently been traced and described by a young Indonesian scholar, Fadly Rahman. The harvest festival, however, has an even longer history, and though the two have not influenced each other, their paths have crossed, in the *kratons*, or courts, of local rulers. Here, for many centuries, farmers brought the pick of the new season's crop as tribute, and the ruler in return feasted them and their families in a display of royal munificence. Meanwhile, in early colonial days, when only very senior Dutch officials were allowed to bring their wives to the Indies, many thousands of young Dutch soldiers, clerks, plantation staff, and adventurers naturally took Indonesian girls as partners, and also enjoyed the food they cooked. These young native women — *nyai*, as they were called — competed to provide the finest dishes for the table, so that by the time the men became middle-aged plantation managers they were well accustomed to such food and were very pleased to be invited to the palace when the sultan wanted to impress them with the traditional hospitality of his region. So I had not been altogether wrong to suspect at least an indirect link between the harvest festival and the *rijsttafel*.

As my fifth and sixth years passed, I was aware that anxiety was gathering over us. The world was being shaken as if by an earthquake, and was threatening to collapse. My parents had to decide where they and their four small daughters would be safest; the Japanese had driven the British from Malaya and Singapore, and were landing in Sumatra. We had already heard of bombing raids on Padang, thirty-eight miles away on the coast. The Mahameru Institute was closed, my father sold practically every moveable thing he had, and my mother sewed her jewels into her clothing. One morning in 1942 we packed

a few small bags, said goodbye to all the family and were hugged by my grandmother. Her last words to me were: "Remember, my beloved granddaughter, when you grow up, don't marry a foreigner." She meant, of course, someone from another island.

The story of the next ten years need not be told in detail. Many survived far worse experiences than we had to face. We were often hungry, or had bad food, but we never starved, and sometimes we ate quite well. For the first two years, we lived with my Sundanese grandmother, where we were able to convert what had been the garage into living quarters. Garages make comfortable, secure homes in the tropics, and many families still live in them today. My father kept ducks in the adjoining field, which he enjoyed and which brought in a modest income, plus, of course, fresh eggs and meat for us.

He and his mother-in-law could not get along, however, and we had to move. My parents were able to get full-time jobs in several places, but something always happened to force us to go. A year before World War II ended, we all had to learn Japanese, though it was obvious the Japanese were losing. On August 17, 1945, my father's heroes, Sukarno and Hatta, declared Indonesia an independent republic. The Dutch made several attempts to recover their lost empire, with the aid of the British. For a while we were refugees in our own country, moving always eastwards, away from the capital (now called Jakarta) and into Central Java, almost a foreign country and with another language to learn. Always, when we were on the road, we met with the greatest kindness at every village where we stopped and asked shelter for the night. Finally, in 1949, the family settled in Magelang, in Central Java. There I, who loved school, was able to complete junior high and gain a place in the senior high school in Yogyakarta, twenty-five miles to the south. It was far enough away to make me feel, almost eighteen years old, that at last I, too, was independent.

Above: Wedding guests attend to the serious business of the day; the ladies have the same food, but served in a separate room.

GRANDMOTHER'S RECIPES

These are based on my grandmother's recipes as recorded, by my mother, and on the best of the snack foods that became familiar as we bought them on all the railway station platforms between Banten and Cirebon where we stopped on our journey in 1942. All are still popular today, and not just on railway stations. I begin with one of my favorite ways of cooking fish.

pangek ikan
braised fish with young vegetable shoots

Another memory of my grandmother's cooking: the wild fiddleheads she gathered on daily walks to inspect her paddy fields, cooked with small freshwater fish in a great earthenware pot. When I first came to England and saw trout at the fish dealer's, they reminded me at once of those little fish, and I started trying to re-create the dish that we called *pangek*. The trout were easy; I took to buying them fresh from trout farms. But the fiddleheads . . . Alas, I could only, very occasionally, find Canadian fiddleheads in jars at the delicatessen counters of large department stores. When there were no fiddleheads, I used small fresh asparagus. I don't, of course, have my grandmother's earthenware pot, so I use a round heavy casserole instead.

6–8 trout or small sea bass, cleaned and
   left whole with their heads on
1 tsp salt
12 oz–1 lb fiddleheads or small fresh
   asparagus or yard-long beans, or a
   mixture of asparagus and yard-long
   beans
2 lemongrass stems, cleaned, each cut
   across into three
3½ c thick coconut milk
handful or more of fresh mint or basil
   leaves (in Indonesia we use *kemangi*)
banana leaves for cooking (optional)

for the bumbu (paste)
6 candlenuts or macadamia nuts,
   chopped
5 shallots or 1 onion, chopped
4 garlic cloves, chopped
2–4 fresh red chilies, seeded
   and chopped
2 tsp chopped fresh ginger
1 tsp chopped galangal
1 tsp ground turmeric
4 tbsp tamarind water (see pp.118–19)
4 tbsp coconut milk
1 tsp salt

Serves 6–8

Rub the fish inside and out with the salt. Set aside. If you are using fiddleheads from a jar, drain the liquid and set the fiddleheads aside. Trim the asparagus if necessary; if using yard-long beans, cut them to the length of the asparagus.

Put all the ingredients for the *bumbu*, or paste, in a blender or food processor, and work into a smooth paste. Transfer this paste to a cooking pot (preferably an earthenware or stainless-steel pan, but in any case not aluminium), and simmer for 5–6 minutes, stirring often. Add the thick coconut milk, and continue to simmer for 10 minutes, stirring occasionally. Adjust the seasoning with a little salt if needed, and transfer the spiced coconut milk to a large glass bowl to cool.

In the same pot, arrange all the lemongrass pieces at the bottom, then 3 or 4 trout or sea bass in one layer, then half the fiddleheads or asparagus or beans. Top these with the rest of the fish, then the rest of the vegetables. Slowly pour in the reserved spiced coconut milk. Arrange the mint or basil on top, and cover the pan, first with banana leaves or foil, then with a saucepan lid, as tightly as possible. Simmer gently, undisturbed, for 35–40 minutes; alternatively, put in a preheated oven at 300°F (150°C) for the same length of time. To serve, remove the banana leaves or foil, and serve the dish hot, warm, or cold.

daun ubi tumbuk
purée of cassava leaves

This cassava leaf purée is among my earliest memories of my grandmother's cooking in Padang Panjang. She called it *gulai daun Perancis*; *Perancis* means "France," or "French," and I have no idea why cassava leaves should be considered French. You cannot get cassava leaves in the West, though cassava roots or tubers can be found quite easily in ethnic street markets or Indian shops.

I have made this dish with curly kale or spinach, but I've now found another substitute in Italian cavolo nero, or black cabbage. I either purée the leaves in a food processor or, as people in Indonesia would do, chop them very finely and cook them for a long time to soften them to a purée consistency. The dried fish or salt cod is optional

Right: *Daun ubi tumbuk* (purée of cassava leaves).

if the puréed leaves are to be used, as I use them, for stuffing fish. For the fish itself, I suggest boned sea trout or sea bass or red snapper; when stuffed, they should be baked in a preheated oven at 350°F (180°C) for 10–15 minutes only. Or if you are good at grilling fish on charcoal, try this one on the barbecue.

8 oz *ikan asin* (see p.276) or salt cod (optional)	1 tsp chopped lemongrass
1 lb cassava leaves or curly kale or cavolo nero or spinach	1 tsp ground turmeric
	1 tsp chopped fresh ginger
2½ c thick coconut milk	1 tsp salt
1 turmeric leaf (optional)	2 tbsp tamarind water (see pp.118–19)
	3 tbsp coconut milk

for the bumbu (paste)
3 shallots, chopped
1–4 large fresh red chilies,
   seeded and chopped

Serves 4–6 as a vegetable dish, or for stuffing a largeish sea trout, sea bass, or red snapper

First, soak the dried or salt fish in cold water for at least 4 hours or overnight, if using. Drain and rinse under running cold water, then chop the fish finely.

If curly kale or black cabbage is used, take off and discard the hard ribs of the leaves, shred roughly, and boil for 4 minutes. Squeeze the water out, and chop finely. If cassava leaves are used, boil for 6–8 minutes, then proceed as for the curly kale. Keep to one side.

Put all the ingredients for the *bumbu*, or paste, in a blender or food processor, and work until smooth. Transfer the paste to a saucepan and simmer, stirring often, for 4 minutes. Add the chopped fish and turmeric leaf, if using, and the chopped vegetables. Stir, then add the coconut milk. Continue to simmer for 35–40 minutes, or until most of the coconut milk has been absorbed. Adjust the seasoning, take out and discard the turmeric leaf. Serve right away with rice, or use as a stuffing for the fish, as suggested in the introduction above.

anyang sayuran
cooked vegetables with spiced roasted coconut

People all across Indonesia eat papaya leaves, but in my family we ate papaya leaves as a possible cure for malaria. My grandmother's *anyang*, which is really the same as *urap* in Java, or *gudangan*, often used not just papaya leaves, but papaya flowers as well. The flowers are quite pretty and taste less bitter than the leaf. I wish I could get them, but alas, as with cassava leaves, no one in Thailand, Indonesia, or Malaysia supposes Westeners might be interested in trying to cook them. Instinctively, I feel that a bitter taste is essential to achieve a good *anyang*, so here I'm using *paria*, or bitter melon, in my mix of vegetables for this dish.

for the vegetables
½ cauliflower, cut into florets
3 carrots, peeled and sliced into
  thin rounds
1 *paria* (bitter melon), halved lengthwise,
  seeds and membranes discarded, and
  flesh cut into thin half-moon slices
1 small cucumber, cut the same way
  as the paria
4 oz watercress, trimmed and rinsed

for the roasted coconut dressing
1 cup freshly grated coconut
1 tsp ground coriander
½ tsp salt
1 garlic clove, crushed
1 tsp *sambal ulek* (p.279) or chili flakes

*Serves 6–8 as a vegetable
accompaniment to a rice meal*

Boil the cauliflower, carrots, and bitter melon separately, in slightly salted water, for 3–4 minutes each. The cucumber is not to be boiled, but the watercress can be, or simply blanched for 2 minutes. Drain all the cooked vegetables thoroughly, and transfer to a bowl with the cucumber.

Dry-roast the grated coconut in a non-stick frying pan over medium heat, stirring most of the time until golden brown. Add the rest of the ingredients for the dressing, and stir again for a minute or two. Transfer the contents of the pan to a large mortar, if you have one, and pound the mixture using a pestle until the roasted coconut becomes a little oily. Alternatively, mix in a blender for a few seconds. Add the dressing to the bowl of vegetables and mix well. Serve warm or cold.

goreng ikan balado
fried fish with caramelized onions and chilies

The word *balado* in the Minang language, or *berlada* in Indonesian, means "with chilies." My grandmother's repertoire did not end just with fish and chilies, but her everyday menu included *dendeng balado* (slices of dry-fried beef with chilies) and *kentang balado* (potatoes with chilies) — just about everything that is cooked this way, deep-fried or stir-fried, and coated with onions and chilies, is *balado*, or *berlada*. You can fry whole small fish — small red snappers and sardines, for instance — or you can use fish filets, cod filet, perhaps, or haddock or plaice. Naturally, in West Sumatra the proportion of chilies is higher than that of onions. Calling this dish "with caramelized onions and chilies" will, I hope, tempt many of my readers to cook it. If I served this with chips and salad, I think I would be the only person to associate it with its true origin, a hill town in West Sumatra. I love cod, so I'm making it here with cod filets. The recipe is equally suitable for bacalao, or salt cod.

4 cod filets, about 4 oz each
½ tsp salt
pinch of chili powder
pinch of ground turmeric
¼ peanut oil, for shallow-frying

**for the caramelized onions
and chilies**
3 tbsp peanut oil or olive oil,
   as preferred
1 lb onions, finely sliced
2 large fresh red chilies, seeded

and chopped
2 garlic cloves, chopped
1 tsp chopped fresh ginger
1 tsp *gula jawa* (palm sugar) (see p.276)
   or demerara sugar
1 tsp salt
2 tbsp tamarind water (see pp.118–19)
   or freshly squeezed lime juice

*Serves 4 as a light lunch, to be eaten
with or without fries and salad*

First, rub the cod filets with the salt, and a pinch each of chili powder and turmeric. Put them in a bowl and keep to one side.

In a wok or heavy frying pan, heat the 3 tablespoons peanut or olive oil until hot, then add the onions, stirring often until they begin to color; this will take 8–10 minutes. Using a mortar and pestle, roughly pound the chilies, garlic, and ginger – there is no need to make this into too smooth a paste. After the onions have been

Right: South Sumatra: fishermen returning to Bandar Lampung from their fishing traps offshore.

frying for 8–10 minutes, add the chili paste and continue stir-frying for 3 minutes longer. Add the sugar, salt, and tamarind water or lime juice, stir again, and leave the pan over low heat for another minute. Remove the pan from the heat.

In another frying pan, heat the peanut oil for shallow-frying, and fry the cod filets for 3–4 minutes before turning them over to cook on the other side for another 3–4 minutes. Up to this point everything can be prepared an hour or so in advance. When ready to serve, heat the caramelized onions and chilies, stirring, for 2 minutes. Add the cod filets from the other pan and turn them over several times to coat them with the onion mixture. Serve hot.

telur dadar padang
my grandmother's omelette

This is one of my grandmother's treats for breakfast. It looks like a cake, and to make the omelette thick she used freshly grated coconut, grated potato, or sweet potato. And she would add a dollop of her *sambal lado* to spice it up. I use *sambal ulek* (see p.279) when I make this omelette at home.

6 duck eggs
2 shallots, finely sliced
1 garlic clove, finely sliced
1 tsp *sambal ulek* (see p.279)
    or ½ tsp chili powder
1 cup freshly grated coconut or grated
    potato or sweet potato
½ tsp salt

1 tbsp milk or cold water
2 tbsp peanut oil

Serves 4 for breakfast or as a light lunch with some salad

Mix together all the ingredients, except the eggs and oil, in a large bowl. Beat the mixture thoroughly with the eggs – it needs more beating than an ordinary plain omelette and should become quite fluffy.

Heat the oil in a wok until hot. (I find a 10 inch non-stick frying pan an easier alternative to using a wok.) Carefully spoon the oil over the sides, or tilt and turn the wok or pan so that the sides are well coated with oil. Pour the omelette mixture into the hot wok or pan, and while it is still liquid swirl it around so that the omelette is not too thick in the center. Let it cook for 2–3 minutes. Turn it over carefully (it should be perfectly circular), and cook slowly for another 3–4 minutes until the middle, which of course is still the thickest part, is firm and the whole omelette is lightly browned. The edges should now be delicately crisp.

Serve hot or cold, cut up into slices like a cake.

STREET SNACKS

Some of these snacks below I had never eaten before we left Sumatra and went to Java. I don't think my grandmother cooked any of them, except perhaps the *pisang goreng*. These are also street foods that I became more familiar with after we came to live in Magelang, in Central Java.

nagasari
steamed rice flour cakes with banana

This sweet snack is, I think, the cheapest of all the snacks you can buy at railway stations and from street vendors, but it is still very good. The vendors, most of whom are women, carry their wares in baskets that they rest on one hip, supported by a length of batik cloth knotted on the opposite shoulder. Another way of carrying assorted snacks – say, four or five different sweets, with a few savory snacks added to the mix – is to arrange them on a *tampah*, a round flat tray of woven bamboo (see picture opposite), which a woman will carry on her head. When they are not meeting trains, these ladies usually call at your home around four in the afternoon, just as most people with young children have woken from their siesta and are ready for tea.

Nagasari are mothers' favorite to feed their toddlers. I remember feeding them to my two-year-old youngest sister, whom I looked after from birth because our mother always went back to her teaching after a short maternity leave. Most Indonesian babies are given mashed banana as soon as they start to be weaned (mine certainly were), so *nagasari* is an ideal food during the next stage, before they progress to rice porridge, then to plain boiled rice accompanied by some other suitable soft food.

The Indonesian Kitchen **27**

Below left: A street seller in a Jakarta suburb.
Below right: Balinese ladies bearing offerings to a village temple.

In Indonesia, you won't find any *nagasari* that haven't been cooked inside a banana-leaf packet. However, I find preparing the banana leaf and making the wrappers time-consuming and quite hard work (see pp.176–7 on wraps and banana leaves). I therefore make my *nagasari* as a cake in a cake pan or in ramekins, and I steam it, either in a large steamer or by simply placing it in a saucepan with enough water around it to reach about halfway up the ramekins or pan.

8 oz rice flour (this must be the most
    finely ground rice powder from Asian
    food stores or supermarkets)
2 oz corn flour
1½–2 c coconut milk

4 tbsp granulated sugar
large pinch of salt
2 or 3 bananas

Serves 8–10

Sift together the rice flour and corn flour into a mixing bowl. Gently heat the coconut milk, adding the salt and sugar to it, and stir to let the sugar dissolve, but do not let the coconut milk come to a boil. Peel the bananas, cut each one in half lengthwise, and cut each half across into three or four pieces. Mix the warm coconut milk into the flour to make a smooth thick batter, then add the bananas.

Using melted butter or vegetable oil, grease the insides of 8–10 ramekins or a 8 inch round cake pan. Pour in the batter, making sure that the banana pieces are distributed as evenly as possible. Steam for 40–50 minutes in a steamer or in a saucepan with the ramekins or cake pan set on a trivet or wire rack, firmly supported with the rim above the level of the surrounding hot water. When cooked, leave the *nagasari* to cool a little, then turn out of the ramekins or pan (if the *nagasari* are sticking to the ramekins, simply serve them with a spoon for scooping). Cut into squares, making sure that each square has a piece of banana in the middle. Serve at room temperature.

pisang goreng
fried bananas

Fried bananas are very easy to make, and Indonesia has many different bananas that are suitable for frying. Yet you can still get bad *pisang goreng*. The trouble, usually, is the oil. Some *warung* owners are not always careful to use fresh good-quality oil — because, of course, it is expensive. Another reason for bad *pisang goreng* is that the bananas used are too ripe, or not ripe enough.

The bananas you get at your local supermarket are perfectly suitable for frying, as they are for making *nagasari* (pp.26–7); alternatively, use ripe plantains, which give a firmer and better texture when they are fried.

4 fairly ripe bananas or 3 ripe plantains
3 oz rice flour
1 oz all-purpose flour
1 oz melted butter
¾ c coconut milk

pinch of salt
peanut oil or clarified butter or olive oil
   for frying

Serves 4–6

Mix together the two types of flour, butter, coconut milk, and salt in a bowl, making a smooth batter. Peel the bananas, and cut each one in half lengthwise down the middle, then cut each piece across into two. If using plantains, cut the halves into three pieces. Coat well with the batter, and shallow- or deep-fry in the oil or clarified butter until golden brown. Serve hot or cold.

rempeyek kacang
savory peanut brittle

I was introduced to these delicious crunchy nut brittles in my childhood. We were traveling from Banten to Cirebon, just after we had all landed in Java from the ferry that had brought us — my mother and father and four small daughters — from Sumatra. We made this long journey in the hope of avoiding the Japanese who had landed in North Sumatra. We knew, of course, that they were already in Batavia, but we avoided them by

going by train through the hills further south, and in fact it was to be weeks or months before we even set eyes on a Japanese soldier. We stopped many times on that journey, and at every station snacks of all kinds, but mostly sweets, were being hawked along the platforms. *Rempeyek kacang* were among the savory snacks, so they were especially welcome — even children don't want to eat sweets all the time.

If you are lucky, you can get really delicious *rempeyek* in Indonesia, with finely chopped chili, garlic, chives, *kencur* (lesser galangal — pronounced *k'ntjoor*), or roughly crushed peppercorns or shredded kaffir lime leaf. I don't use these extra ingredients for my *rempeyek*, except sometimes the finely crushed kaffir lime leaf, which also appears in the recipe for Aromatic Crab Cakes on pp.96–8.

Many Indonesians find *rempeyek* hard to make properly, or say they do. I have never found them difficult, but a little practice may be necessary before you get them quite perfect. Here is a *rempeyek* recipe that has never failed me.

For best results, it is worth cutting the peanuts in half, laborious though this chore may be, unless you can find very tiny peanuts or ones that have been split. Ordinary whole peanuts don't hold together so well in the finished product, and as a result that absolutely perfect crunch will not quite happen. It is important, too, to go to an Asian food store, to get really fine rice flour; the rice flour sold in most supermarkets is definitely not fine enough.

2 candlenuts or macadamia nuts
1 garlic clove
2 tsp ground coriander
1 tsp salt
5–6 oz raw peanuts (still in their skins), halved

4 oz very fine rice flour
peanut oil or rapeseed oil for frying

Makes 50–60 rempeyek (enough for up to 20 people)

Using a mortar and pestle, pound the candlenuts or macadamia nuts and the garlic together into a paste, or put in a blender with ¼ cup water, and blend until smooth. Transfer to a bowl, then add the coriander and salt. Mix in the rice flour, and add 1 cup water (use only ¾ cup if you have already added water to the nut mixture), a little at a time, stirring and mixing thoroughly. Sprinkle the peanuts into the batter, and stir through.

Right: *Rempeyek kacang* (savory peanut brittle) and *rempeyek teri* (savory rice flour crisps with dried anchovies) (recipe on p.208).

To fry *rempeyek*, you need a non-stick frying pan and a wok. Heat some oil in the pan, and enough in the wok to deep-fry the rempeyek. Take a tablespoon of the batter, with some peanuts in it, and pour into the frying pan so that it forms a single flat shape like a biscuit. Continue until the frying pan is full – you will probably be able to fry 8–10 *rempeyek* at a time. When they have been frying for between 1 and 2 minutes, transfer the *rempeyek* to a tray lined with paper towels. Repeat this process until all the batter has been used.

Now carefully transfer the hot oil to the wok. You will probably need to add some more oil. Let the oil become really hot before you start deep-frying the half-cooked *rempeyek*, perhaps 10–12 at a time, in the wok. Deep-fry until crisp and golden – this will take a few minutes. Take them out with a slotted spoon and allow to cool on paper towels. Continue until all the *rempeyek* have been deep-fried.

Once the *rempeyek* are completely cool, store in an airtight container, where they will remain crisp for up to 2 weeks.

klepon
sticky rice flour cakes with brown sugar filling

Klepon is very much a Javanese name. Elsewhere in Indonesia, these little balls of sticky rice paste are called *ondé-ondé*, which is very confusing for the Javanese. What they call *ondé-ondé* is a Chinese snack, also made with sticky rice flour, but usually filled with a sweet red-bean paste, and with an outer shell that has sesame seeds in it. Chinese *ondé-ondé*, moreover, are deep-fried, while *klepon* are boiled, then rolled in freshly grated coconut. Klepon are usually sold in banana-leaf containers of a particular shape (see picture opposite), each containing three or five *klepon*.

Like the *nagasari* on p.26–7, this is a favorite children's snack, although adults like it, too. The ones sold by street vendors are always bright green, colored with juice extracted from pandanus leaves (see p.275). Pandanus leaves (*daun pandan*) are now found in many Chinese and Thai food stores, and I have also seen tiny bottles containing pandanus extract for sale. You just add a few drops of it to the *klepon* dough, as if you were using vanilla essence. This is fine, but if you can find neither the pandanus leaf nor the commercially produced extract, do not be tempted to use artificial food coloring. I leave my *klepon* white when I have to.

8 oz sticky rice flour	½ fresh coconut, husk and shell removed
3 tbsp very thick coconut milk	½ tsp salt
2 or 3 drops pandan essence (optional)	
3–4 oz *gula jawa* (palm sugar) (see p.276) or muscovado sugar	*Makes 18–21 klepon (enough to serve 6)*

Sift the flour into a bowl. Make a well in the middle, and pour in the very thick coconut milk and add the pandan essence, if using. Start kneading to bring together into a dough. Continue to knead, gradually adding ¼ cup cold water, a little at a time, until the dough is pliable but not sticky.

Take a bit of dough, about as big as a small marble, flatten it on a pastry board, and fill with a small piece of the *gula jawa* or ½ tsp muscovado sugar. Shape into a ball, with the sugar inside. Repeat until all the dough has been used.

Bring a saucepan half-filled with water and a pinch of salt to a boil. Drop in the *klepon* one by one until you have 10 or 12 in the water. Boil for 10–15 minutes until they float to the surface. Remove with a slotted spoon, and drain in a colander.

Once all the *klepon* are cooked, remove any brown outer skin from the coconut and grate the flesh. Mix the salt into the coconut, and roll the *klepon* in the grated coconut until they are well coated. Arrange on a serving dish, sprinkling any remaining coconut on top. Serve warm or cold as a snack.

pergedel jagung
corn fritters

Indonesians love these fritters as much as they love grilled corn on the cob, and they will snack on either at any time of the day. The *pergedel* sold on railway platforms, as far as I remember, are pretty large ones, but even when they've eaten two or three of these and are feeling quite full already, an Indonesian family will say, "We've not eaten yet!" They still must have a proper meal with rice. Street vendors' *pergedel jagung* are usually made with fresh corn on the cob and are quite chewy. For cooking at home, especially if you don't want the corn popping and spitting oil while you fry the fritters, an effective precaution is to mash the corn a little with the back of a spoon, to break open each kernel. I don't put the corn in a blender, as that would make it too smooth; the fritters wouldn't have the right texture and would taste quite different. This recipe combines corn with mashed potatoes and lots of chopped parsley. For a treat, to serve with before-dinner drinks, add some roughly chopped shrimp or small whole peeled shrimp to the batter.

4 fresh corn on the cob or 2x 12 oz cans
   sweet corn, drained
8 oz new potatoes, peeled
3 tbsp chopped spring onions
4 tbsp chopped fresh flat-leaf parsley
2 tsp ground coriander
1 tsp *sambal ulek* (see p.279)
   or ½ tsp chili powder
1 heaping tbsp rice flour

1 tsp salt
1–2 eggs, lightly beaten
8 oz peeled and deveined raw shrimp,
   roughly chopped, or small peeled
   shrimp (optional)
peanut oil or rapeseed oil for frying

Makes 12–16 fritters (enough to serve 4)

Below: Central Java: deep-frying fritters in a domestic kitchen, Yogyakarta.

Using a sharp knife, shave the corn kernels into a bowl. Mash lightly with the back of a large spoon to break them down but not squash them. If using canned sweet corn, rinse, drain, and mash lightly, also with the back of a spoon. Boil the potatoes for 8 –10 minutes, drain, then mash or put through a potato ricer. Mix the corn and potatoes in a bowl with the other ingredients (except the oil), adding the eggs and shrimp last, if using. Mix well and taste. Add more salt if necessary. Divide the mixture into 12–16 rounds, laying them on a floured plate in a single layer. (Use two plates if necessary.) Cover with cling wrap. Chill until ready to cook.

When you are ready to serve the fritters, heat enough oil for shallow-frying in a non-stick frying pan. Shallow-fry 6 or so fritters at a time, pressing each one with a fork to flatten slightly. Fry on one side for 2–3 minutes, then turn over and fry for another 3 minutes. Carefully remove the fritters from the pan with a spatula, and drain on a plate lined with paper towels. Repeat the process until all the fritters are cooked. Serve hot right away, or warm or cold as snacks with drinks.

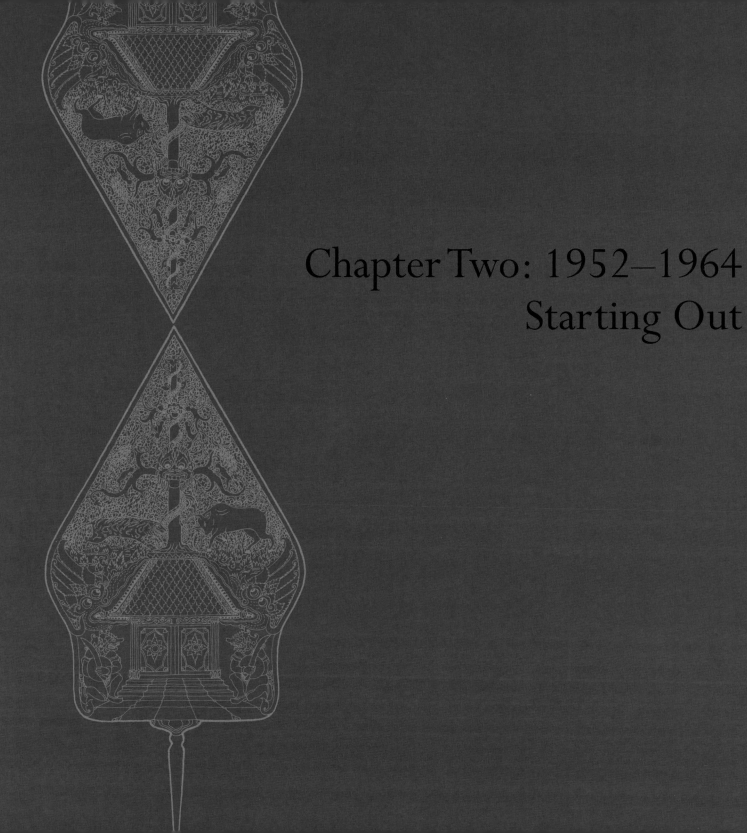

Chapter Two: 1952–1964
Starting Out

As a senior high school student, I boarded in the house of the mother of one of my mother's colleagues. Yogyakarta in those days was an important town, but far smaller than it is today. The house, a large one where up to a dozen students lived (mostly girls, two to a room), was in Jalan Pakuningratan, a quiet street a few minutes' walk from the northern end of Jalan Malioboro, the town's center. I was to live there for nearly ten years, until I married. From the house to my school was a ten-minute bike ride; at one or one-thirty, when morning school was over, I pedaled back for lunch, then hurried off again to spend the afternoon playing tennis, rounders, basketball, or baseball. After six months, I was chosen to be captain of women's sports, but the real compliment was that sometimes I was invited to play baseball with the boys.

I don't think anyone lingered over their meals in our boarding house; the cooking was nothing special. We were all up and about by six, but so is everyone in the tropics – or they should be, for the sun is just over the horizon, the light is bright but the air still cool, and schools and offices open at seven or seven-thirty. If we didn't want the food the servants had cooked, we would ask one of them to pop around the corner and buy some *nasi gudeg*, a traditional Yogya street-food dish, famous among generations of students. Or we could go into the kitchen where there was usually leftover cold rice, to be made into *nasi goreng* and topped with a fried egg. At midday and dinner, the same regime: we were free to eat wherever we wanted, usually at a Chinese restaurant nearby, where we could have noodles and *babi kecap* (pork sliced and cooked in soy sauce), though as Muslims we obviously weren't supposed to eat pork. The Balinese students were Hindus; if they wanted pork, they had to go out for it – our *ibu*, or "mother," the middle-aged lady who ruled the house, would not allow pork in the building, nor would the servants. In the Chinese restaurants, there were plenty of non-pork dishes that did not trouble our consciences, as long as we remembered to tell the waiter to ask the chef not to use pork fat. The Chinese prided themselves on having lived in Java for generations without losing their identity, but their chefs all knew how to cook Javanese food.

A popular quick lunch dish was and is, and I think always will be, *gado-gado*, a cooked vegetable salad with many variations and accompaniments. Off Malioboro there were many little *warungs* where you could perch on a stool and watch the owner as he or she made up your portion as directed, then ladled over it a most delicious hot spicy peanut

sauce. Any meal without rice is regarded, anywhere in Asia, as merely a snack. Most of us ordered our *gado-gado* with thickly sliced boiled potatoes, but we regarded these as just another vegetable. If we wanted rice, and were going to take our lunch back to the boarding house, we bought *lontong*, rice compressed into a solid mass by being cooked in a banana-leaf packet. A slightly fancier version, called *ketupat*, encloses the rice in little purse-like containers woven from long, narrow strips of coconut leaf.

The school curriculum in Indonesia has always included lessons on healthy and sensible eating, so we had at least a vague knowledge of nutrition and realized that we had to have protein as well as carbohydrate. Fresh meat and fresh fish were too expensive to eat every day, but soy beans were cheap, and tofu (which Indonesians call *tahu*) and *tempe* (which English speakers spell "tempeh," to remind us that the word has two syllables) were part of almost every *gado-gado*, and were cooked in many other ways, too. Soy beans boiled in their pods make a good snack, but their most valuable nutrients are locked into cells that the human gut cannot digest. These nutrients are amino acids, which combine with other amino acids in rice to make proteins that our bodies cannot make for themselves. One way to release them is to process the beans into a kind of milk, which can be drunk or made into tofu; another is to ferment cooked soy beans with a mold that binds them together into a solid mass. This fermented soy bean cake is tempeh, and with rice, tempeh, and a few greens, you can keep going almost indefinitely. You will find more about tempeh on pp.120–4.

For anyone who was studying hard for exams and didn't have time to go out, there were all the street vendors, many of them passing the house and calling their wares. Men carried portable kitchens slung across one shoulder, selling noodles or satays. Women balanced bamboo trays – the *tampah* again – on their heads, or supported baskets in colorful batik cloths knotted on one shoulder, the way I used to carry my infant sisters astride a hip. These ladies sold delicious snacks: *pisang goreng*, *lemper*, *klepon*, *nagasari*, and other steamed cakes, *kue putu*, *kue apem*, and others, all made from sticky rice flour. Our particular favorites among these were made and sold, throughout my time in Pakuningratan, by a doctor's wife who lived a few doors away. The family were well off, but she needed an occupation to fill her time, and to encourage her to teach her domestic helpers to be better cooks.

Page 36: Gods, heroes, clowns: *wayang kulit*, the Javanese shadow play.
Above: A Sundanese dancer rehearsing.

There was plenty of social life in Yogya to tempt students. In Magelang, my father disapproved of such activities, but here I was free to do as I pleased. Our amusements were indeed very innocent. Our landlady, or *ibu*, and her elderly mother, whom we addressed (in Javanese) as *eyang*, or "grandmother," were from an aristocratic family with connections to the *kraton*, the sultan's palace. When they were invited to parties in the *kraton* district, they often took one or two of us students with them. On these occasions, we were not only fed, but entertained as well, by performances of Javanese dance, *wayang kulit* (shadow puppets, where the show usually lasted until dawn) or *wayang wong* (traditional theater performed by live actors). The stories were usually episodes from Javanese versions of the Hindu epics, the Mahabharata and Ramayana. I could never resist a good story, and I loved the spectacle, the sonorous music of the gamelan orchestra, the splendid costumes and the poetry of the speeches – elegant High Javanese for gods and heroes, crude but witty Low Javanese for clowns and mechanicals, just like Shakespeare. Soon, I was sitting up with *eyang* all night, listening to performances broadcast by the local radio station, Radio Republik Indonesia Yogyakarta, and discussing the finer points of performance and storytelling with the old lady. I think she probably regarded the Minangkabau as lacking in high culture, but found me responsive and teachable.

The *kraton* area lay at the southern end of Malioboro, and faced north, away from the sea and towards the mountain Merapi, a living volcano. The public spaces, notably the sultan's principal audience hall, or *pendopo*, were on this side of the complex, and before them lay the *alun-alun*, a great open space with two spreading sacred *waringin*, or banyan trees, in its center. No permanent buildings were allowed here, but it was often invaded by fairground stalls and the smoke of a hundred food vendors cooking, as the crowds gathered for a *pasar malam*: literally, an evening market, but devoted more to enjoyment, meetings, food, and chatter than to regular business. Most evenings, in fact, this was a good place to look for supper any time after five o'clock; the street vendors were there in force. Almost all the food they sold was cooked right there, in front of the customers. My favorite was *martabak*, a pancake with savory stuffing – there is also a sweet version of it, *martabak manis*. There were different kinds of *soto*, spicy soups made with chicken (*soto ayam*) or beef (*soto daging* or *soto Madura* – the island of Madura is famous for its

Left: *Wayang wong*, the ancient Hindu legends performed by human actors in Jakarta.
Above: *Wayang golek* figures – stick puppets of carved and painted wood.

cattle, and for its bull races), many different satays with *sambal kecap* or *sambal kacang* (peanut sauce) and small savory snacks such as *bakwan*, *lemper,* and *arem-arem*, all sold in little containers of folded banana leaf, pinned with slivers of bamboo. *Sambal kacang* also accompanied the cooked vegetable salads, *pecel* and *gado-gado*. Every kind of fruit that was in season was there: durian, mangoes, mangosteens, rambutan, *jambu air*, *jambu klutuk, salak,* and at least six, often more, varieties of banana. There were fruit salads — Javanese people love *rujak*, a salad of sour, crunchy fruit dressed with spices and hot chilies, a sensation in the mouth and far removed from Western ideas of a fruit salad. There were iced drinks made with all sorts of natural juices, and, as often as not, luridly colored with dyes of dubious origin. *Es* (ice) was crushed or shaved into most of them: *es kopyor*, *es kolang-kaling*, *dawet*, and many other concoctions of sweetened coconut water or coconut milk. These were invariably sweetened with sugar syrup made from caramelized coconut sugar, or what the Dutch call *stroop* — sugared water colored with fruit essences.

Nowadays, on more recent visits to Indonesia, I have seen all sorts of milk shakes (most Indonesians no longer regard themselves, and are not regarded, as "lactose intolerant"), iced coffee and iced tea, and even bottled tea. On a journey in the tropics, my recommendation is alway drink *air kelapa muda*, coconut water from a young nut. Make sure that you buy from a vendor with a pile of freshly harvested green coconuts — better still, ask someone to climb up a tree and cut one for you — and see the top of the nut chopped off in front of you. You can pour the water into a glass, or drink it through a straw or straight from the nut, which is best of all if you don't mind a lot of it going down your chin.

In short, an hour or two in the *alun-alun* on a bright evening will soon fill you with everything you fancy, and load you with little packages to take home for all those people whose supper you promised to bring. This is also a wonderful place for

Left: Rambutan tied in bundles on a market stall.
Above right: Bali: a man climbs a coconut palm.

people-watching, and if you are clearly a foreigner you can be sure that someone, usually a little group of young men, will hail you and assume you speak English.

I graduated from high school in 1955, and enrolled in the English Department at Universitas Gajah Mada, the university the sultan had founded only a few years earlier. I enjoyed my three years of study there, but my way of life continued much as before, and this long period of continuity, even a certain amount of routine, did a lot to help me recover from the traumas of my younger years. I obtained my BA in 1958, and embarked on postgraduate studies. I stayed on in the boarding house, where I was by now one of the oldest inhabitants; I was comfortable there, all my friends knew where to find me, and the dozen or so boarders made a congenial little community.

I found I was eating more and more often in Chinese restaurants, perhaps because I had more money now or perhaps because I was looking for new adventures in food. Shunning pork, I limited my orders to beef, lamb, chicken, duck, and seafood – this still gave me plenty of choice. I loved thinly sliced beef, stir-fried with spring onions and bamboo shoots. I never went to a restaurant alone, of course, and with a small party we could order a whole crisp-fried chicken or duck, forerunners of the Sichuan chicken and Peking duck I would later eat in London. Many of my favorite dishes were Javanese adaptations of Chinese, such as the fried stuffed wontons which Indonesians call *pangsit goreng*, stuffed usually with crabmeat or shrimp, chopped up and mixed with diced water chestnut, chopped Chinese chives or spring onions, and flat-leaf parsley. More authentically Chinese, I think, were the wonton soups, crab soups with sweet corn, and a great range of noodle soups.

Now that I was a postgraduate student, I took a job as secretary and translator, first for the Professor of Social Psychology, and later for the Professor of English. At the same time I was offered two more jobs, both of which I accepted: as head librarian for the English Department and as a part-time junior lecturer. The little spare time I now had I filled with tennis and cycling, to keep myself from putting on weight – I made most of my own clothes, often a new dress every week, so I wanted to stay the same shape. Anyway, I needed all the cash I could get, for I was now supporting my parents so that they could afford to pay for my sisters' education. My father had high ambitions for all of them, just as he had for me. We had quarreled, at the start of my course, because he wanted me to study Indonesian and other Asian languages, whereas I wanted to do English language and literature. For my postgraduate thesis (regretfully, never finished), I worked on the novels of Jane Austen, which were very popular with us English Department young ladies — we recognized ourselves in them, and our society, with its strict social codes and cattiness.

By now I was an experienced broadcaster, taking part in poetry readings and plays for the Yogya radio station. I was also asked to interpret for English-speaking foreign visitors. Whenever President Sukarno went on tour around his islands, all the ambassadors from the Jakarta embassies followed, wishing no doubt to know what he was up to. I was always in the team selected to interpret his speech. Sukarno was a virtuoso orator, playing on his audience to work them to a pitch of ardor, then pricking the bubble with a joke that had them ecstatic with laughter. And doing this again and again, so that at the end you were left emotionally exhausted, yet deeply satisfied, and intensely proud to be an Indonesian. But I couldn't lose myself in wonder; I had to interpret every word the man said, to satisfy "my" ambassador, who probably understood Indonesian quite well, and was liable to pick me up on any point where he thought I might be wrong. I, too, went home excited after these occasions. I was planning a future for myself at United Nations Headquarters in New York …

I was determined that while I was young I would escape, at least for a while, the confines of tradition and genteel poverty by leaving Indonesia and seeing how the rest of the world lived. The way to do this was to study abroad, on a scholarship from the British, the Americans, or the Australians. I had plenty of examples in the departments I worked in: people went away for a year, or two, or three to world-famous universities, returning with degrees, professional qualifications, even doctorates. The English and History departments shared a building, a picturesque tumbledown eighteenth-century Javanese nobleman's palace just outside the walls of the *kraton*. It seemed now to be packed with young men and women back from the United States, some delighted to be home, others, in their own words, "States-sick" and wishing they could go back. As an English Department alumna and Austen fan, of course, I wanted to go to England. At various times, I was offered a scholarship to Australia and another to the United States. I turned them both down.

In January 1961, the British Council Representative arrived, by car, on an official visit to Yogya. One of the events that marked this was a small party, at which I was introduced to him and also to a new arrival who had traveled with him from Jakarta: a young man who had graduated from Oxford only six months before, and who was to spend the next three years lecturing in the History Department, under contract to the Indonesian government. Soon afterwards, he came into the English Department library, sat right down on my desk (there was a chair that visitors might, if I thought them worthy of it, be invited to sit on) and cheerfully addressed me as Sri. I was startled, then, for no reason I could think of, pleased … It took him more than a year to find the courage to ask me to go out with him on our first date, and the film we went to was as unromantic as it could possibly be – it was a documentary about the London Blitz – but, to cut an old story short, within three months we were engaged. Almost simultaneously, the long-awaited offer of a scholarship came from the British Council: a postgraduate course at Edinburgh University, in Linguistics.

I felt that fate was playing games with me. Roger at first said, "Take it. It's only a one-year course; we can get married when you come back." I put off sending my letter of acceptance to the British Council. A day or two later, he said, "On second thoughts, I'd rather you turned it down. You might change your mind and marry a Scotsman!" "Well," I said, "I might. So you'd better write to the Council in Jakarta and tell them I'm not going to Edinburgh – then you can ask my father's permission to marry me."

Roger had met my parents not long before, when they invited the expatriate staff of the English Department to lunch on the front terrace of our house in Magelang. Now I told him to wait in Yogya while I went to tell them of our proposed marriage. It was clear at once that my father was going to take a lot of persuading. My mother was much more understanding. "Let me talk to your father," she said. "Give me a day or two. I'm sure I can bring him round." For a while I cherished the dream of eloping to Singapore. On the agreed day, Roger appeared, with an armful of gladioli that he presented to my mother. I ushered him into my father's presence, and left them together for almost an hour. I knew Roger's grasp of the Indonesian language was rudimentary … Both men finally emerged, however, smiling broadly. So our Singapore trip was off – and the wedding was on! My mother and I embraced each other. A new world was born.

In the end we had a rather grand wedding, stretching over three days and culminating (of course) in a great midday wedding feast at my parents' house in Magelang, with a gamelan orchestra, several hundred guests from many countries, and far more good food than the assembled multitude could possibly eat. This was not the end: we returned to Yogya in time for a brief rest before the evening reception, for our students and colleagues and friends. This took place in the Malioboro branch of Toko Oen, a chain of Chinese-owned restaurants that sold Chinese, Indonesian, and Dutch food, as well as sweets, cakes, and ice cream. It was considered very chic to have your wedding party there, and there was even a limited amount of alcohol for those who wanted it, though certainly no champagne. At ten o'clock, we said goodbye to each of the hundred-odd guests, then, tired and happy, sought the village at the foot of the volcano, twelve miles away, where we had done much of our courting. It was a thousand feet above sea level, and the early August nights were chilly; in Australia, somewhere far to the south of us, it was winter. The friends who had lent us their cottage had thoughtfully laid a log fire in the fireplace, and it was soon burning brightly.

Left: The gamelan orchestra that played for our wedding.

We had, of course, taken care to get married early in the university vacation, and our honeymoon was a leisurely one. We drove, in the somewhat rickety car Roger had bought from a departing American professor, to East Java, and a week or so later to Bali. Roger, who was by now halfway through his three-year contract, had been there once or twice before, but I had never seen it. He had told me he wasn't sure if he liked Bali, or if I would like it, but who can resist an opportunity to honeymoon in a place that is, at least by reputation, so incontestably romantic?

Bali in 1962 was very different from what it became twenty or thirty years later. The landscape, indeed, was beautiful, but we did not think it more beautiful than Java. It had enjoyed good times before the war, when tourism flourished, but now there were few hotels, no proper airport, and almost no visitors. Though we had Bali pretty much to ourselves, and the Balinese friends we visited were very hospitable, we were not sorry to drive back along the south coast road, potholed as it was, to Gilimanuk at the island's westernmost point, there to manuever the car gingerly up two planks onto the old landing craft that was the ferry across the strait to Java.

We returned from these adventures in good time for the start of the new term, settling into the tiny house that had been allotted to Roger on the university campus soon after his arrival. It was not altogether an easy time for me: though all my best friends stayed loyal and approved my marriage, I knew some of my contemporaries were either shocked or envious, or both, and one or two showed it. The first official communication that I received from the university informed me that I would retain my university posts until my husband's contract ended, but that I was barred from promotion or any increase in salary. I couldn't complain at such treatment because Indonesians needed the jobs and the pay – and soon I was no longer an Indonesian, for Roger and I went to Jakarta, and in the British Consulate I took the oath of allegiance to Elizabeth II. In return, with surprising speed, I received a British passport.

During our brief engagement, I had told Roger one . . . not lie, exactly, but half-truth: "I'd better tell you now," I said one evening, "I can't cook." I don't remember now quite why I said this; perhaps I looked forward to having someone else perform the daily task in the kitchen, or perhaps I wasn't sure if he would like my Indonesian food. As we knew we both liked Chinese food, we ate mainly in Chinese restaurants – no change for me there. As soon as we were established in our own house, however, I started to want very much to cook for myself and not have to eat the bad food, adapted from the Dutch, that his *koki* put before us each evening. She was an aged Javanese who had worked for the Dutch for many years, and plainly regretted their departure. She was a good-hearted soul, but soon I was more or less bribing her to stay out of the kitchen and let me get supper. It was a very, very simple kitchen, but better than many

I had cooked in before; it had a three-burner kerosene stove, which worked – this was more than you could say for the kerosene-powered refrigerator Roger had shipped from England. There was a Chinese student in the English Department who I knew was a first-rate cook and very enthusiastic. I had him teach me a few Chinese dishes, and Roger obviously enjoyed all of these. Little by little, I extended my repertoire, modifying the very chili-hot dishes, and

Left: Sri's sisters and friends at the wedding feast.

noticing what food he selected from the buffet table when we were invited to students' weddings or Western-style parties given by my married friends. I tried cooking some Western recipes: not English ones at first, for those would invite comparison with his mother's cooking, which he had told me was very good. A few months after the wedding, I gave my first dinner party, inviting the new professor of English and his wife.

In those days, the only foreigners in Yogya were doctors, priests, or academics. Eating around, we encountered many interesting food habits. Though I had not cared for the Japanese when I last encountered them, I found our Japanese neighbors charming and hospitable. We ate *sukiyaki* at the orthodontist's house and, while his wife and I drank tea, Roger and the orthodontist polished off a bottle of Johnny Walker. Our next-door neighbors, to begin with, were New Zealanders, and with them we drank a 1960 New Zealand wine which had spent many months in a hot store room; it was undrinkable, but we drank it. After they left, a Russian moved in, with a Czech wife. Dropping in one evening, we were more or less hijacked into staying to dinner, and having eaten our way through a huge Russian meal were told that now we would, for the sake of comparison, have an equally large Czech one, both washed down with a lot more whisky. We ate Thanksgiving dinners with the Americans and fondue with the Germans, curries with another English lecturer and his Burmese wife, and pasta, not with the Italians (there weren't any), but with another New Zealander whose wife was Swedish. We ate very little Indonesian food, unless I cooked it or we were invited to a big party, which was almost always to mark some occasion – in other words, it was a *selamatan*. Indonesians didn't give many dinner parties, and very rarely invited foreigners to eat in their homes because they were shy and afraid that their guests might not like their food. I practiced assiduously my dinner-party technique, as well as my cooking, and by the end of my first year as a wife had some reputation as a hostess, but I knew I must widen my gastronomic horizons as soon as I left this little enclave of Indo-global food culture. For the time being, I cooked Padang food remembered from early childhood, Javanese food I learned from students, and Chinese, mainly Cantonese, taught to me by our Chinese friend, who came to our house to show me how to use five-spice powder. When I first

went food shopping in London a year or so later, this was the only ready-mixed Asian flavoring I could find; for all the other spice mixes, and such essentials as *kemiri*, galangal, *daun salam,* and chili sambal we had to make special trips to Den Haag. Indonesian food, it seemed, had conquered the Netherlands, and in time it would reach Britain — as Roger and I did, early in 1964.

It was still possible then to travel between Europe and Southeast Asia by sea; Roger had come to Singapore from the port of Birkenhead, on a cargo boat, taking five weeks. He flew for only his journey's last stage, from Singapore to Jakarta. Now it was time for us to leave. We were to sail with Lloyd Triestino from Tanjung Priok, the harbor of Jakarta, to Naples, then by train to London — first class all the way, and paid for by the Indonesian government. We packed a crate of teak furniture, pictures, books, clothes, and bric-a-brac, dispatched it by some mysterious route that would, many months later, bring it safely to our front door in Surrey, and made our final journey in the old Opel estate wagon that had served us, if not always faithfully, at least nobly. We spent a couple of days with my parents at the house in Magelang, and on the next morning packed the car and said goodbye. I hugged my mother with much the same feelings that I had had when saying goodbye to my grandmother more than twenty years before; we promised to come back soon, but perhaps I knew in my heart that it would be many years before we returned to Java, and then I would come to lay flowers and pray at her grave.

We stayed a few days in Jakarta with an old friend in the British Council, handed over the car to its new owner, and negotiated the complicated process of leaving the country. Our ship, the MV *Asia*, was a microcosm of Italy moored at the dock; my first taste of real Europe was to be two weeks aboard, then a week in Naples, and another in Rome, in the sunshine of a northern winter. In Italy, I found a warmth that I still feel today.

Left: Italy, with vineyards and morning cloud: the village of Rolle in the Veneto, seen from the balcony of the room where this book was written.

STUDENT FOOD

In this chapter, the recipes are for dishes familiar from my student days in Yogyakarta: street food, popular items from the city's small restaurants, some traditional family favorites and a few Central Javanese classics. Every cook has his or her trade secrets, and I have incorporated mine in many of these recipes to make them easier to shop for and prepare, and somewhat faster to cook, while still retaining their essential character.

mee kuah
street vendor's egg noodle soup

As this chapter is about the food I ate when I was a student in Yogya, I must recall this particular noodle soup. All the street vendors would appear at around eight or nine in the evening, each uttering a different cry or shout, or banging a plate to make a signal that everyone would immediately recognize. We students in the boarding house called in a different vendor each evening: one evening the satay man, on another occasion the *soto* or *gule* seller, and on Thursday or Friday, usually, the noodle man. I asked him once why he called his fare *mee kuah* and not *bakmie kuah*. He told us that *bakmie* would indicate a noodle dish that had some pork in it — the *ba* in *bakmie* is short for babi, meaning "pork," while *mee* or *mie* (both pronounced "mee") is the word for "noodles." He carried his wares on one shoulder, suspended from a *pikulan*, a yoke of thick split bamboo. One end carried the large saucepan for the soup, and the other all the rest of his kit and ingredients, including his bowls and bucket of water to wash the bowls after each customer had used one. His tea towel always looked rather unclean, so this was the reason most people called him to their houses: it meant they could use their own soup bowls. The taste of the noodle soup was always good. Nowadays, street vendors are no longer so popular, especially for noodle soup. The idea of it has been taken and copied by companies who produce instant noodles in packets. These packets contain a coil of noodles, a sachet containing powdered broth, another of MSG, and perhaps a third sachet containing dried vegetables, needing only to be quickly rehydrated with hot water. I'm sure this is not as tasty or nutritious as our old-fashioned fresh *mee kuah*, made with fresh vegetables and freshly made stock, but this is what young people are eating now, something instant and cheap.

At home, I'm still making my noodle soup the old-fashioned way. My repertoire of noodle dishes is quite wide, and includes noodle soups from several Southeast Asian countries. Making good noodle soup my way will take only a few minutes, however, provided, of course, you have prepared the broth or stock in advance (see recipes for making stock on pp.130–1).

The next step is to prepare, say, three different vegetables which are in season, cut up small enough to be eaten comfortably with a soup spoon, and some thin slices of chicken or beef. Stir-fry the meat in 1–2 tablespoons vegetable oil, together with just a little chopped shallot, garlic, and fresh ginger, for 4 minutes, add the vegetables and continue stir-frying for another 2 minutes, then add the stock. Season with salt and freshly ground black pepper, and continue boiling the stock with the meat and vegetables in it for 3–4 minutes. In another saucepan, cook the noodles in boiling water: about 3 minutes for dried noodles; 1–2 minutes for fresh noodles, which you can buy from most Chinese shops. Drain and divide the cooked noodles into as many bowls as you are serving, then pour in the soup, dividing the vegetables and the slices of meat equally among the bowls. Serve piping hot. The usual garnish for this is crisp-fried shallots (see p.275) and some chopped fresh flat-leaf parsley.

soto ayam
javanese chicken soup

This soup can be eaten as an appetizier or as a one-bowl supper dish with rice; however, in Indonesia, as in several other Southeast Asian countries, a clear broth such as this is usually put on the table, with the other dishes, at every meal. You ladle some of this into your own small bowl, and take a spoonful whenever you want. So instead of drinking water, tea or other beverages, you enjoy a clear, tasty, and nourishing soup.

2 chicken breast filets
4 garlic cloves, chopped
5 candlenuts or macadamia nuts,
   chopped
a little peanut oil
4 oz peeled and deveined raw shrimp,
   cut in half lengthwise
pinch of ground turmeric
½ tsp chili powder (optional)
1 tsp grated fresh ginger
1 tsp light soy sauce
3½ c beef or chicken stock (p.130) or
   vegetable stock (pp.130–1)

4 oz beansprouts, rinsed and drained
salt and freshly ground black pepper

for the garnish
1 hard-boiled egg, sliced (optional)
1 potato, thinly sliced and fried until crisp
4 spring onions, cut into thin rounds
several sprigs of fresh flat-leaf parsley
lemon wedges or slices
crisp-fried shallots (see p.275)

*Serves 4 as a soup or 2 as a one-bowl
lunch or supper dish*

Season the chicken breasts with a quarter of the chopped garlic, salt, and pepper. Put in a saucepan of boiling water, and poach, covered, for 20 minutes. Take out the chicken and allow to cool.

Using a mortar and pestle, pound the candlenuts or macadamia nuts and the remaining garlic into a paste. In a heavy saucepan, fry the paste in a little oil for 1 minute. Add the shrimp, turmeric, chili powder (if using), ginger, and soy sauce. Shred the poached chicken, discarding the skin, and add to the sauce. Pour in 1 cup of the stock, cover, and simmer for 5 minutes. Add the remaining stock, adjust the seasoning and simmer for 5 minutes more. Just 2 minutes before serving, add the bean sprouts.

Arrange slices of hard-boiled egg, if using, and fried potato in soup bowls, and sprinkle with chopped spring onions and parsley. Top with slices or wedges of lemon. Bring the *soto* to the table in a large serving bowl, and ladle it into the bowls. Sprinkle fried shallots on top. This should be served very hot.

If you eat *soto* as a supper dish, make some plain boiled rice to go with it; you may also want to add a little more chicken. If you think the chili powder will make the dish uncomfortably hot, then leave this ingredient out. If you are cooking for people who disagree among themselves how hot their food should be, then make your *soto* without chili, but provide a side dish of hot sambal for the spice-lovers; for example, *sambal ulek* (see p.279) or *sambal terasi* (pp.175–6).

gule kambing
an aromatic lamb stew

Originally, this was a goat stew, with a lot of sauce, and Indonesians still eat it today the way people used to at the street vendor's stall near my parents' house in Magelang: they put the white rice in a deep plate, and ladle the meat over it with plenty of sauce. Customers are then offered some sambal in a bowl, so that they can help themselves. A teaspoonful of the sambal will be more than enough for a plateful of rice and *gule*. Other garnishes will be added to the *gule* – crisp-fried shallots, chopped fresh flat-leaf parsley.

Here are two methods of cooking *gule* at home, which I have tested many times to bring them as near perfection as may be. Both use the whole leg of lamb. When I was in Australia, however, early in 1993, teaching Indonesian cooking at several cookery schools there, I used the Australian cuts of shank and filet of lamb, cut into even-sized medallions. The filet of lamb was, I think, from the best end of neck, or possibly the rump.

1 leg of lamb, about 5–6 lb
2½ c hot water
1½ in piece of cinnamon stick
2 salam leaves (see p.279) or kaffir lime
   leaves or bay leaves
1 lemongrass stem, cut into three
1–1½ c thick coconut milk

for the bumbu (paste)
6 shallots or 1 onion, chopped
4 garlic cloves, chopped
6 candlenuts or macadamia nuts
2–4 large fresh red chilies, seeded and
   chopped
½ tsp ground white pepper
½ tsp cayenne pepper or paprika
2 tsp chopped fresh ginger

1 tsp chopped galangal or
   ½ tsp laos powder
1 tsp ground turmeric
2 tsp ground coriander
2 cloves
1 tsp salt
4 tbsp thick tamarind water (see
   pp.118–19) or 2 pieces of *asam
   gelugur* (see p.274)
2 tbsp peanut or olive oil

for the garnish
2 tbsp crisp-fried shallots (see p.275)
a handful of fresh flat-leaf parsley
some *sambal terasi* (pp.175–6) (optional)

Serves 6–10

METHOD 1

Cut the lamb into ½ inch cubes, removing and discarding any fat or sinew. Put all the ingredients for the paste (except the *asam gelugur*, if using) into a blender or food processor, and blend until smooth. Transfer the paste to a large heavy saucepan, and fry gently, stirring often, for 6–8 minutes until aromatic. Add the meat, and stir continuously for 2 minutes, then add the hot water, cinnamon stick, lemongrass, and salam or other leaves. If using *asam gelugur* instead of tamarind water, put in the pot now. Cover the pan and continue to simmer for 40 minutes. Uncover, and add the coconut milk. Continue cooking over low heat, stirring the stew often, for 20–25 minutes, depending on how runny or thick you want it to be. Adjust the seasoning. Take out and discard the cinnamon stick, lemongrass, and leaves, and the *asam gelugur*, if used. Serve piping hot as explained above.

METHOD 2

Bone the leg carefully, and with a cleaver cut the bones into several pieces. Keep to one side. Cut as many medallion-sized pieces as you can from the best part of the leg filet. Remove any fat and sinew, and cut the rest of the meat into small cubes. Put the medallions of lamb in a glass bowl, and rub them with a mixture of ½ teaspoon salt and some freshly ground black pepper. Set aside while you blend all the ingredients for the paste. Transfer the paste to a large heavy saucepan, and fry gently, stirring often, for 6–8 minutes. Add the bones and small meat cubes; stir around for 2 minutes. Add the hot water, cinnamon stick, lemongrass and salam or other leaves. Cover and simmer for another 40 minutes. Remove the lid, add the coconut milk, and cook, uncovered, over a low heat for 20–25 minutes, stirring often. Adjust the seasoning. Up to this point, this can be prepared well in advance.

Just before serving, heat the sauce until it is nearly boiling, then strain into a smaller saucepan. Discard the bones. The smaller cubes of meat can be kept for other uses (if you chop them finely, they can be used as *martabak* filling, see pp.59–60). Pan-fry the lamb medallions in olive oil for 3–5 minutes each side, turning once. To serve, arrange the medallions on warm dinner plates, reheat the sauce and ladle onto the plates. Garnish the meat, and serve right away.

martabak
savory filled wontons

When I was still living in Yogyakarta, I never dreamt of making *martabak* myself at home. It was a pleasant afternoon walk from where I lived to the *alun-alun*, the open space outside the *kraton*, the sultan's palace, where every day from six o'clock in the evening there was a lively food market. There would be a dozen or so food vendors cooking their wares in front of you, and one of these was the *martabak* man. You could also have different kinds of *soto*; as well as these you would find sellers of fresh fruit, and there were satay men and noodle vendors. But when I got to England, I felt that I must learn how to make *martabak* myself. Wonton pastry, or wonton skins, as they are called in Chinese markets, were the answer, as I could not learn to make the elastic pastry that the vendor in Yogya thumped and stretched while his customers, admiringly, watched. So here is my recipe for home-made *martabak*.

2 x 6 oz packet wonton skins (see p.279)
1¼ c rapeseed, peanut, or sunflower oil,
    for shallow-frying

for the filling
2 tbsp olive oil
2 large onions, finely sliced
2 garlic cloves, finely chopped
2 in piece of fresh ginger, finely chopped
1 tsp ground coriander
½ tsp ground cumin
½ tsp ground turmeric or curry powder

2 in piece of lemongrass stem, outer
    leaves discarded, finely chopped
1 tsp salt
1 lb lean ground beef
4 spring onions, finely chopped
3 eggs, beaten

Makes 30–36 martabak

To make the filling, heat the olive oil in a wok or heavy frying pan, and fry the onions, garlic, and ginger until they are soft. Add the other filling ingredients, except the beef, spring onions, and eggs. Fry for another half-minute, stirring all the time, then add the meat. Mix well and cook, stirring occasionally, for about 15 minutes. Let the mixture cool for between 30 minutes and an hour. Put the mixture in a bowl, add the chopped spring onions, and mix well.

When you are ready to cook the *martabak*, add the beaten eggs to the filling and mix well. Lay a few wonton skins on a flat plate or tray. Put a tablespoonful of filling onto each wonton square. Put another square on top, and press the edges down so that they are more or less sealed. The finished *martabak* should be flat and filled with meat almost to the edge.

Heat the oil for shallow-frying in a heavy frying pan over high heat. Fry the *martabak*, four at a time, for about 2 minutes each side; turn once only. The casing should be quite crisp around the edges, but not in the middle. Serve hot or cold.

pangsit goreng dan sop pangsit
fried wontons and wonton soup

Another favorite in Chinese restaurants in Yogya. Usually, of course, the filling will be mostly pork with very few shrimp. A good *pangsit*, although it's deep-fried, should not be oily at all. The Chinese are very good at controlling the temperature of the oil for deep-frying, so a restaurant's *pangsit goreng* will come to you piping hot, with a small bowl of very hot chili dipping sauce. At home I make the filling with chicken and shrimp, and, though I'm still fond of *pangsit*, when I make them I much prefer to boil them and serve them in a clear broth (see pp. 130–1 for making good stock).

3 garlic cloves, very thinly sliced
peanut, rapeseed oil for frying
   (for *pangsit goreng*) or
   3½ c clear stock (if you
   are making wonton soup)
3½ oz chicken thigh filet, ground
8 oz raw shrimp, peeled, deveined, and
   ground

4 shallots, very thinly sliced
1 tbsp finely chopped fresh chives
2 small eggs
1 tsp corn flour
salt and freshly ground black pepper
small packet wonton skins (see p.279)

Makes 24 pangsit

Fry the shallots and garlic lightly in a little oil until soft. Mix with the ground chicken and shrimp, chives, eggs, and corn flour, and season with salt and pepper. Take about a spoonful of the mixture and roll it into a ball. Put the ball of mixture on a wonton skin, fold the skin over to make a triangle, and give the two sharp angles a twist. Deep-fry the *pangsit* in a wok or deep-fryer, four or five at a time, for about 2 minutes until golden brown and crisp. Serve hot or cold with a chili dipping sauce, as an appetizer or as a snack.

For making wonton soup, the amount of broth you must prepare obviously depends on how many soup bowls you will need to fill and serve. Apart from that, all you need do is to put the filled wontons, four or five at a time, in slightly salted boiling water in a saucepan, for 2 minutes; keep the water at a rolling boil. Drain each batch in a colander, and continue boiling the rest of the filled wontons. If you are not ready with your broth yet, keep the boiled wontons in a single layer on a plate. (You can pile them up, but the layers must be separated by cling wrap, otherwise they will stick to each other.) Now prepare your broth for the soup, by adding some chopped spring onions and parsley. Season the soup with a teaspoonful of light soy sauce, and some black pepper. Bring the broth to a boil, just as you are ready to serve the soup. Put three or four filled wontons as one serving into a large soup bowl, ladle the boiling broth into the bowl, and serve right away, piping hot.

gado-gado
cooked mixed vegetables with peanut sauce

The best *gado-gado*, and I still remember it well, used to be sold at a *warung* in Yogyakarta, in a small alley not far from the main street, Malioboro. This was in 1960. For my fellow students and me, it was the main meal of the day. At two or three o'clock in the afternoon, after attending lectures in the decayed nobleman's house that in those days was the Faculty of Arts and Letters, we would set off on our bicycles to return to our lodgings on the other side of town. The late lunch break at the *warung* eating *gado-gado* was the turning point of the day when we could gossip, relax, enjoy the passing street scene, and eat fresh crisp vegetables with a stinging hot peanut sauce, a gourmet dish for a few rupiah. This *bumbu*, or sauce, was made to our individual orders while we watched. We

each chose our vegetables, and the whole *gado-gado* was served with *lontong*, hard-boiled eggs, fried tempeh and tofu, and *krupuk* or *emping*. We were not hungry again until nine o'clock in the evening.

When I moved to England in 1964, I had to go to the Netherlands to get most of my Indonesian ingredients, including the *bumbu gado-gado*, or peanut sauce. Today, you can find all you need in almost any fair-sized town. *Gado-gado* is excellent for a one-dish lunch or supper – a very healthy vegetable dish that you can present as an artistic platter of well-arranged salad, with the delicious peanut sauce as the dressing. The choice of vegetables is wide, and you don't need to cut and slice your vegetables to make them look like the traditional *gado-gado* unless you really want to.

for the peanut sauce
1 quantity *sambal kacang* (p.174)

for the vegetables
This is one example of a good combination of vegetables, but you can adapt it or construct your own

4 oz cabbage or spring greens, shredded
8 oz French beans, cut into ½ in lengths
4 carrots, peeled and thinly sliced
4 oz cauliflower florets
4 oz beansprouts, rinsed and drained

for the garnish
some lettuce leaves and watercress
2 hard-boiled eggs, quartered
1 potato, boiled in its skin, then peeled and sliced, or 8 oz of cut-up *lontong* (p.132) (optional)
½ cucumber, thinly sliced
1 tbsp crisp-fried shallots (see p.275)
2 large *krupuk* (see p.278) or a handful of fried *emping* (see p.276), broken into small pieces (optional)

Serves 4–6

Boil the vegetables separately in slightly salted water for 3–4 minutes, except the beansprouts, which need only 2 minutes. Drain each one separately in a colander.

To serve, arrange the lettuce and watercress around the edge of a serving dish. Pile the vegetables in the middle of the dish, then arrange the eggs and sliced potatoes or *lontong*, if using, with the cucumber slices on top. Alternatively, arrange the vegetables, eggs, potatoes or *lontong*, and cucumber in separate piles on the serving dish, leaving room for a bowl of the peanut sauce in the center.

Heat the peanut sauce in a small saucepan until hot; add more water if it is too thick. Adjust the seasoning with a little salt if necessary, and pour the sauce over the vegetables. Sprinkle the crisp-fried shallots on top, and scatter over the *krupuk* or *emping*, if using. Serve at room temperature or cold, but not chilled. If you want to serve hot *gado-gado*, it can be reheated in a microwave oven. When reheating, however, do not include the lettuce and watercress, cucumber slices, fried onions, *krupuk* or *emping*. Add these garnishes immediately before serving.

gudeg yogya
traditional yogyanese chicken

This staple is also the everyday food of all students in the city's high schools and the oldest university in Indonesia, Gajah Mada University, my alma mater. For us, around a dozen Gajah Mada students living in a family boarding house, it was a substantial breakfast that we could find around the nearest street corner. In fact, our landlady's kitchen provided us with a reasonably good breakfast, but it was the same every day: *nasi goreng*, with a leathery fried egg, or rice porridge if we asked for it. So the *gudeg* was different. Bringing it back and eating it became a kind of protest, getting what we really wanted and at the same time showing our independence of mind and appetite.

If you can get fresh green jackfruit near where you live, *gudeg* can be made at home and will taste almost as good as the Yogya *gudeg* of my student days. This, then, is my version. Instead of fresh jackfruit (available only occasionally in some Thai and Indian shops in Britain), you can use canned green jackfruit, available from almost any Asian store. If, however, you are using fresh young jackfruit, *nangka muda*, you need to cut off a thick layer of peel, as if peeling a pineapple. Next, cut the flesh into small segments. (Warning: the sticky juice that comes out when you are peeling and cutting the jackfruit will stick to your hands, and can be removed only by rubbing your hands with cooking oil, then washing them with soapy water or detergent. If the juice gets onto your clothes, it is almost impossible to remove, and will leave a dark stain.) The jackfruit segments must be boiled in plenty of water, with a teaspoon of salt, for 30–40 minutes, then drained and left to cool before the next stage of cooking. Canned jackfruit need only be drained and rinsed.

Right: The Hindu temple complex and ruins at Prambanan, Central Java.

3½ c thick coconut milk
4½ c thin coconut milk
3 salam leaves (see p.279) or bay leaves
2 in piece of galangal
1 whole chicken, about 3¼ lb, roasted
    for 50 minutes, then cut into
    8 portions, discarding some of the
    bones and the skin
1½ lb parboiled jackfruit
    segments or canned green jackfruit,
    drained and rinsed
6–8 hard-boiled eggs, peeled

for the bumbu (paste)
5 shallots, chopped
4 garlic cloves, chopped
1 tsp chopped fresh ginger
8 candlenuts or macadamia nuts,
    or 10 blanched almonds, chopped
2 tsp ground coriander
1 tsp crumbled shrimp paste (see p.279)
1 tsp ground white pepper
1 tsp sugar
1 tsp salt

Serves 6–8

Blend all the ingredients for the *bumbu*, or paste, gradually adding ½ cup of the thick coconut milk. Continue blending until smooth. Transfer to a saucepan, bring to a boil and simmer, stirring often, for 6 minutes. Add the thin coconut milk, the salam or bay leaves, and the galangal. Continue to simmer for 20 minutes. Add the chicken and jackfruit, increase the heat and simmer, stirring occasionally, for another 30 minutes. Now add the remaining 3 cups thick coconut milk, and adjust the seasoning. Continue to simmer, stirring often, for 20 minutes or until almost all the liquid has been absorbed by the chicken and jackfruit.

    Add the boiled eggs, and continue cooking for another 4–5 minutes. Before serving, discard the leaves and galangal, and serve hot with plain boiled rice.

ayam goreng kalasan
original kalasan fried chicken

Every visitor to Yogyakarta goes to see the temple complex at Prambanan, about nine miles out of town on the Solo road. The road and the temple site are crowded now, but when I was a student at Gajah Mada University they were much quieter. Prambanan was a favorite picnic spot. A small eating house in the nearby village of Kalasan was already well known for its special fried chicken. We used to progress sedately from Yogya on our high Dutch bicycles, and if we felt particularly rich that day we might treat ourselves to fried chicken at the *warung* near the temples. Times have changed, but the original *warung* was still there when I visited Prambanan in 1993. Similar businesses have now sprung up and expanded into other parts of the country. Already, in 1987, I had eaten this style of fried chicken at a restaurant called Ayam Goreng Nyonya Suharti, right next door to the Ambarukmo Palace Hotel in Yogyakarta. Nyonya Suharti has now become a chain, with restaurants all over Indonesia.

What follows is my attempt to re-create this typical Yogyanese fried chicken. One ingredient that might present a problem if you are not in the tropics is coconut water, and this is absolutely essential. Water out of thick-shelled old coconuts from the supermarket will do, but you need quite a bit — the contents of several nuts. In Indonesia, the water is from *kelapa muda*, the young coconuts that grow everywhere and are full of water because their flesh has not begun to form. Many Thai food stores now sell young coconuts, so you may be lucky.

1 free-range chicken, 3¼–4½ lb, cut in half or into 4 pieces	2 salam leaves (see p.279) or bay leaves
3½ c coconut water	2 tbsp all-purpose flour
5 shallots, finely chopped	salt and freshly ground black pepper
2 tsp finely chopped fresh ginger	peanut oil for deep-frying
1¼ in piece of galangal	
½ tsp ground turmeric	*Serves 2–4*

Put the coconut water in a deep saucepan. Add to it the shallots, ginger, galangal, turmeric, salam or bay leaves, and 1 teaspoon salt. Mix well, then put in the chicken halves or quarters. Leave to marinate for 2–4 hours, then simmer the chicken in the marinade for 1–1¼ hours over medium heat. Leave to cool in the remaining cooking juices. When cold, take the chicken pieces out and dry them with paper towels. You can now cut the chicken halves into smaller pieces, as preferred.

On a large plate or a tray, season the flour with salt and pepper. Rub the flour all over the chicken pieces. Heat the oil in a deep-fryer or wok to 325°F (165°C) – a small cube of bread dropped into the oil should brown in 50–60 seconds – and fry the chicken until golden brown. The pieces should be crisp outside and still soft and tender inside. Serve hot right away, or cold for a picnic.

bakmie goreng
chinese fried noodles

My fond recollections of fried noodles from Chinese restaurants derive, again, from my time as a high school and university student in Yogyakarta. The Chinese restaurant near my boarding house in Yogya was always full of customers, and indeed their servings were lavish and their noodles excellent, though oily. As my friends and I didn't eat pork, we asked that our food not be fried with pork fat, and said we preferred chicken anyway. The noodles came with lots of chicken meat on top, including the liver. For eight of us, the chef must have used the meat of a whole chicken, and put the carcass in the pot to make his admirable stock. He also gave us plenty of vegetables and a generous garnish of crisp-fried shallots (see p.275).

Apart from the noodles, salt, and water listed here, all the ingredients are the same as those that accompany the rice in the recipe for *nasi goreng* on pp.135–6.

1 lb fresh or dried egg noodles
1 tsp salt

Serves 4–6

Below: Jakarta: selling *nasi goreng* at a streetside *warung.*

Bring 10 cups water and the salt to a boil in a large saucepan. Add the noodles. If you are using fresh noodles, boil for 1–1½ minutes; if using dried noodles, boil for 3 minutes. While they are boiling, tease the noodles apart using a large fork or a wooden spoon, so that they do not stick together. Put the noodles in a colander, and rinse under cold running water until they are cold, to stop them overcooking. Drain in the colander, turning them several times so that all the water drains off. Proceed, without delay, as described in the recipe for *nasi goreng* on pp.135–6.

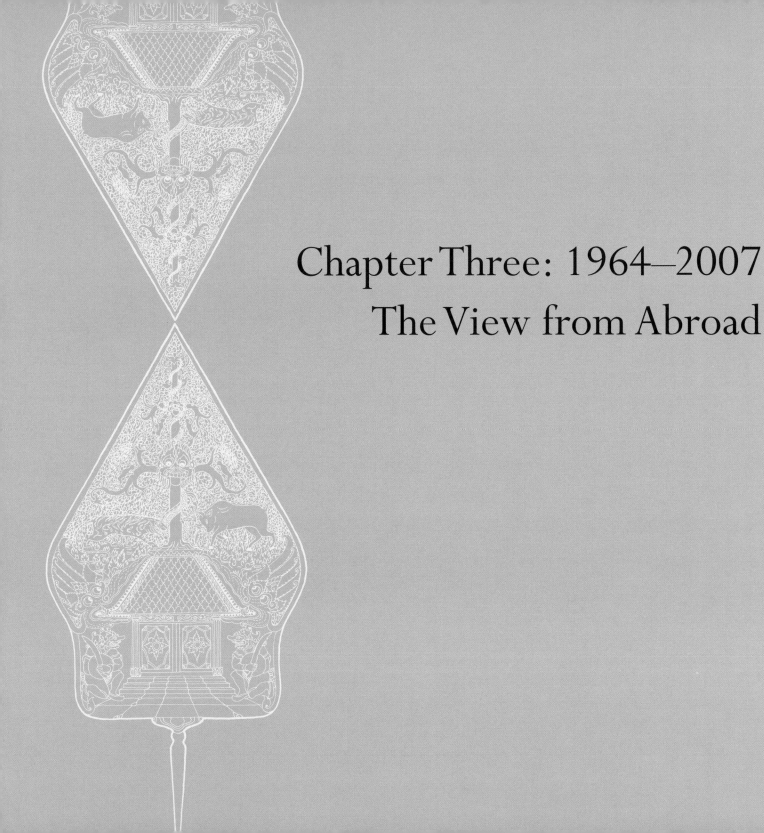

Chapter Three: 1964–2007
The View from Abroad

Although I was brought up in a small town, I am a city person at heart, and the two cities that excite me most are Venice and London. Each, in its own way, has made its living for the past thousand years or more by continually reinventing itself and its food. Both have shown an extraordinary talent for survival; each is intensely conservative in its own way. Venice made its wealth in the Middle Ages through trade with the Orient. It was one of the gateways through which spices, particularly pepper, cloves, and nutmeg, entered western Europe before the Portuguese opened the sea route round the Cape of Good Hope. Any Italian cookbook today shows that these exotic flavors are needed as much as ever in the modern kitchen. On recent visits, I've also been rather pleased to see that Venetians, and no doubt their foreign guests, are snacking on slices of fresh coconut, kept cool in the market stalls under little fountains of iced water. It's hardly surprising that Indonesians and Italians appreciate each other's food, especially when you consider that Italians have been growing and eating rice at least since the mid-fifteenth century. And all that fish! Not only are all those splendid sea creatures in the Rialto clear-eyed and, to all appearances, wonderfully fresh, but also each batch is tagged and named, with the sea area in which it was caught. It is sad, though, that so much fish now has to be harvested in distant seas and brought to market frozen.

As for London, it is perhaps the greatest city of the world for eating out, at least in my experience; New York and Singapore may rival it, but they are young, and London has been reborn many times. Southeast Asian restaurants are a good example of this continual reinvention. The Thais arrived first and are unlikely to be challenged; they are not only the most dynamic community in the region, but have long been the most open to the outside world. They remained independent throughout the colonial period, and they avoided direct involvement in World War II and the Indo-China conflicts that followed. The most grievously afflicted in those conflicts —Vietnam, Laos, and Cambodia — are making progress in the eating-out business, especially Vietnam, which has been influenced but not overwhelmed by its reluctant past associations with China, France, and the United States. There were few, if any, Vietnamese restaurants in London when I arrived. Today, the "All in London" website directory lists 240 Thai restaurants, 48 Vietnamese, 18 Malaysian, six Indonesian, five Singaporean, three Philippine, and one Burmese. I don't know how accurate the numbers are, but the rank order certainly seems

about right. It doesn't, of course, reflect the numbers of Thais, Burmese, etc. living in Greater London; it reflects only their success in attracting London restaurant-goers.

An Indonesian food lover who has chosen permanent exile: is that how I think of myself? Perhaps I have become a bit of a missionary. My mission is to show my readers the real goodness of Indonesian food – and my dream is to convince my countrymen and women of its excellence and make them proud of it. What do I have to show for forty-odd years in the West? A dozen or so books; some journalism, a long succession of cooking demonstrations and classes around the world, some radio interviews and guest appearances on TV channels; two grown-up married sons who have inherited my love of good food and are talented cooks; my fair share, or rather more, of travel and restaurant-going and privileged stays in luxury hotels (all in the name of "research," naturally); some consultancy sessions with big food producers and supermarkets, which I don't think bore much fruit; acquaintance, leading usually to mutual respect and often to real friendship, with a vast number of people in every field and corner of the food industry and food studies – I owe them much.

Page 68: Young jackfruit.
Above: Slices of fresh coconut for sale near the Rialto, Venice.

Most of my everyday cooking is pure improvisation, interrupted from time to time by inspiration – "I need some more shallots and lemongrass. Roger – !" Wimbledon Village High Street is a good location, and its history, as we have watched it unfold over the past twenty-odd years, says a lot about the social history of food in Britain. When we first arrived in England and started looking for an apartment, we went round all the best suburbs, and the place I really wanted to live in was either Hampstead or Wimbledon. But it was all too clear that these hilltops represented the commanding heights of the economy and were far beyond our reach. Twenty years later, we finally made it – as tenants of a semi-derelict shop, which happened to have a large apartment above it. We were obliged to live in the apartment, under the terms of the lease. This dated from 1904, the year in which our side of the street was built.

In that summer of 1984, as we bustled around to open London's first Indonesian food store and delicatessen (an experiment never, as far as I know, repeated), Wimbledon Village had two butchers; two grocers; a branch of a well-reputed chain of grocery stores; a long-established baker, opposite us on the High Street; several pubs and three or four off-licences; one Greek restaurant; and two Indian.

It turned out that we had timed our arrival quite well. Over the next few years, the "traditional" businesses, which included most of the food shops, closed. Big new supermarkets, with big parking lots, were within fifteen minutes' drive, and the small traders couldn't compete. The luxury shops did better, particularly the ladies' dress boutiques, which today populate the street and share most of the space with the coffee bars, fast-food joints, ethnic restaurants (Indian, Thai, French, Italian, modern European) and jewelers. Pubs and bars thrive, and Sunday, which used to be the quietest day of the week, is now the busiest.

This isn't exactly "gentrification": High Street has always been surrounded by wealthy middle-class homes. The movement has been away from the raw materials of dinner, selected by the prudent housewife and weighed in front of her before she took out her housekeeping money, towards semi-prepared meals which busy young men and women assemble from the deli counter, arrange quickly in tiny kitchens with microwaves and often, presumably, eat alone. I don't criticize them for this, much less would I patronize them – they have no choice, except in the processed foods for which they shop, which,

Top: *Daun salam*, salam leaves.
Above: Fresh turmeric root.

in this town, are likely to be expensive luxury items from the Mediterranean, the Americas, or farthest Asia. Weekends are more convivial, when young ones flock to the bars, and on summer evenings restaurant tables spread across the pavement. It's an affluent version of the street food my friends and I used to eat in Yogyakarta, and I hope that they have as much fun as we had.

My shop, Mustika Rasa, the "crown of taste" (or "top taste," as my son Daniel translated it for customers), was in a way a pioneer in these changes, although I suppose I was just lucky in being able to ride the wave. It kept me, and Roger and Daniel whenever they were available, extremely busy during its brief existence. Irwan, the elder son, was a student in Manchester by that time. The shop opened in September 1984 and closed shortly after its third birthday. I cooked takeaway food for the shop, catered for local residents' parties, served pre-booked dinners in my own dining room, gave Indonesian cooking classes and, for a year or two, supplied Indonesian snacks and recipe dishes to Harrods Food Hall. My big problem was that I never quite caught up with myself: I could not find, train, and keep skilled, trustworthy staff, and, although the place was always awash with good food and swimming in cash, the bank overdraft never seemed to diminish. Luckily, our bank manager kept faith in us. Most of the high street freeholds were owned by large property companies, and in seeking to increase their profits these landlords approached rent reviews like hungry diners scenting a feast. Our landlord was one of the biggest, and – we found out just in time – regarded us as too small fry to be worth keeping. We were auctioned off, with several of our neighbors, and found ourselves fortunate freeholders within a few months of the shop's opening. Otherwise, I think we would have been not the cooks, but the dinner.

The 1980s were indeed life-changing for all of us. Our first decade together in London had been fairly sedate; I worked for the Indonesian Service of the BBC in Bush House; Roger taught foreign business students at a polytechnic. Irwan was born in 1966; Daniel six years later. For each baby, one of my younger sisters was brought to London to spend three years with us as au pair, continuing her studies and helping to look after the youngest. By the time Daniel was three years old, I had succumbed to my inner voice and the repeated entreaties of one of Roger's university friends who was now a literary agent: "Write an Indonesian cookbook, Sri – I'll find you a publisher." *The Home Book of*

Indonesian Cookery was published by Faber in 1976, and, although it made no great splash, it set off enough ripples to catch the eyes of several people – one in particular – who would set me on an entirely new course.

The one was Alan Davidson, the most remarkable individual whom I have ever come to know well. He had just retired from a career in the diplomatic service, during which he wrote several books on the fish of various oceans and how best to cook and eat them. His final posting was as British ambassador to Laos, where he collected material for *Fish and Fish Dishes of Laos* and *The Seafood of Southeast Asia*, at the same time helping many Lao refugees to cross the Mekong to relative safety in Thailand, and to settle, eventually, in England. Through bad scheduling, I missed my chance to interview him in Bush House for my Indonesian listeners, so instead I invited him and his wife, Jane, to dinner at my house. It turned out that he also wanted to meet me, having read *The Home Book* and realized that I could tell him about Indonesian foodways in his post-retirement role as a food writer and academic. I was very flattered to be invited to attend a weekend meeting of such people at St. Antony's College, Oxford, where he was a visiting fellow; the historian Theodore Zeldin, a fellow of the college, was co-organizer of this event. It was billed as a symposium, and was attended by a small but select list of invited members. Here I met for the first time Elizabeth David, Jane Grigson, Jill Norman, Claudia Roden, Paul Levy, Yan Kit So, Anne Willan, Doreen Fernandez (the doyenne of Philippine food writers) and, in succeeding years, many others. The Oxford Symposium on Food and Cookery soon became an established feature of the late Oxford summer, and it now attracts 180 or more food professionals, academics and devoted others every year – a wonderfully mixed, convivial group.

What mattered most for me, however, was that my meeting with Alan proved the turning point in my fast-developing passion for researching, cooking, and teaching people about the food of my birth country, Indonesia. When Faber decided not to reprint my first book, I offered it to Alan. At that time he and Jane, with Elizabeth David, Richard Olney and others, were launching a journal of food studies and food history called *Petits Propos Culinaires* (always known as *PPC*). Years later, he wrote about the circumstances of its birth:

It was at this point that Jane and I met Sri Owen and learned that the *Home Book of Indonesian Cookery*, at that time her only published work, was reaching the end of its natural life and that the publishers, Faber, had reluctantly concluded that it would not be viable in paperback form. Since we had a special interest in the food and cooking of South-East Asia, and were confident that Sri's book would have a future as a paperback (all the more so if a substantial amount of the background information which Faber had not wished to include could be restored to it), we responded positively when Sri asked us whether we might take on the book. We had never published a book before, but we supposed that it would not be very difficult. With the warm support of Rosemary Goad at Faber, we set to work with Sri and her husband, Roger, to bring *Indonesian Food and Cookery* into being.

With a lot of new material on Indonesian ingredients, more recipes, and a much-improved cover design, *Indonesian Food and Cookery* (always referred to as *IFAC*) was published in 1980. It was the first title to appear from Prospect Books, a publishing venture newly launched by the Davidsons and their partners. The cover design and the line drawings that enhanced the text were by one of their Laotian protégés, Soun Vannithone. The book was launched with a party in the Davidsons' house in Chelsea. I cooked all the food for it, and watched carefully to see how the guests reacted to my Indonesian dishes. What I saw and heard only confirmed my determination to follow my passion for cooking and entertaining. From this memorable beginning, the book had a long life in Britain and several other countries, and went into a second, enlarged edition. I felt it was giving me a signal, telling me it was time to start a new career in earnest. But this did not happen at once.

I knew I had a lot to learn and that I needed to travel. Our two boys, veterans of camping trips across Europe and well accustomed to restaurant-going, were now aged nine and fifteen. It was high time for them to meet their Indonesian family. I had not been back for seventeen years, prevented by the need to earn a living and by some ill health in my thirties. Some of those years had been traumatic for Indonesia, but the country now had a stable government, and most of my sisters, and their husbands, were clearly benefiting from a new climate of economic expansion. In that summer of 1981, all the signals seemed set to "go." We were away for six weeks, with stopovers in Singapore, then in Kuala Lumpur and Melaka in Malaysia, and, in Indonesia itself, longer stays in Jakarta, Yogya, Pontianak in West Kalimantan (where two of my sisters were living) and, of course, Bali. The family reunion was fine, Irwan and Daniel liked some of the places we went to and didn't like others, and we all managed to stay healthy nearly all the time. I didn't feel, though, that I had learned a great deal more about food, and I wasn't sure yet that I had another book in me.

Back in England, I followed the example of several of my neighbors and started selling home-cooked dishes from my freezer. We also bought one of the first genuinely useful home computers, a Commodore 64, and started taking in word-processing jobs, which at least paid the hire-purchase installments on the machinery. We word-processed some of the first articles for *The Oxford Companion to Food*, the immense project which Alan had embarked on and which would take him twenty years to complete. I did some technical translation and sometimes interpreted for Indonesians who found themselves in court. The BBC had told me that my current contract could not be renewed. I knew I couldn't sit at home all day, waiting for my husband to return from work and my children from school. That was when I decided to open a shop … When the shop closed, three years later, I was exhausted but felt I had proved myself a professional, as cook and writer, and I was ready to get going. In the spring of 1988, Roger took early retirement from his polytechnic. With shop rents coming in, we could again afford a little modest traveling.

Roger and I were enjoying a siesta under a magnificent painted ceiling in Siena when a phone call came from London to tell me that Doubleday had accepted my proposal for two books: one on rice; the other on Indonesian regional food. These kept us busy for the next three years. For *The Rice Book*, we visited about fifteen rice-producing countries and met growers, traders, and scientists in almost all of them, bringing home a huge pile of books and notes, and hours of taped interviews, together with an overwhelming impression of the goodness and general niceness of everyone concerned with rice. Their generosity and eagerness to tell us everything we needed to know resulted in *The Rice Book* winning the André Simon Memorial Award in 1993. Conspicuous among them were the rice growers of the Murrumbidgee Valley in New

South Wales, who were reluctant at first to take our project seriously, but were browbeaten by Australian food writer Cherry Ripe into showing us around. Their hospitality was thereafter unbounded. We returned to Australia for longer visits to meet some of the people who were bringing Asian food to the great city restaurants and in the process reinventing the ways Australians cook and eat: David Thompson, Tetsuya Wakuda, Neil Perry, Gay Bilson, Damien Pignolet, Maggie Beer, Tim Pak Poy, Cheong Liew, Beh Kim Un, Serge Dansereau, Stephanie Alexander – the list could go on. Australia and Indonesia: such near neighbors, so utterly different in almost every way – yet Australians are becoming less European and more Asian in their food, as well as their holiday destinations. One year we went around the world, landing in Vancouver, Canada, half an hour before we took off from Sydney, according to my watch.

The North American west coast, from Vancouver south to San Francisco, seemed in a way like an echo of Australia in the Asian notes of its cooking and the depth and flavor of its wines. Air travel is making the Pacific a modern equivalent of the ancient Mediterranean, or of the Indian Ocean in the early modern age, a focus of world trade

Right: Launch party for *The Home Book of Indonesian Cookery* in the Faber offices in Bloomsbury, 1976.

with food playing a leading role – not only bulk foodstuffs such as wheat, soy beans and fish, but food culture as well. At one Oxford Symposium on Food and Cookery I met Julia Child, who encouraged me to join the International Association of Culinary Professionals (IACP), the heavyweight title of a large organization, the center of gravity of which is firmly in the United States. This took us to various great American cities for its annual conferences, and opened up a world of new friends and contacts. This, of course, is one of the IACP's principal reasons for existing, but it also brought us invitations into many homes and participation in many shopping trips and meals in restaurants. These were at every level from intimate to vast and very formal. I recall a bitterly cold morning, 6 a.m. in the Philadelphia fish market, where I learned much about the economics of fish. In Portland and Seattle, I became acquainted with Dungeness crabs. In Cooperstown, in upstate New York, I cooked with Philippine food writers and chefs for a feast on the Fourth of July. In San Francisco, Roger and I ate at Charles Phan's Slanted Door restaurant and shopped in the Asian food market in front of City Hall. New York City has drawn me back many times, to eat adventurously (for example, in Romy Dorotan and Amy Besa's Cendrillon restaurant), take part in a conference, shop in Union Square and at Dean and Deluca's, and teach at Peter Kump's school and the French Culinary Institute (where I was allowed to demonstrate Indonesian dishes and accompany them with Bisol Prosecco from the Veneto). So one of the dreams of my student days came true – although, as always with dreams, it wasn't quite the way I'd dreamt it.

For the next book, we spent four months in Indonesia, visiting remote areas I had never expected to see, and returning, more than fifty years after I left, to my birthplace and the scenes of my childhood in West Sumatra – though nothing of the town as I had known it remained. And if a small provincial town had become unrecognizable, what of Jakarta, which in 1960 had one set of traffic lights and few buildings more than two stories high? In 1981 we had seen the results of rapid development, with skyscrapers, shopping malls and gridlocked traffic between innumerable stoplights. Twelve years later, the dual carriageways, towering office blocks of glass and steel, massive hotels with lobbies apparently copied from *Star Wars*, the shops selling world-famous designer clothes and handbags (genuine or not, I cannot say) – all became even more of a fantasy

Top: Fresh chilies on sale in Padang market.
Above: Petai beans, Bogor market, West Java.

world after dark, illuminated in ever-shifting color.

The food scene had changed, too, though once we got out of town we soon saw that old ways still survived. In the countryside, few people could afford imported foodstuffs or modern kitchen equipment, and the traditional social order went on pretty well unchanged, with its calendar of feasts, the resulting competition for status, and the obligation among neighbors to return favors. Migrants to the towns, if they prospered, wanted to be up to date, but at the same time were nostalgic for the food that they had eaten with parents and grandparents. (Perhaps I'm an extreme example of this.) These contradictory longings were seized on to provide copy for the voracious new media. I already knew that a number of women's magazines were appearing and apparently flourishing; one of my sisters regularly sent me *Selera* ("Taste"), and it had prepared me for some of the developments I now saw at first hand. The middle classes had continued their steady rise, in numbers and income, and even if they couldn't afford to travel overseas they were much more aware of the outside world, which came to them in TV programs via big antennas disfiguring their rooftops and in the imported goods in the shops. The TV shows included cooking lessons and documentaries about other countries' food habits. For people who could afford them, there were gastronomic tours to Australia, Singapore, Hong Kong, and elsewhere. As the tourist trade developed within Indonesia, there was an urgent need for cooks and chefs to run the kitchens of thousands of new hotels and restaurants. Hotel schools, state-run and private, sprang up in many large towns, and the rather despised and often unpaid role of cook, amateur or professional, started to acquire status of its own. Chefs' associations appeared and are now well established; we met members of the Indonesian chefs' organization, IJUMPI, and spent a day with students of the Hotel School in Bandung. We also met and interviewed many hotel general managers, food and beverage managers, and executive chefs. At the time these were mainly European, but Indonesians (in particular, Balinese) are now in charge of prestigious hotel kitchens in their country and elsewhere.

Detlef Skrobanek is clearly not an Indonesian name, but few other Europeans have done as much as he has to bring Indonesian food into the modern world, both as creative cook and promoter. For my benefit, he produced a magnificent tasting menu in a private dining room of the Jakarta Hilton, in which every course was based closely on a traditional Indonesian dish, revised, elaborated, and beautifully presented, but with its native flavors and textures retained. I also received a copy of *The New Art of Indonesian Cooking*, which he wrote with Julia Roles and Gerald Gay. It makes my mouth water just to turn the pages, but I have to confess I have never attempted to cook from it; my *New Wave Asian* shows just a little of its influence; *The New Art* is very much a book for the celebrity chef. But Detlef and others have put heart into their Indonesian colleagues, it seems. On successive visits to the country, I have been happy to find well-cooked Indonesian items on many hotel and restaurant menus across a wide price range. I've also eaten good Indonesian food in restaurants in Australia, and encountered a Balinese chef in the Royal Hotel d'Angkor in Cambodia.

Another big figure in the Indonesian food world whom I have come to know over the past fifteen years or so is William Wongso, entrepreneur extraordinaire, passionate about Indonesia and its traditions, and, like Alan Davidson, always in search of young talent that he can nurture and encourage. In our regional researches he introduced us to people and restaurants all over the country, took us around the whole Jakarta area and further afield in his 4x4, showed us food courts he was nurturing in department-store basements and on huge new housing developments, and gave us advice, ideas, knowledge, food, and drink – little snacks in backstreet *warungs* he happened to know of, fine dining in Chinese restaurants behind discreetly sober doors in the old business quarter, meetings of the Jakarta Wine Club of which he was founder and president, a lunch in his Italian restaurant that would be hard to match in Italy itself. His current flagship, the Kafe Artistik, represents the new wave in Indonesian cuisine. I hope the rest of the fleet can keep up with him.

Indonesian Regional Food and Cookery duly appeared in 1994. A year later, we came back from a holiday in Scotland to find a letter saying that the book had been awarded a Premio Langhe Ceretto and we were invited to go to the Ceretto family's winery in Italy's Piedmont to collect it – and to cook an Indonesian dinner for a little party of sixty or so guests. This was irresistible, and we set off on another transcontinental drive to Turin, Alba, and the hills of the Langhe. This expedition brought me not only fun, satisfaction, a cash prize, and several dozen bottles of excellent wine; it also gave me friends in Italy, the country of mainland Europe with which I had felt an affinity since I first came ashore in Naples thirty years before. My Italian circle expanded a few years later when Roger and I joined Slow Food, which in turn led me, in 2000, to be invited to Rome to cook an Indonesian dinner for a group of Italian academics.

Through Slow Food I became known to the Prosecco wine-growers of the Veneto, who wanted to expand their export market into Asia and wondered how their wines would match with Asian foods. I cooked for forty or so of their members in a hotel in Vittoria Veneto, and got into conversation with Gianluca Bisol, the only one who was prepared to talk to me in English. (My attempts to learn Italian, which seems to me an easy language compared with French, have somehow never taken root.) Close contact has been maintained ever since between our two families, and the larger part of this book has been written, and almost all its recipes tested, in the Bisol *foresteria* among the vineyards and rolling hills of Valdobbiadene.

Here the recipes are for experimental "New Wave" dishes, based on Indonesian traditions, adaptations of old recipes, and experiments with new and unfamiliar ingredients – unfamiliar, at any rate, in the Indonesia I was brought up in. Here I start to follow my instinct that "fusion food," though it has become unfashionable in name, need never be bad food. Traditions and fashions are continually changing as people adopt new styles of cooking and adapt old ones. The instinct to experiment and try something new is always there, especially if you are a cooking teacher and writer. So this chapter ranges widely, from memories of my father's cooking to my discovery of Italy – and the unexpected harmonies between Italy and Indonesia, including, but not limited to, those countries' shared love of ice cream.

INDONESIAN ICE CREAM AND DISCOVERING ITALY

Indonesians have been eating ice cream ever since the first refrigeration plants arrived there, more than a century ago. The magic of putting something cold into your mouth when everything around you is always sticky-hot – how could they resist it?

I certainly couldn't, when I was a student in Yogyakarta, though it had to remain an occasional treat, too expensive for every day. My favorite was *es krim kopyor*, mixed with the curious, slightly spongy but wonderfully flavored flesh of a scarce kind of coconut; the ice cream was the most expensive of all because these coconuts were in such demand. Before Roger and I left for England, I promised myself that in London I would permit myself two extravagances: as much chocolate and as much ice cream as I could possibly want, whenever I wanted them.

Fortunately for my figure, and for our trembling bank account also, after a month of reckless self-indulgence my craving for ice cream and chocolate dwindled to the point where the thought of either made me feel quite ill. But in the meantime I had glimpsed, and tasted, something that was to become, over many years, much more important to me. I have mentioned that we came to Europe on an Italian liner, the *Asia*, from Jakarta to Naples, a two-week voyage that landed us in Italy in mild January sunshine. I was attracted to this place at once, and beneath the obvious differences I slowly became aware of many points of contact with my own country. In fact, after my first six months in England I began to look back on Italy as a place I should like to go back to and learn more about.

It was five or six years before an opportunity arose. By that time our first child, Irwan, was three years old, Roger was a lecturer at a London college and I was kept busy at the BBC. My next-to-youngest sister had graduated and had come to London to improve her English and help look after little Irwan; she would be returning home soon. I wanted her to see something of Europe, but good hotels were beyond our reach, so we bought camping gear and set off in our second-hand Peugeot 403. At the end of our first day, we arrived in Paris in one of the most torrential downpours that even I, brought up in the tropics, have ever witnessed. Somehow we found our way to *le camping* in Versailles, and in darkness put up the tent on the only patch of fairly dry ground we could find – drained as it was by being on a steep slope. The following day was better, but still overcast, and even Paris looked unattractive; that afternoon we packed up all our gear, stuffed the soaking tent back into its bag and heaved it onto the roof rack, and set off towards the south. We drove all night, and at dawn found ourselves in the little town of Argentat on the River Dordogne, on the banks of which was a green and level campsite with hot showers. The sun shone, the birds sang, I cooked a good lunch and the tent dried quickly. After that night in Versailles, we knew we could face anything. So we decided, after a few more sunny days in France, to go to Italy.

Once again, it was a revelation. We continued our practice of driving at night and arriving somewhere in the early morning, always finding a coffee shop or trattoria that was just opening and would give us breakfast. Milan, Florence, Pisa, Rome, Venice, Ravenna – I must be combining, in memory, several such trips, for we made at least three, the last in an old VW camper van. But the place that stands out in my memory is Siena, which we have returned to again and again, and which always astonishes. Young Irwan, nonchalant in a stunning jumpsuit created by my sister – scarlet, with two broad stripes, white and black, from right shoulder to ankle – was immediately made welcome by the old ladies who sold corn for the pigeons in the Campo, and in every restaurant to which we went. I knew that Italians love children, but seeing them show such understanding and affection to my child made me realize how many good qualities they share with my own people. Appreciation of fresh, healthy home-cooked food, for example: I was not at all surprised, years later, when the Slow Food movement was launched in Italy.

From that first trip, I also recall a voyage round Lake Como, where we had an excellent fish lunch on board the steamer: fried trout, fresh from the lake, with crunchy almonds scattered over it. Almost thirty years later, Roger and I repeated the experience, on board the same boat and with the same menu, just as good – even the price was still reasonable. A few days later, we ordered mixed grilled fish in a restaurant, and thought them a little flabby, though well cooked. I am still puzzled by a note at the foot of the menu which informed us that, "for the sake of hygiene," all the fish had been frozen. Perhaps there are no more fish in the lake, and these had been farmed, in Romania or Tanzania; perhaps the restaurant had taken to buying fish in bulk and storing it, to keep costs down. At least they were honest with us, and I would certainly rather have good frozen fish than be poisoned. Whenever we go to Venice, I take care to spend an hour or two in the Rialto markets, unrivalled for fresh produce and especially for fish. Even in our camping days, I bought fresh fish there and cooked it outside our tent in the evening, drawing interested and I think rather envious looks from passers-by. The only fish market I know in England to compare it with is the new Billingsgate, but that is a much more commercial operation; the Rialto is for everyone, in the city center where it has been for many centuries, and every fish is tagged and named, with the sea area in which it was caught and, of course, whether it is fresh or has been frozen and thawed out for immediate use.

Now – another thing Italians are famous for, of course, is ice cream …

Right: Italian ice cream displayed for sale in a shop, or *gelateria,* in Siena, Italy.

es krim adpokat
avocado ice cream

The avocado was brought to Indonesia from South America in the eighteenth century, but avocados have never become popular favorites there. People with enough space in their gardens grow these handsome trees as ornaments and for shade. In my childhood, one stood in the garden of my parents' house, and my mother had acquired the Dutch habit of mashing up the fruit with condensed milk as a dessert. Fortunately, we didn't have to eat this very often; I found the sickly sweetness of it quite revolting, and avoided avocados altogether for many years afterwards. When I came to Europe, however, I tasted guacamole and realized that there were possibilities; I began experimenting with avocado ice cream. Time passed, and I became acquainted with Myrtle Allen of the celebrated Ballymaloe House hotel in Ireland's County Cork. When her daughter-in-law Darina invited me to teach a short course on Southeast Asian cooking at Ballymaloe Cookery School, I proposed, as one of my recipes, avocado ice cream made with coconut milk, to which Darina responded with enthusiasm, but pointed out that the Irish are accustomed to an abundance of their excellent cream. She suggested that we make my ice cream both ways. Both were well received, but I think most of them preferred the dairy cream version. It just shows that what you're used to in childhood you cherish all your life. Anyway, I still love my fresh coconut milk ice cream -- and I have never overcome my suspicion of condensed milk.

2½ c thick coconut milk
   and a pinch of salt, or 1¼ heavy
   cream mixed with 1¼ c milk
4 small ripe avocados, each weighing
   about 6 oz
8 tbsp freshly squeezed lime or

lemon juice
10 level tbsp confectioners' sugar

Serves 4–6

In a heavy pan, gently heat the coconut milk with a pinch of salt, or the heavy cream and milk, until it is at simmering point. Transfer to a bowl to cool.

   Halve, stone, and peel the avocados. Chop the flesh and mix with the lime or lemon juice in a glass bowl.

Left: Two ice creams: the green is *es krim adpokat* -- avocado, and the white is *es krim duren* -- durian (recipe on p.93).

When the coconut milk or cream-and-milk mixture is cold, pour into a blender, then add the avocado and confectioners' sugar. Blend until smooth and creamy. Transfer the mixture to a sorbetière or ice cream maker. Churn according to the manufacturer's instructions until the bits that cling to the side of the container are frozen. Scoop into a freezerproof plastic container, and put in the freezer. Keep frozen until required. Transfer to the refrigerator 45 minutes before serving; this allows the ice cream to soften a little so that it can be scooped easily and neatly served.

es krim ketan hitam
black sticky rice ice cream

The three most hectic and exhausting, but in many ways most rewarding, years of my life were those when I ran my Indonesian delicatessen in Wimbledon Village High Street. I cooked not only for the shop, but also for dinner parties in my dining room above it. This ice cream was much in demand for those parties, and I would have offered it to Harrods if I had had the equipment to produce it in large quantities. After three years, I decided the shop had achieved its prime purpose of making Indonesian food better known in London, and I returned to traveling and writing. In 1995, Ceretto, a family firm of winemakers in north-west Italy, picked *Indonesian Regional Food and Cookery* as one of its recipe books of the year. Roger and I were invited to the gala presentation dinner, which would be attended by sixty people. I was only slightly anxious about the fact that I would be the principal cook; more worrying was the fact that my dinner would follow one on the previous evening cooked by the celebrated Signora Lidia, who presided over the kitchen of Ristorante da Guido in Costigliole d'Alba. Roger and I drove to Alba with a carload of supplies, and returned a week or so later laden with fine wines. Both dinners were a success, and my gamble of serving black rice ice cream to the world's acknowledged ice cream masters had paid off. The Italians loved it. I admit, though, that I did not try to make ice cream for sixty; one of the Ceretto staff contacted a professional ice cream maker, and I simply gave him my black sticky rice porridge made to the following recipe.

3½ oz black sticky rice
1 oz plus 2 tbsp white sticky rice
6 c fresh coconut milk or 3 x 14 fl oz
   cans coconut milk plus 1 c water
½ tsp salt
1 small cinnamon stick

3 tbsp grated *gula jawa* (palm sugar)
   (see p.276) or granulated sugar
2 tbsp liquid glucose or light corn syrup
2 c heavy cream

Makes 10–12 generous helpings

Combine the black sticky rice and white sticky rice in a bowl. Cover well with cold water and leave to soak for 4–8 hours. Drain.

Put the drained rice and all the remaining ingredients except the glucose or light corn syrup and heavy cream in a heavy saucepan. Slowly bring to a boil, and continue boiling slowly until the rice grains are soft and stick together to make a mass of dark purple porridge. This will take about 1 hour 35 minutes, or perhaps a little longer. Leave the porridge to cool completely.

To make the ice cream, add the liquid glucose or light corn syrup and heavy cream to the porridge. Mix well, then put the mixture in a blender or food processor. Blend until smooth, then churn in a sorbetière or an ice cream maker according to the manufacturer's instructions until the bits that cling to the sides of the machine are frozen. Scoop the ice cream into a freezerproof plastic container and freeze until required. Transfer the ice cream to the refrigerator 1 hour before serving to soften.

es krim jambu klutuk dengan keju dan cabai
ricotta, guava, and chili ice cream

This recipe first appeared in *Cool Green Leaves and Red Hot Peppers* (1998), by Christine McFadden and Michael Michaud, I have borrowed Christine's recipe with her permission. Two of the ingredients in particular made me want it: ricotta, the celebrated Italian cheese, and guavas, my favorite fruit since I was a child. In Indonesia we call them *jambu klutuk* – alas, they are not too easy to get in London, and if you do find them they are almost always white. Canned guavas, however, are obtainable in Aisan shops and good supermarkets, and are almost always pink. They taste good and make good ice cream as long as you drain off and discard the syrup. Christine uses the Habañero chili, a variety I don't think is generally known or cultivated in Indonesia. Knowledgeable Indonesians would probably just call it "a chili from Mexico," and would no doubt approve of it. I'm borrowing also Christine's description of this ice cream, as I find it very intriguing. Here's what she says:

This is a schizophrenic combination of cold, hard guava ice cream spiked with habañero chili — one of the hottest varieties of all. The taste experience is sensational — the initial chill in the mouth is combined with the heady fragrance of guava and followed, seconds later, by a subtle slow burn.

Ricotta cheese is great for making ice cream. It saves making an egg-based custard, and, mixed with a little cream or yogurt, gives a relatively smooth and creamy result.

5 oz granulated or superfine sugar
1 Habañero chili, seeded
4 guavas, about 1¾ lb in total
strained juice of 2 freshly squeezed limes
9 oz ricotta cheese

6 tbsp heavy cream or
  Greek-style yogurt

Makes about 4 cups

Put the sugar and 1 cup water in a small saucepan with the chili. Stir over low heat until the sugar has dissolved, then boil for 5–7 minutes until the bubbles look syrupy. Leave to cool, then fish out the chili.

Quarter the guavas, peel and cut into chunks. Purée in a food processor or blender with the lime juice and the cooled syrup. Push the mixture through a sieve to get rid of the seeds.

In a large bowl, beat together the ricotta and cream or yogurt until very smooth. Mix in the guava purée, whisking well. Freeze in an ice cream maker, according to the manufacturer's instructions. Alternatively, pour the mixture into a shallow freezerproof container, cover with cling wrap and freeze for about 2 hours or until beginning to harden around the edges. Put into a bowl, whisk until smooth, then freeze again until firm. About 30 minutes before you are ready to serve, transfer the ice cream to the refrigerator to soften a little and make it easier to scoop.

Right: Two ice creams: the purple is *es krim ketan hitam* — black sticky rice (recipe on p.88), and the pink is *es krim jambu klutuk dengan keju dan cabai* — ricotta, guava, and chili (recipe on p.89).

es krim jeruk purut
kaffir lime ice cream

Another borrowed recipe, this time from Celia Brooks-Brown's book *Entertaining Vegetarians* (2003). Not only the juice and zest of limes, but also the shredded leaves of the kaffir lime tree combine to give it a wonderfully fresh and aromatic sourness, and I am sure that you will follow my example and make it often because every guest who tastes it will want more, drawn by its exquisite aroma and flavor.

There is one tiny problem. Although you should be able to find kaffir lime leaves in good Asian, especially Thai, food stores, the health inspector occasionally pounces on them and refuses to issue an import licence. This is because small insects have stowed away among the leaves (though they are presumably dead by the time they reach their destination). If for this or any other reason you cannot get the leaves, kaffir limes themselves (see p.277) are almost always available. The juice and zest from one of these will pretty much make up for the absence of shredded leaf (roll the kaffir lime under the palm of your hand to soften slightly and make juicing easier). The seven "ordinary" limes that appear in the list of ingredients are there to give the citrusy flavor that mingles so well with the cream.

2½ c heavy cream
2½ c whole milk
8 oz superfine sugar
6 kaffir lime leaves, finely shredded

grated zest and juice from 7 limes
("ordinary" green limes, not the knobbly skinned kaffir variety)

Makes 8 generous helpings

In a large glass bowl, mix the cream, milk, and 6 ounces of the sugar. Stir until the sugar has dissolved. Transfer the mixture to a freezerproof plastic container with a lid, and put it in the freezer. Leave it there for 2 hours.

In a small bowl, mix the lime juice, shredded kaffir lime leaves, and the remaining 2 ounces sugar. Stir until the sugar has dissolved, put this in a small freezerproof plastic container with a lid and keep in the freezer for 2 hours.

After 2 hours, bring out both the plastic containers from the freezer. Pour their contents into a large glass bowl, and with a large metal spoon, vigorously mix these already frosty fluids until they all blend evenly together. Pour the mixture into one or two plastic containers suitable for ice cream and freeze until required. Transfer to the refrigerator about 45 minutes before serving to soften slightly.

es krim duren
durian ice cream

Most of my readers will know about durian, and may well be enthusiasts. In that case, they will probably regard complaints about the smell as trivial, and writers' attempts to excuse it as irritating. (In fairness to hotels, airlines etc. which won't allow it on their premises, the smell can become rather overpowering in a confined space.) I have to say that my husband, Roger, is a little unusual in that he actually likes the smell, but doesn't like the texture of durian pulp. Perhaps it's not surprising that this is his absolute favorite ice cream, though our two sons continue to hold their noses. For us tropic-dwellers who tasted our first durian at the age of about three, this is, simply, the king of all fruits. For seventeen long years, from my first arrival in Europe until our first return trip to Indonesia, I don't think I got so much as a smell of one. Every visit we make to Southeast Asia now has to be carefully synchronized with the expected durian season, which is often unpredictable and short. You can imagine that I was very excited, some twenty years ago, when I managed to find a whole durian in my favorite Thai food shop in the Upper Richmond Road in Putney, and could afford to pay too much for it. Even I couldn't finish the whole durian in the few days before it faded, so I made it into ice cream. Roger took to it at once. One advantage of durians from Bangkok is that, by and large, they have fairly small seeds and, by any standards, excellent flavor and aroma.

Some years ago, I was invited to attend a weekend devoted to theatrical shows, lectures, discussions, and several good dinners, all on the theme of "food in performance." The organizers asked if I would like to bring one or two exotic things along for people to taste, so I made *lemper* (pp.134–5), which went down very well, and three quarts of durian ice cream. That was the most I could make at short notice, and

Below: Durian on sale in Chiang Mai.

anyway I didn't know if people would love it or hate it. There were more attendees than I had expected, and they each got about an egg-cupful. Wild enthusiasm, and anguished requests for more. Well, here at least is the recipe. It's very simple.

4 durian seeds with the custardy creamy
   pulp (see above and p.276)
2½ c heavy cream

¼ c whole milk
1 tbsp confectioners' sugar

Makes 4 cups

Remove and discard the durian seeds. Purée all the flesh and the other ingredients in a blender until you have a runny custard. Pour the mixture into a sorbetière or ice cream maker and churn according to the manufacturer's instructions until it starts to freeze on the sides of the machine. Transfer to a freezerproof container, and keep in the freezer until required – but remember to put the container of ice cream in the refrigerator 40–60 minutes before serving to allow it to soften slightly.

es krim kelapa muda
coconut ice cream

This was the ice cream I most enjoyed when I was a student. To start with, anything frozen is always a bit suspect in hot countries: you need to be confident that it was hygienically made. Yogya in the 1950s had just one reliable ice cream shop, selling a good range of its own products. The best coconut ice cream was, and is, *es krim kopyor*. This is made from coconuts which, for some reason still not fully understood, turn out to be filled not with a layer of firm white flesh and a quantity of liquid, but with a mass of soft, filmy flesh that has a most delicious flavor. These *kelapa kopyor* cannot be recognized until the shell is opened, so in a sense every coconut is a bit of a lottery, though I have never heard of anyone finding one in a Western shop. Many coconut trees never produce a *kopyor* nut. There is said to be a new variety that yields 80 percent of its nuts as *kopyor*, but I will believe this when I see it.

Alas, there is no prospect of *es krim kopyor* being available just yet in North America. The recipe I give here, however, produces very good results. All the other ice cream recipes in this section are ones I borrowed, or developed myself, because they use Indonesian ingredients. This is the only one based on an original recipe that I found in Yogyakarta. Ideally, to make it you need *kelapa muda*, young green coconuts with flesh that is still soft and almost completely white. In the West, the best available young coconut flesh is to be found in Chinese or Thai supermarket freezers. Use this when making this coconut ice cream, and make the coconut milk from freshly grated mature coconut flesh (see p.115) or from shredded coconut (see p.116). If only canned coconut milk is available, by all means use that: the result will still be good, though not quite as good. One important thing to remember when using coconut milk, even in sweet dishes, is that you need to add a large pinch of salt (sometimes more). This enhances the creamy taste of the coconut.

4¾ c freshly made thick coconut milk
    (made from 7 oz shredded coconut;
    see p.116)
6 oz superfiine sugar

6 oz frozen young coconut flesh,
    thawed, then finely chopped
½ tsp salt

Makes 8 generous helpings

Heat the coconut milk to simmering point, then add the sugar, young coconut flesh, and salt. Stir until the sugar has dissolved, then remove from the heat and leave to cool completely.

Put the mixture in a blender and purée until smooth. Transfer to a sorbetière or ice cream maker, and churn according to the manufacturer's instructions until the bits on the edges of the machine have frozen. Transfer the mixture to a freezerproof container and store in the freezer until needed. Alternatively, for those who don't have an ice cream maker, pour the mixture into one or two freezerproof plastic containers with lids, and put in the freezer for 2 hours. Take out, and stir the contents thoroughly with a large metal spoon to break up any large ice crystals, then return to the freezer until needed.

Whichever method you use, remember to put the ice cream in the refrigerator 45 minutes to an hour before serving, so that it softens a little.

MODERNIZED RECIPES

The following recipes are my attempt to re-create or to "modernize" the cooking of Central Java in the 1950s.

pergedel kepiting dengan daun limau purut
aromatic crab cakes

My fondest recollection of eating crab was of my father's hot chili crab. He was a very good cook, taking after his mother. As I've said so much about her cooking, I should not forget that of her son. While I was still living with my parents, my father used to bring home live crabs from the market. Men of my parents' generation were not expected to even enter the kitchen, let alone cook. But my father had always been fascinated by food, and my grandmother let him cook, out of doors, while we lived in Padang Panjang. As in many countries nowadays, outdoor barbecuing seemed to be the prerogative of men — my father was allowed to supervise the spit-roasting of a whole goat, and any other outdoor work, such as tending *lemang*, sticky rice cooked in bamboo tubes. His crab repertoire was not large; having killed and dismembered his crab, he would expertly pick out the white meat and pass it to my mother, who would make crabmeat scrambled with eggs, and crabmeat fritters.

Before I give you the recipe that I have developed from those basic fritters, I would like to continue with a word or two on the subject of buying crabs. Unfortunately, in the west, unless you live in coastal towns, it is difficult to get really good live crabs. If you have a very good fish dealer near your home, you may sometimes be lucky. You can get dressed crabs easily enough from speciality delis, but for this recipe you don't need dressed crab, only the best white crabmeat. The best crab I have ever tasted (apart from my father's chili crab) was a Dungeness crab we had at a friend's house in Portland, Oregon. And honorable mention must go to the chili crab we had at the Courtyard Restaurant in Singapore's Raffles Hotel. I fear I have not inherited my father's talent for cracking shells and extracting the meat. I now buy crabmeat fresh from my local fish dealer.

16–20 oz fresh or frozen crabmeat,
  white meat only, or white and brown
  meat from 2 good-sized live crabs to
  make the same weight
8 oz peeled new or waxy potatoes,
  boiled until tender,
  then mashed and a large pinch
  of salt added
3 tbsp finely chopped spring onions
3 tbsp finely chopped fresh
  flat-leaf parsley
2 tbsp finely chopped kaffir lime leaves
1 tbsp finely chopped lemongrass,
  inner part only

1 tsp finely chopped fresh ginger
½ tsp ground turmeric
1 tsp (or less) chili flakes
1 tsp ground coriander
1 tsp baking powder
1 tbsp rice flour or all-purpose flour
½ tsp sugar
½ tsp freshly ground black pepper
1 egg, lightly beaten
about ½ c peanut or olive oil for frying

*Serves 4 as an appetizer (makes 12
small or 20 smaller crab cakes)*

Mix together all the ingredients for the crab cakes, except the egg and oil. When they are all blended by hand or with a fork, add the lightly beaten egg and mix this into the crab mixture. Check the seasoning, in case you need to add a little more salt and pepper. Divide the paste into 12 or 20 portions, mold each portion into a ball, and chill for 30 minutes.

Heat the oil in a large non-stick frying pan until hot. Flatten each crab ball to make a round flat cake. Cooking in batches of 6–8 crab cakes at a time, fry on one side for 2 minutes, then turn over and fry on the other side for 2 minutes or a little less. Remove using a slotted spoon, and drain on paper towels.

To serve, arrange three or five crab cakes on each serving plate, and decorate with a handful of mixed salad dressed with your favorite piquant dressing.

terung isi
stuffed eggplant

In previous books I have published several recipes for stuffed eggplant, made with three or four different varieties. Indonesians, and our neighbors from other parts of Southeast Asia, love the small round ones which in English are often called "apple eggplants" (see p.276). These are often available from Thai or other Asian food shops. They have an intriguing bitterness and, even when stuffed and steamed, they can still be quite hard to bite. Roger has never really taken to them, though the conventional purple eggplants are his favorite vegetable. Other friends have told me that they prefer to use my stuffings in the eggplants to which they're accustomed. So here is my new recipe, for purple eggplant stuffed with red and yellow peppers, anchovies, and flat-leaf parsley. They look pretty and taste delicious. If you leave out the anchovies, or replace them with black olives or capers, this dish becomes a very tasty main course for vegetarians, served with vegetarian fried rice or fried noodles.

4 purple eggplants, washed and dried
2 red peppers, washed and dried
2 yellow peppers, washed and dried
1 tbsp virgin olive oil
4–6 anchovy filets in oil, drained and chopped

2 tbsp finely chopped fresh flat-leaf parsley
2 tsp freshly squeezed lime or lemon juice
salt and freshly ground black pepper

Serves 6–8 as a vegetable dish

Preheat the oven to 350°F (180°C). Brush the whole eggplants and peppers with the oil. Put on a baking tray, and bake in the oven for 35–40 minutes.

Allow to cool a little, then cut the eggplants in half lengthwise. Carefully scoop out the flesh without damaging the skins. Put the flesh on a chopping board, and slice it lengthwise into thin strips. Cut the peppers in halves, too, but do this over a large bowl, so that the juices from the peppers are saved. The seeds need to be removed; if some of them get into the cooking juice, strain the juice into another bowl. Discard the pepper skins, and cut the peeled peppers into long strips, similar to the eggplant strips. Arrange the strips of eggplant and pepper in the skins of the roasted eggplants, using, as near as possible, the same amount of each of the different colored strips.

Put the rest of the ingredients in the bowl with the reserved juices from the peppers. Mix well, and check the seasoning. Add more freshly ground pepper, salt, and lime or lemon juice if necessary. Pour the dressing onto the stuffed eggplants, which can now be served warm or cold. If you want to serve them hot, put them back into the oven to warm up, but for only about 5 minutes.

udang besar istimewa
special jumbo shrimp, stuffed and poached

As this is where I'm bringing together my newest recipes, I've chosen for this dish the tastiest (and easiest) way of combining the ingredients for the marinade. Once the shrimp are stuffed with minced small shrimp, they are poached in a sauce of your choice: try the *sambal goreng* on pp.172–3 or the *kalio* sauce used for Beef Rendang (see pp.178–80). You will need enough jumbo shrimp to serve each person two as an appetizer or three or four as a fish course accompanied by salad and/or grilled polenta.

4 tbsp olive oil

for the marinade
2 tbsp virgin olive oil
5 garlic cloves, crushed
½ tsp *sambal ulek* (see p.279)
   or chili powder

1 tbsp tamarind water (see pp.118–19)
   or freshly squeezed lime juice
½ tsp salt

*Serves 4 as an appetizer or main course
(enough for 8–12 jumbo shrimp)*

Mix together all the marinade ingredients in a glass or ceramic bowl. Prepare the jumbo shrimp as follows: remove and discard the heads, then the legs. Devein the shrimp. With a sharp, pointed knife, slit the underneath of each shrimp lengthwise, turn it over and, with your hand, press the back of the shrimp to make it lie flat. Dry the shrimp with paper towels, and put in the bowl with the marinade. Mix well, and leave to marinate in the refrigerator for at least 2 hours.

for the stuffing
14–16 oz peeled and deveined small
   shrimp (usually sold from the freezer of
   any Thai or Chinese supermarket),
   thawed completely, rinsed and minced

4 garlic cloves, crushed
1 tbsp light soy sauce
½ tsp chlli powder
2 tbsp finely chopped fresh flat-leaf parsley
1 tbsp finely chopped fresh chives
1 egg, lightly beaten

In a bowl, mix together all the ingredients for the stuffing, except the egg. Knead for a minute or so with your hand, then add the lightly beaten egg and, using a large metal spoon, mix this in well also.

Now start filling the marinated shrimp with the stuffing. Push and spread the stuffing well into the cut sides of the shrimp. Arrange them on a plate in a single layer, cover with cling wrap and chill for an hour.

When the shrimp are ready for cooking, heat the olive oil in a non-stick frying pan. Fry the stuffed shrimp, four at a time, for 1 minute only, turning them once. Remove from the heat and drain on paper towels.

When you are ready to serve the shrimp, assuming you have your sauce ready in a saucepan, heat this to boiling point. Poach the shrimp, four at a time, in the sauce for 2 minutes. Remove after 2 minutes using a slotted spoon, and put on a plate. Continue poaching the rest of the shrimp in this way. Just before serving, heat the remaining sauce, adjust the seasoning and carefully put the shrimp into the hot sauce. Turn them around once with a slotted spoon, then immediately remove the pan from the heat. Serve the shrimp hot as suggested above.

Note: If you find it's tricky to stuff the shrimp, make the stuffing into dumplings, and fry and poach these as for the shrimp. Serve together with the sauce.

ayam panggang asam pedas
marinated and roasted chicken

Asam means "sour"; *pedas* is "chili-hot." The marinade for this chicken is certainly quite hot, but the resulting roast-chicken taste will be just nicely piquant, with a slight sweetness and sourness. The marinade is what we called *sambal rujak*, which is sometimes mistakenly called *bumbu rujak*. These are actually two very different things. *Bumbu rujak* is similar to *bumbu sambal goreng* (Sambal Goreng paste, see p.172), with a few additional ingredients – tomatoes, for example. Like *sambal goreng*, it can be cooked with or without coconut milk, as preferred. The recipe that follows on p.107 is for Duck Roasted in Bumbu Rujak. *Sambal rujak*, on the other hand, is a relish used as a piquant dressing for half-ripe fruit. Fruit dressed this way is called *rujak*, a fruit salad with a chili-hot dressing. When *sambal rujak* is used to marinate a chicken, the chicken should really be boned (i.e. the bones should be removed). I buy my free-range chickens from my friend

Anne Petch, who owns and runs Heal Farm in Devon. Whenever I ask her to bone my chicken, she does it beautifully because she herself uses a lot of boned chickens that she stuffs in various ways and sells as "three-bird roasts" or "five-bird roasts." These are deservedly popular at any time of year, but especially at Christmas time. But back to business -- you can, if you prefer, marinate the chicken without boning it. In traditional Indonesian cooking, I don't recall that we boned our chickens. If you do take out the bones, then you will need two extra skinless chicken breast filets.

1 chicken, boned or not boned
2 skinless chicken breast filets (if you are
   using boned chicken)
2 green cooking apples, peeled, cored,
   and diced

for the marinade
1 tbsp *kecap manis* (see p.277) or other
   dark soy sauce
2–4 fresh bird's-eye chilies,
   finely chopped (optional)

1 tsp *sambal ulek* (see p.279)
   or ½ tsp chili powder
1 tsp crumbled shrimp paste (see p.279)
1 tbsp grated or chopped *gula jawa*
   (palm sugar) (see p.276) or 1 tbsp
   demerara or muscovado sugar
3 tbsp tamarind water (see pp.118–19)
   or freshly squeezed lime juice
½ tsp salt

Serves 4–6

Preheat the oven to 300°F (180°C).

In a bowl, mix the ingredients for the marinade together well. If using boned chicken, lay it flat on a baking dish, with the two breasts in the middle. Scatter the apple cubes on top. Rub the marinade all over the chicken, on the extra breasts and apple, and under the skin. Tie or sew the chicken back together with string, to make it look like a whole chicken. Rub the remaining marinade all over the outside. If using a whole chicken with bones, rub the marinade all over the outside and inside of the chicken. Put the apple in the cavity of the chicken, and wrap the chicken loosely in foil. Roast in the oven for 50–60 minutes. Open up the parcel, increase the temperature to 400°F (200°C), and continue roasting the chicken for another 15 minutes or until browned or even slightly charred on top.

Serve hot or cold, carved into thin slices, as a main course accompanied by roast potatoes or boiled new potatoes, or steamed rice. Vegetables with a coconut dressing such as *gudangan* (pp.194–5) will go well with this dish.

tahu dan tiram berkuah
mild curry of tofu and scallops

The Javanese use the name *tiram* to refer to almost any shellfish with a hard shell. Alan Davidson, in his *Seafood of Southeast Asia*, says that the Indonesian name for oyster is *tiram*. In fact, in the Indonesian language, *tiram* can also mean "mussel," "cockle," or "scallop." Here, I'm using it to mean "scallop." Tofu and scallops go beautifully together, the different soft textures mingling as they do in this special curry sauce that I have developed for this book. There is certainly nothing traditionally Indonesian in this recipe, which evolved during my study of other cuisines. It is lovely as an appetizer, or as an accompaniment to Coconut Rice (p.131) or mashed potatoes.

14–16 oz Chinese-style tofu or firm long-life Japanese tofu, cut into small squares no larger than the scallops (or scallop halves, as appropriate)
½ c hot water or fish stock
½ c coconut milk or light cream or Greek-style yogurt
1 lb fresh scallops without their shells (leave whole if small, but cut in half if using large scallops)

to marinate the tofu
½ c hot water
2 tsp finely chopped lemongrass, soft inner part only
2 kaffir lime leaves or lemon leaves, finely shredded
½ tsp chili powder
½ tsp salt

for the bumbu (paste)
3 shallots or 1 small onion, chopped
2 garlic cloves
2 in piece of fresh ginger, peeled and sliced
3 large fresh red chilies, seeded and chopped
1 tsp *terasi* (shrimp paste) (optional)
2 candlenuts or macadamia nuts, chopped (optional)
1 tsp ground coriander
1 tsp paprika
½ tsp ground turmeric
½ tsp salt, or more to taste
1 tbsp freshly squeezed lime juice
2 tbsp olive or peanut oil

Serves 6 as an appetizer, or 3–4 as an accompaniment to rice or potatoes

Combine the ingredients for marinating the tofu in a bowl. Add the pieces of tofu, and marinate for 1–2 hours. Drain the tofu, and set aside. Reserve the marinade.

Put all the ingredients for the *bumbu*, or paste, in a blender or food processor. Add 2 tablespoons cold water, and blend until smooth. Heat a heavy saucepan over medium-high heat, add the paste and fry for 4 minutes, stirring continuously, until fragrant – take care not to burn the paste. Add the reserved tofu marinade, including the solids. Add the ½ cup hot water (or fish stock if you have some handy). Bring the mixture to a boil, reduce the heat, and simmer gently for 20 minutes. Add the coconut milk or cream or yogurt. Simmer, stirring, for 2 more minutes. Check the seasoning, adding a little more salt or lime juice if needed. Up to this point, the sauce can be made up to 24 hours in advance and kept in the refrigerator until needed (but it cannot be frozen).

When you are ready to serve, bring the sauce to a rolling boil, stir and put in the reserved tofu. Continue to simmer for 4–5 minutes, then stir in the scallops and remove the pan from the heat. Leave the pan covered for 1 minute before transferring the contents to a serving bowl. Serve hot, as suggested in the introduction.

panggang bebek bumbu rujak
duck roasted in bumbu rujak

This recipe could equally well have been placed in the section that describes boiled dishes, or perhaps in the section that deals with grilling. As it is meant as an extra recipe to show the difference between *bumbu rujak* and *sambal rujak* (see also the introduction to Marinated and Roasted Chicken on p.102), I have put it here. This is another recipe that is popular in West and Central Java.

1 duck, about 3–4 lb, halved lengthwise
3 tbsp peanut or coconut oil,
   to fry the paste
4½ c coconut milk

for the bumbu (paste)
10 candlenuts or macadamia nuts,
   chopped
6 shallots, chopped
6 garlic cloves, chopped
2 tsp chopped galangal

2 tsp chopped lemongrass, soft inner
   part only
4–6 large fresh red chilies, seeded and
   chopped
1 tsp crumbled *terasi* (shrimp paste)
2 tbsp tamarind water (see pp.118–19)
1 tsp soft brown sugar
2 tsp salt

Serves 2 or 4

Wash the duck halves. Cut off and discard any loose skin, and remove excess bones and any excess fat. Pat the duck dry with paper towels.

Put all the ingredients for the *bumbu*, or paste, in a blender, and blend until smooth. Heat the peanut or coconut oil in a saucepan, and stir-fry the paste in it for 4 minutes. Add the coconut milk, bring to a boil, and add the duck halves. Stir to coat the duck all over with the paste and coconut milk. Cover the pan, and cook the duck over medium heat for 45 minutes. Remove the lid from the pan, increase the heat, and continue cooking the duck until the sauce becomes very thick. Check the seasoning, adding more salt if necessary. Up to this point, this can be prepared well in advance. Take out the duck and keep to one side on a plate. Transfer what remains in the pan of the very thick sauce to a bowl.

When you are ready to serve, grill the duck halves, preferably over charcoal, but otherwise under a grill on the highest possible setting, for 3–4 minutes on one

Left: Well-drilled ducks line up to go home after a day foraging among the rice stubble in Bali.

side. Turn over and grill the other side while brushing the reserved sauce onto the duck. Grill for another 4 minutes until quite brown or even just a little charred, but not burned. Serve hot with rice, pasta or potatoes, and cooked vegetables or salads.

panggang bebek dengan kuah bayem
thirty-minute duck breast with spinach sauce

In the recipe for *bebek betutu* on pp.228–9, I describe a traditional Balinese way of cooking a duck. This is my adaptation of it. Cooking the duck breast this way will result in a nice crisp skin and very tender, slightly pink slices of duck. Slice the meat after cooking, and serve right away with some green salad. This duck is equally good with rice, pasta, or potatoes. Making the accompanying spinach sauce is simple – you simply add a little water and some fresh spinach leaves to the marinade.

4 duck breasts
1 quantity *bumbu* (paste) as for Bebek
    Betutu (Traditional Slow-cooked
    Balinese Duck, pp.228–9)

2 oz fresh spinach leaves, rinsed,
    drained and shredded

Serves 4

In a heavy saucepan over medium heat, fry the *bumbu* (paste) for 6–8 minutes, stirring often, until fragrant. Transfer to a glass bowl and let cool.

When the paste is completely cold, make two incisions in the skin of each duck breast. Add the duck breasts to the marinade, stirring well so that each breast is well coated. Leave to marinate in the refrigerator for at least 4 hours, or overnight.

When you are ready to eat, preheat the oven to 400°F (200°C). Drain off and reserve the marinade. Put the duck breasts, skin-side up, on a rack in a roasting pan. Half-fill the pan with hot water (do not allow the water to touch the duck), and roast in the oven for 20–25 minutes.

To make the spinach sauce, put the spinach, ¼ cup water and the reserved marinade in a saucepan. Cook gently for 3 minutes. Serve immediately, as suggested above.

Chapter Four:
Staples and Basics

COCONUT

Some of our most important food plants — rice and bananas are good examples — are the result of centuries of patient selection and breeding by our forebearers. Coconuts, on the other hand, seem to have been given to us ready-made. Their origin is still a bit of a mystery. The first coconut palm must have evolved somewhere, but where? Botanists now think that it was on the coast of southern or southeastern Asia, and that the species established itself quite quickly through a simple competitive advantage: coconuts float in salt water, and can still take root and flourish when they are washed ashore, many months later and perhaps hundreds of miles away. There is only one genus and species, *Cocos nucifera*, though humankind has bred many varieties by selecting for better resistance to disease, different proportions of coconut water to soft or hard flesh, and other qualities. One distinctive form is the Malayan Dwarf — short trees make harvesting easier.

Coconut is reckoned to be one of the world's two most popular flavors — the other, of course, being chocolate. For most Indonesians, chocolate is a luxury, but coconuts are an absolute daily necessity. In a well-tended landscape of rice fields, the villages are marked by the coconut groves that shade them, the palms overreaching every building except perhaps the minaret of the village mosque. On deserted sandy beaches, they lean seawards and provide shade from the tropical sun. Few or none of these trees are "wild" in the sense that nobody owns them, though the shoreline palms may be self-sown: only the sea, or humans, can carry nuts to a new location where they can germinate. Inland, coconut palms are always cultivated and cared for. As every tree bears multiple flowers each month, and each nut takes about ten months to become ready for picking, a coconut palm is a storehouse of present and future wealth for its owner, wealth that requires some skill and nimbleness to obtain. Many palms are 80–100 feet high, and you cannot just wait for nuts to drop off; by the time they do that, they are too old to be worth much. You can climb the tree yourself, or you can pay a professional to do it for you — either a man with a sharp, heavy knife, or, in some areas, a well-trained good-natured pig-tailed macaque.

Every part of a coconut can be used for something. Its fibrous outer covering, called *sabut* in Indonesia, is used to make brushes, mats or ropes, or to scrub the bottoms of pans

Page 110: Stems of lemon grass, some with ends cut for use as lemon grass brushes.
Right: Fresh coconuts split open.

and woks. The only other use of the fiber that I have heard about, though not witnessed, is for smoking meat and fish, which is done in the Philippines with the fiber of young coconut. There are also Philippine recipes that specify smoked coconut milk, made by burning older nuts still in their shells; this gives the flesh, and the milk extracted from it, a smoky taste. The *tempurung*, the hard brown inner shell of the coconut, with all the fiber removed, can be cut in half to provide two useful bowls, and you can add handles to make ladles or other simple kitchen utensils. Young coconuts are picked mainly for their water, which is used in drinks and in cooking (see *ayam goreng kalasan*, pp.65–6), and for their very tender flesh, which is scraped out and mixed with the water for drinks, can be made into ice cream or is sometimes used as an ingredient in soups. Until recently, young coconuts were almost never available in northern Europe because they are large and heavy, making the cost of transporting them by air prohibitive.

Anyone who goes food shopping in an Indonesian market will find coconuts in abundance, at different stages of development, each suitable for whatever purpose the cook has in mind. Young green coconuts, the ones we call *kelapa muda*, we buy not so much to cook with as to drink the clear sweet coconut water and to eat the tender young flesh. Coconuts that are a little more mature are *kelapa setengah tua*, "middle-aged": the outer skin is getting somewhat brown, but the flesh is still quite soft and not fibrous or gritty on the tongue, and it can be easily grated using a hand grater. It is used to coat different kinds of rice flour cakes, such as *klepon* (see pp.33–4), is served with *pisang goreng* (p.26), and is an ingredient of *sambal kelapa* (p.175).

The next stage is *kelapa tua*, old coconut. In the West, these have long been available in supermarkets and elsewhere. They are still the best source of good coconut milk – *santen*, as we call it. To break open the nut, wrap it in an old plastic shopping bag and hit it, all over and from every angle, with a blunt instrument: the back of a Chinese meat cleaver is ideal. If you start by robustly tapping it, there is a fair chance you will loosen the bond between the shell and the flesh or kernel without cracking the latter; the kernel will then emerge unbroken, which makes it a lot easier to peel off the brown rind. Usually, though, the whole nut gives way and cracks open, any water inside runs out (another reason to use a plastic bag), and you have to prize the flesh from the outer shell with a short, flexible, and (preferably) blunt knife.

If you are going to use the grated coconut as a garnish for sweet cakes or *pisang goreng* (fried bananas), or to make ice cream or a *sambal kelapa* (coconut relish), you must now remove the brown outer skin or rind from the white flesh with a potato peeler or a sharp knife. If you are using grated coconut to make *santen* (coconut milk), however, you don't need to discard this brown rind because the color will not affect the finished dish. So, for a savory meat dish such as *rendang* (see pp. 178–81), you can skip the peeling. If your sole aim is to make coconut oil, likewise, don't peel; however, for puddings, cakes, or ice cream, pure white flesh is essential.

Making and storing coconut milk

The small pieces of coconut flesh can be grated by hand or in a food processor. For 12 ounces coconut, you will need about 2½ cups fairly hot water to make coconut milk. (This must be boiled water that has been left to cool a little; not water from the hot tap.) Process or blend for a few seconds, or leave to soak for 2–3 minutes, then put the wet coconut into a sieve over a large bowl. Squeeze a handful at a time to force out the "first extraction," or thick coconut milk, and let it pass through the sieve into the bowl. Put the squeezed grated coconut back into the blender to be processed again to make the "second extraction" of the coconut milk, which is the thin coconut milk. By mixing the two, you get what I call the "standard' coconut milk that I usually use for my recipes. If a recipe calls for either of the extractions to be used separately, then obviously you don't mix them.

The milk will keep in the refrigerator for not more than 48 hours. During this time, a thick "cream" may come to the top; this can simply be stirred back into the liquid.

Coconut milk by itself cannot be frozen, but most dishes that are cooked with it can be. With *rendang* and *kalio* (pp. 178–81), there is no problem because the milk is totally absorbed into the meat; therefore they can be frozen. Dishes in which the milk is not totally absorbed should not be kept frozen for longer than a week or so. All frozen cooked food must, of course, be well thawed before it is reheated.

Other coconut products

SHREDDED COCONUT

Store-bought shredded coconut makes good coconut milk, and it saves you the effort of dealing with a whole nut. Well-known brands bought in supermarkets are good, but expensive if you need a large quantity. Avoid any that contain added sugar. Most Asian food shops sell unsweetened shredded coconut in large bags much more cheaply. To make coconut milk, proceed as described above, but if you are using a blender, mix for 20—30 seconds. If you are not using a blender, simmer the shredded coconut and water in a pan for 4—5 minutes. Allow to cool a little, then sieve and strain as above.

Above: Freshly-grated coconut.

CANNED COCONUT MILK

I have often, and over many years, used canned coconut milk from Thailand, and found it very satisfactory and a great labor-saver. In the past two or three years, however, I have become suspicious of it because it thickens so fast in cooking. Coconut milk should become thick and oily only after boiling for at least 45 minutes, but my hitherto-trusted brand now thickens after barely half that time. I therefore try to use it less, and to make my own coconut milk more often.

You can now buy canned coconut milk that is "half-fat." Presumably this is meant to appeal to the diet-conscious; it is true that coconuts do contain some undesirable fats, but on balance they are more healthy than harmful. I lament the fact that in an earlier book I made the mistake of saying that they contain cholesterol. Obviously they do not; cholesterol is not found in any plant, except in negligible quantities. The half-fat product can be used for most dishes requiring coconut milk, but not for *rendang*; in cooking *rendang* you need the oil that is left during the last hour of cooking, when the water in the coconut milk is being driven off by evaporation. This oil makes the *rendang* nicely brown, and its outer layer slightly crisp. The oil from the coconut milk will appear about an hour before the *rendang* starts to brown, so the sauce will be very oily as it reaches the stage at which the dish is called *kalio*. *Kalio* sauce always looks like an oily curry sauce. If you want to stop at this point, and don't want the *kalio* to become *rendang*, but think you've got too much oil, then spoon out the surplus oil and reserve it for cooking something else – *oseng oseng* (pp. 219–20), for example, where you need just 2 tablespoons of this already quite spicy oil. The oil from *kalio* hardens like butter in the refrigerator, and can be kept for up to a week.

CREAMED COCONUT

This is like a hard, whitish margarine. It has its uses, but I would not recommend it for any of the recipes in this book, unless a very small amount is needed near the end of cooking in order to thicken the sauce.

TAMARIND

Tamarinds are the seed pods of a large tree which is found in most areas of the Old World tropics, and which was taken by the Spanish to their New World possessions. Outside the tropics, you can buy tamarind in most Asian food stores, either fresh and in the pod, or shelled and pressed into dark brown plastic-wrapped blocks. Tamarind is valued both for its unique flavor and for its sourness, but it is not much to look at. A ripe pod most resembles a row of three or four dull matt-brown chocolate spheres that have fused together; if you crack this shell open, you see a confused fibrous sticky brown mass of seeds and pulp. It is this pulp that is pressed into blocks and sold. It can simply be added to the cooking pot as it is, but in that case it is usually heated in a frying pan until slightly charred, and it must be removed before serving. Recipes more often call for tamarind water. This is made by putting a lump of the pulp into warm water and kneading it with the fingers to release the richly flavored brown extract. The fibers are then discarded.

The question is, how much tamarind should be added to how much water? Reputable writers give widely different figures, but I suggest that tamarind pulp, broken from the block, should be soaked and kneaded in eight to ten times its own volume of warm water. If the recipe demands thick tamarind water, you should double the quantity of pulp. The water itself does not "thicken," but it does become darker in color, making the flavor stronger. In any case, strain off the solids and discard them before adding the tamarind water to the other ingredients. Some authorities say that boiled tamarind loses its flavor; in my experience the loss, if any, is very small.

Making tamarind water

If you are using a lot of tamarind water, it is worthwhile boiling a whole 7-ounce block of tamarind in about 2¼ cups water. Boil for 20 minutes, using a wooden spoon to stir the tamarind often and break up the block. After 20 minutes or a little longer, put the tamarind and its cooking water into a sieve set over a glass bowl, and allow to pass through. You will now have a bowl of thickish brown tamarind water. This can be stored in an airtight jar in the refrigerator for about 10 days, before mold starts to grow on it. It is then not safe for further use and must be discarded. You can, however, freeze

Left to right: Frozen tamarind-water cubes; fresh tamarind pods.

tamarind water in ice-cube trays; it will keep in the freezer, with no loss of flavor, for up to 2 months. Put a measured amount — one, two, or three tablespoonfuls — of tamarind water in each ice-cube compartment, and when the cubes are well frozen, transfer them into a self-sealed freezer bag. Then it's easy to take just one cube to go straight into your cooking pot.

A very satisfactory alternative to tamarind water is *asam gelugur* (see p.274).

TEMPEH
(in Indonesia, spelled *tempe*)

Tempeh is an extremely nutritious food made from fermented soy beans. By itself, cooked tempeh has a pleasantly neutral flavor and a semi-soft texture, but no one could say it was exciting. The Javanese, however, who probably "invented" tempeh and who are now its principal exponents, have developed many excellent ways of adding flavor and texture to make it a real gourmet ingredient. In Western countries, vegetarians and vegans eat it because it makes available the amino acids in soy beans that combine with other amino acids in grains – notably rice – to make proteins that the human body requires throughout life. Plain boiled soy beans are not fully digested in the human gut, so their amino acids mostly go to waste. Meat-eaters like myself, however, also eat tempeh because it is low in saturated fats and calories, and rich in iron and calcium – and because it tastes delicious when it's well cooked.

Tempeh has been credited with saving many lives in times of war and famine, and with keeping poor people healthy and well fed at all times. If you buy it in health food shops, you may find that it's surprisingly expensive. By making your own, you will pay well below the shop price and have the reassurance of knowing exactly what went into your tempeh: soy beans, water, a little vinegar, and the mold *Rhizopus oligosporus*, the strands of which bind the beans together in a firm but tender mass.

Making tempeh at home
WHAT YOU NEED

It is not difficult to make your own tempeh, and the result is usually better as well as cheaper than the commercial product. As with other processes involving fermentation, you are more likely to get good results by making quite large quantities; fortunately, blocks of uncooked tempeh can be frozen for up to six months. The most important pieces of equipment are a large saucepan (to hold about 2½ gallons if you are processing a 4½ pound bag of soy beans) and a warm place in which to store the tempeh for 24–30 hours while it ferments. It needs to be kept at a temperature of about 85°F (30°C). An airing cupboard may be suitable, and you can use a heater to boost the warmth a little as

Right: Fresh uncooked tempeh.

long as you do not raise it above 95°F (35°C). But if you start making tempeh regularly, find or make a small enclosed space and fit a heating device inside it: a couple of electric light bulbs, wired up to a simple thermostat on which you can set the desired temperature, are all that is required. Make sure that your enclosure is well ventilated: molds need oxygen, just like other living things.

You also need a supply of food-quality plastic bags, preferably resealable. A good size is about 6 x 9 inch; this gives you a block of tempeh weighing about 1 pound. A 4½ pound bag of soy beans makes eight blocks of tempeh this size. Each of these bags must have a lot of very small holes punched in it so that the mold inside can breathe; these should be about ½ inch apart, or less. If you can buy bags with ready-made holes in neat rows, you are fortunate. I always have to make the holes myself, and always end with a stiff wrist. I use a bradawl with a sharp point, and stack the bags in tens so that each jab pierces through twenty layers of plastic. As I use only eight bags for each batch of tempeh, after four batches I have eight bags with holes "in the bank" and can skip the hole-jabbing next time round.

The final problem to solve is that of sourcing your tempeh starter. Tempeh mold is something like bread yeast, but unfortunately bread yeast will not turn soy beans into tempeh. In tropical countries, the air is well laden with spores of all sorts of yeasts and molds, and a professional tempeh producer will keep a starter culture going from one batch to the next. Though it is theoretically possible to do this in a cool climate, the process is tricky and unreliable, and could be risky. I buy my tempeh starter culture from a specialist producer. Such firms are not found on every street, but with the internet, a good telephone book, and a few telephone calls you should be able to locate one fairly easily. I buy my starter in the minimum quantity the firm will supply: 2 ounces of an off-white powder, which I store in the refrigerator. The supplier says it should be used within six months, but I have made good tempeh with it after a year. This amount of starter should make at least 90 pounds of tempeh.

Finally, you need soy beans. The best place to buy these is an Asian food store or supermarket, where 2¼ pound and 4½ pound bags are very reasonably priced.

Above: Fresh tempeh for sale in Padang central market.

MAKING TEMPEH

Put 4½ pounds soy beans into a large pan, and pour in cold water to wash them free of any chemical foam that may appear. Drain, then refill the pan with cold water so that the beans are well covered – they will absorb almost their own weight of water, so put in plenty. Bring to a boil and, as soon as the water is boiling, turn off the heat, cover the pan, and leave for at least 4 or up to 24 hours.

The remaining processes of dehulling the beans, boiling them for 1 hour, cooling them, inoculating, and finally packing them take altogether at least 2 hours, although while the beans are simmering they need only occasional attention.

To dehull and split the beans, put them, in their pan with the water they were boiled in, on a low table or, better, in the sink under the cold tap. Plunge your hands into the beans and squeeze and rub them vigorously with your fingers and between your palms. After a few minutes of this, pour in cold water, swirl the beans around and let bean skins and froth rise to the surface. Gently lift and tip the pan so that this debris is discarded. Continue adding water, kneading and squeezing the beans, then swirling to let the rubbish rise to the surface so that it can be tipped out of the pan, until the water in the pan is clear and the quantity of skins greatly reduced. You will need to go through the cycle at least 10–12 times. You will never get rid of all the skins or split every bean in half, but it is important to split as many beans as possible – if a high percentage of beans are left whole, the tempeh will be loose and may fall apart when it is cooked.

Now add enough fresh cold water to cover the beans well, then pour in about ½ cup white distilled vinegar. Put the pan back on the stove, put the lid on, and bring to a boil. Reduce the heat to low and let the beans simmer quietly, covered, for 1 hour. There is no need to stir or do anything else, except make sure that the water does not begin to boil.

At the end of the hour, spread an old tablecloth or sheet on the kitchen table, preferably making several layers of cloth. Pour off as much of the hot water from the pan as possible, and strain the beans in several batches in a colander. Spread the beans on the tablecloth, covering the available surface evenly – the layer should not be more than 1 inch thick. The aim now is to reduce the temperature of the beans to about body heat and to remove surplus water without making the beans too dry. Keep turning the beans over, piling them and spreading them out again. Give them a few blasts with a hair dryer if you want. If you realize that a lot of beans are still whole, you can do some more squeezing and rubbing at this stage, but bear in mind that there will always be some skins and some whole beans left, so you don't need to be too rigorous about this.

When all the beans are cool and damp, but not cold or quite dry, put them in a large bowl and inoculate them with about a teaspoonful of the powdered starter. As the quantity of starter is so small, stir it into the mass of beans with your hands, shifting handfuls around so that the starter is spread to all parts of the mass.

Fill your pre-pierced plastic bags with the beans, so that every bag, when zipped up or otherwise sealed, makes a flat cushion about ¼ inch thick. If the bags are much thicker than this, the center of each block may not get enough oxygen. Gently pat each bag flat so that the beans are uniformly and closely packed, right to the edges and into the corners. Arrange the bags on wire racks in single layers so that air can get all around each one, and put them in a warm cupboard to ferment.

Once they are there, leave them undisturbed. Absolutely nothing will happen for at least 20 hours, though a little moisture may condense inside the plastic. After about 24–28 hours the spores of the mold will start to form a whitish veil across the soy beans. Once the process is under way it generates its own heat, and therefore you can reduce the temperature in the enclosure. The tempeh is soon white all over, a few beans showing through; you can now pick up a solid block, the beans knitted together by the spores, the substance slightly warmed by the life within and having a faint but pleasant smell not unlike newly baked bread.

As soon as you are satisfied that the tempeh is "done," store it either in the refrigerator, if it is to be cooked and eaten in the next day or so, or in the freezer. Take care to separate the blocks from each other until they are well chilled through, otherwise the mold will start to discolor and darken. A little discoloration is harmless, but if your tempeh turns black and starts to soften, you must throw it away – chemical changes are taking place which will produce toxins. Tempeh will keep for up to six months in the freezer.

Right: Nine steps to making tempeh:
1 Soy beans twelve hours after initial boiling.
2 Beans topped up with cold tap water.
3 Squeezing, grinding and rubbing the beans to split them.
4 Swirling the beans around to let the skins float to the top.
5 Pouring off the water and bean skins.
6 Spreading the cooked beans to cool and partly dry.
7 Inoculating the beans with the tempeh starter.
8 Bagging the beans.
9 28-30 hours later: blocks of finished tempeh.

RICE

The staple foods of most people in South and East Asia are rice and fish. Fish, clearly, come in huge variety and are cooked in a vast number of ways. Rice is different: it is usually boiled or steamed, nothing more. Yet it would never occur to us to find rice monotonous – on the contrary, if we have not eaten rice, we have not had a proper meal and, however much we ate, it would merely be a snack. True, we all love snacking, but we must have at least two, preferably three, rice meals each day. And the rice must be pure white, its outer husk completely removed, even though we know that this contains most of the nutrients. Brown rice is for children and sick people; healthy people seen eating it lose their self-respect.

Rice itself has our respect, partly for what it gives us, but partly, too, because we are a little afraid that it might abandon us. Season after season, when things go well, it gives us a bountiful harvest, far more productive than any other grain. It grows quickly, so we can usually take two harvests a year, or at least have time for a crop of vegetables between one monsoon and the next. It is also a great builder of families and communities. For most of the year, each family manages its small farm with the labor of its members, but at certain times, particularly transplanting and harvest, it must call on its neighbors for help, and be called upon in turn. The village as a whole keeps a roster of these vital events, ensuring that sufficient hands are available when needed. Farmers must also agree on the distribution of the one vital resource, the water that irrigates the fields, and they must mutually see to the upkeep of waterways and dykes. A landscape of flooded rice fields, whether on hill slopes crowned with forest or in flat country where villages are marked by tall palms, demands knowledge, management skill, and immense labor to create and maintain.

Rice, in fact, demands total commitment from the people who live by it; the gifts it offers are never certain. This is why most Southeast Asians have always seen rice as a goddess, a woman who must be persuaded and cajoled, and never taken for granted. Today, of course, things are changing fast, but rice is still the one food that must be treasured, never wasted and always treated with honor.

Above: Bali: winnowing newly-threshed rice.
Right: Rice terraces in the valley of Yeh Ayung, near Ubud.

Cooking rice

My grandmother used the absorption method when she cooked her rice. She called her rice *nasi tanak*; to make it, she used an iron saucepan with a thick bottom. The rice was washed in several changes of water before it went in, measured in cupfuls — for each cup of rice, a cup of water, then an extra ½ cup of water at the end, regardless of the quantity of rice. As I remember, the rice always came out soft and fluffy, with a thin layer of *intip* sticking to the bottom of the pan. She would take out the *intip* carefully, to be dried in the sun. When dry, the *intip* was deep-fried in a wok to make a crisp rice cake. This she usually served as a tea-time snack, either sprinkled with a little salt or spread with home-made *tengguli*, a sugar syrup made with *gula kelapa*. (This is the same as *gula jawa* (see p.276), but she never called it by that name.)

To cook rice this way, you need about 10 minutes from the time the water starts to boil until the water is completely absorbed by the rice. Next, reduce the heat as low as possible and continue cooking, with the pan now tightly covered, for another 10 minutes. If you want your *intip* quite thick and brown at the bottom, leave the pot on the stove with a slightly higher heat for another 5 minutes. If your pot is not non-stick, put the pan, still tightly covered, on a soaking wet towel for 5 minutes. Transfer the rice to a bowl and take out the *intip*, with luck and practice, in one piece.

The Javanese do it differently. They start by cooking their rice in a saucepan. When all the water has been absorbed, the rice is transferred to a conical woven bamboo basket called a *kukusan* that is put on top of a *dandang* (see left), and steamed for 10 minutes. They then immediately put the rice in a large wooden bowl, and stir it with a wooden spoon while at the same time fanning it quite vigorously. This is to make the rice develop the most desirable texture, which, in Javanese and Sundanese, is called *pulen*, beautifully soft and aromatic. I once had a *dandang* and *kukusan* when I was living in Yogya. Later, I acquired a rice steamer made in Amsterdam, but now of course, like most rice-eaters, I have an electric rice cooker.

In this book, I use only Thai fragrant, basmati, white sticky, and black sticky rice. All of these can now be found without much difficulty in Western countries, although sticky rice (especially black) is still not available in many supermarkets. Still, it should not be too difficult to find almost any kind of rice.

Left: Steaming rice in a traditional *kukusan* above a *dandang* on a charcoal stove, in a village near Yogyakarta.

STOCKS

kaldu daging sapi dan ayam
beef and chicken stock

This is a clear stock I always make for *soto ayam* (Javanese Chicken Soup, pp. 53–4). It is a clear stock with not too many things in it to distract from the taste of beef and chicken. You need to use only the carcass of a chicken, including the wings. The important thing is that you must clean it by washing the inside of the carcass, where bits of liver and lungs may still be stuck between the bones, under a cold, running tap. If your butcher will give or sell you some good beef bones to add to the stock, it will taste good and be very clear. Otherwise use about 8 ounces beef cut from good brisket or topside. Put the chicken carcass and the bones from the beef, or the beef cut, with cold water in a large saucepan. Bring to a rolling boil and let boil for 5 minutes. Drain the carcasses and the beef through a colander. Rinse the saucepan, return the chicken bones and beef to the pan, and cover with cold water again. Add 1 teaspoon sea salt. Bring to a boil slowly, and let it boil for an hour or so, skimming off any froth from the surface from time to time. Strain the stock and let it cool in a large bowl before refrigerating it for use in, for example, *soto ayam*.

kaldu sayuran
vegetable stock

The recipe here will give you a clear, tasty, uncomplicated vegetable stock. You need 2 carrots, thoroughly washed, and each cut into three pieces; 1 onion, unpeeled but washed and quartered; 3 tomatoes; 1 garlic clove; and a bunch of fresh flat-leaf parsley. Put all these in a large saucepan, add 1 teaspoon salt, and fill the saucepan halfway with cold water. Bring to a boil, reduce the heat slightly, and simmer, covered, for an hour or so. Strain, and keep the stock in the refrigerator until needed.

As an alternative, here is what most Western chefs would call an "Asian" stock. This is quickly made from the following ingredients: a 1¼ inch piece of galangal, 1 or 2 lemongrass stems, 3 kaffir lime leaves and 1 chopped onion. Put in a saucepan and add about 8 cups water. This needs to be boiled for only 5–8 minutes, just to release the aroma of the galangal, lemongrass, and kaffir lime leaves. If you boil them for too long, your stock will become slightly bitter. Strain, discarding the solids; store in the refrigerator until needed. This stock is mainly used for vegetarian soups, or any other dish where you don't want to use meat or chicken stock.

RICE

nasi gurih
coconut rice

Nasi gurih, also known as *nasi uduk*, is rice cooked in coconut milk. Colored with turmeric, it becomes *nasi kuning*. In Indonesia, we do not always soak the rice first, nor do we stir-fry it in oil or butter. The method I suggest here, though, will appeal to a lot of people because it ensures that the rice does not become too soft and clingy.

2 cups long-grain rice, soaked for 1 hour, washed and drained
2 tbsp olive oil or clarified butter

3 cups coconut milk
1 tsp salt

Serves 4–6

In a heavy saucepan over medium heat, stir-fry the rice in the butter or oil for 3 minutes. (Add 1 teaspoon ground turmeric here if you are making *nasi kuning*.) Add the coconut milk and salt. Bring to a boil and cook, uncovered, until the rice has absorbed all the liquid.

Reduce the heat, cover the pan tightly, and cook for another 10–12 minutes undisturbed. Alternatively, the rice can be "finished" by steaming in a rice steamer or by cooking in the oven or a microwave. Serve hot.

lontong
compressed rice

Lontong is always eaten cold, for example, with satay; it soaks up the hot satay sauce, and its coolness and soft texture contrast with the hot spices and the meat. In Indonesia, the rice is cooked in a cylinder of banana leaf, or else in a little packet woven from coconut fronds. The latter is called *ketupat*. *Ketupat* are particularly associated with Lebaran festivities at the end of Ramadan.

After my arrival in England in 1964, I struggled for many years to make *lontong* at home with foil instead of banana leaf. Then I discovered that just one type of boil-in-the-bag basmati rice is ideal for making perfect *lontong*. Unfortunately, almost all boil-in-the-bag rice nowadays is parboiled, making it useless for *lontong*, as the partly cooked grains cannot compress and merge together. Do your best to find a brand that isn't parboiled. Check, too, that the bags (made of a special plastic with tiny holes) are the right size – the rice should fill them one-third full, not much more or less. If they are too big, machine or hand-stitch a seam across them to reduce the size, then follow the cooking instructions below.

2 or 3 x 3½ oz bags boil-in-the-bag pure   *Serves 8–10*
    basmati rice

Fill a large saucepan, or better still a spaghetti pan, two-thirds full of cold water. Bring to a boil, add a pinch of salt, and let the water come to a rolling boil. Put in the boil-in-bag rice, quickly return the water to a boil, and continue boiling for 90 minutes, replenishing the hot water when necessary with boiling water from a kettle, so that the rice remains covered all the time. At the end of 90 minutes, drain the bags of rice, then lay them flat on a plate. Leave to cool completely. The *lontong* will be at their best after they have been refrigerated overnight.

To serve, cut up the "cushions" of compressed rice into chunks or wedges about 1¼ inch thick using a large, sharp knife wetted with water. Discard the bags.

lemper
javanese sticky rice rolls

For me, *lemper* has now become my personal Indonesian sushi — I make it in so many different ways, wrapped with smoked salmon or filled with shiitake mushrooms (ideal for vegetarians and vegans) instead of the traditional chicken fillings. The Sumatrans have their own sticky rice roll in the form of *lemang* (p.234), and the people of Sulawesi have their *lalampa* (pp.136–7)

Here's one recipe for *lemper* — it makes at least 10–12 slices; more if the slices are thinner. You will need either a Swiss roll pan or a sushi rolling mat, to spread and flatten the rice before you roll it up. Usually, one slice is sufficient per person.

2 cups sticky rice, soaked in cold water
  for 40–60 minutes, and drained
2 cups coconut milk
½ tsp salt

for the stuffing
2 chicken breast filets
4 shallots, chopped
3 garlic cloves, chopped
3 candlenuts or macadamia nuts,
  or a few blanched almonds

1 tsp ground coriander
½ tsp ground cumin
½ tsp soft brown sugar
1 kaffir lime leaf (optional)
½ tsp salt
½ tsp ground white pepper
2 tbsp peanut oil or olive oil
½ c thick coconut milk

Makes 10–12 slices

Boil the rice in the coconut milk with ¼ teaspoon salt until all the liquid has been absorbed by the rice. Transfer the rice to a steamer or double saucepan, and steam for 15 minutes. Turn off the heat, but leave the rice in the steamer until you are ready with the stuffing.

Poach the chicken breasts in boiling water with a large pinch of salt for about 20 minutes. Take them out, and leave to cool on a plate. When they are cool, shred the poached breasts finely, discarding the skin.

Blend the rest of the ingredients for the stuffing with half of the coconut milk until smooth. Put the liquid in a small saucepan, bring to a boil, reduce the heat slightly, and simmer for 8 minutes. Add the shredded chicken and the rest of the coconut milk. Continue simmering until all the coconut milk has been absorbed by the meat, but the mixture is still moist. Adjust the seasoning, and leave to cool.

Line the Swiss roll pan with a sheet of wax paper, and spread the cooked rice on this, pressing it down (with another piece of wax paper) to fill the pan evenly. Spread the cooled chicken stuffing evenly over the rice, then roll it up as if you were making a Swiss roll. Cut into slices with a large knife that has been wetted in hot water. Serve warm or cold as a snack, or with drinks.

Alternatively, you can roll *lemper* with a Japanese sushi rolling mat. Line the mat with foil, then line this with slices of smoked salmon. Spread the rice evenly on top of the salmon, then the chicken filling on top of the rice. Lift the two edges of the rolling mat, so that the opposite edges of the rice come together. Now roll the bamboo mat so the rice shapes itself into a nice compact roll. Remove the foil wrapping and cut the roll as above. *Lemper* should not be refrigerated, but if, because of the salmon, you have to chill it, then leave it uncut. The rice will harden in the refrigerator. Take the *lemper* out of the refrigerator and cut the roll at least 1 hour before it is to be served. This will allow the rice to regain its natural texture.

nasi goreng
fried rice

This is one of the better known Indonesian dishes, although it originated in China. I must include the recipe here, for it has become an everyday dish that can be served with whatever you have, be it cold meat or leftover roast, or a vegetable stir-fry. There are right and wrong ways of making *nasi goreng*. A bad one is oily, garnished only with a leathery fried egg. This is the kind of thing that gives Indonesian food a bad name. A good *nasi goreng* is light and hot; the rice grains moist but separate, and quite fluffy; and the garnish fresh and attractive to look at.

The rice should be cooked 2–3 hours before it is to be fried, so that it has time to get cold. Freshly cooked still-hot rice will go soggy and oily if you fry it. Rice that has been left overnight is too stale to make first-rate *nasi goreng*. Next, the cold rice must be mixed in with the other ingredients when those ingredients are already cooked and still hot. From then on, the mixing and stir-frying must be done over low heat and must continue until the rice is hot but not burned.

If you are going to use seafood or meat, it is best to stir-fry this separately. You can use the same spice mixture as given here for the fried rice, if you wish. Mix the meat or seafood into the rice in the final 2 minutes before serving; or simply spread on top of the rice on the serving dish.

2 tbsp peanut oil	4 oz button mushrooms, cleaned and
1 tbsp butter	quartered
3 shallots or 1 small onion, very finely	2 tbsp hot water (optional)
chopped	salt to taste
1 tsp *sambal ulek* (see p.279)	1 lb long-grain rice, cooked by
or ½ tsp chili powder	the absorption method (see p.129)
1 tsp paprika	or in an electric rice cooker, and
2 tsp tomato purée or ketchup	allowed to cool completely
2 tbsp light soy sauce	
3 carrots, very finely diced	*Serves 4–6*

Heat the oil and butter in a wok or large frying pan. Stir-fry the shallots for 1–2 minutes, then add the other ingredients, including the hot water (if using), but not the rice. Continue stir-frying for about 6 minutes until the vegetables are cooked. Add the rice, and mix thoroughly so that the rice is heated through and takes on the reddish tinge of the paprika and tomato. Adjust the seasoning. Serve hot on a warmed serving dish – by itself as an accompaniment to a main course; garnished with sliced cucumber, sliced tomatoes, watercress, and crisp-fried shallots (see p.275); or topped with seafood or meat as described above.

lalampa
sticky rice cakes stuffed with tuna

Lalampa are sticky rice cakes from Minahasa, in northern Sulawesi; they are made in exactly the same way as *lemper* (pp.134–5), but the filling is tuna fish.

for the filling

2 tbsp rapeseed or peanut oil

8 oz shallots or onions, finely chopped

8 garlic cloves, finely sliced

1 tbsp grated fresh ginger

1 tsp salt

1 lb tuna steak, chopped, or 1 lb canned
  tuna, drained

3–6 ripe tomatoes, skinned and seeded,
  then chopped

4 oz chopped spring onions

2–3 fresh red chilies, seeded and
  finely chopped

4 oz chopped fresh basil or mint

freshly ground black pepper

Makes about 20 lalampa

To make the filling, heat the oil in a wok or saucepan. When hot, add the shallots or onions, garlic, and ginger. Stir-fry for about 8 minutes, then add the rest of the ingredients and continue stir-frying for another 3 minutes. Leave the filling to cool before using it to stuff the rice.

for the rice

1½ lb white sticky rice, soaked in cold
  water for 20–40 minutes,
  then drained

3 c thick coconut milk

1 pandanus leaf, cut across into three
  (optional)

½ tsp salt

Heat the coconut milk in a large saucepan until almost boiling. Remove from the heat, and add the salt and pandanus leaf, if using. Stir, add the rice, and stir again with a wooden spoon. Cover the pan and leave undisturbed for 10 minutes, by which time all the coconut milk will have been absorbed by the rice. Transfer the rice to a steamer, placing it over a bottom pan which already has very hot water in it. Bring the water quickly to a boil and steam the rice for 10 minutes.

Turn off the heat, and transfer the rice to a large tray. Leave to cool a little, and discard the pandanus leaf, if used. When the rice is cool enough to handle, divide it into 20 equal portions. Put one portion onto a square of wax paper or foil, flatten the rice, and put a tablespoon of filling on top. Roll the rice, with the filling inside, to make a sausage shape, then unroll the paper or foil so that you can use it for the next one. Repeat the process until you have 20 *lalampa*.

In Indonesia, each *lalampa* would be wrapped with banana leaf; they would then be grilled, in batches, over charcoal. They are turned once or twice, to prevent the banana leaf wrappers from charring too quickly, then unwrapped and served right away. I just arrange them (unwrapped) on a flameproof dish and put them under a hot grill for about 2 minutes each side, turning them only once. (You can wrap each *lalampa* in banana leaf before grilling, if you wish; the leaf gives the rice a pleasant tinge of green and a subtle extra flavor. Discard the leaf before serving.) Serve hot or cold, as a snack, or with drinks.

nasi kebuli
biryani with fried chicken

1 lb long-grain rice, soaked in cold water
   for 1 hour, then rinsed and drained
2 c peanut oil

pinch of grated nutmeg
2 cloves
1½ tsp salt

for the stock and fried chicken
3¼–4 lb roasting chicken,
   cut into 8–10 pieces
4 shallots or 1 onion, chopped
2 tsp ground coriander
1 tsp ground cumin
2 in piece of lemongrass stem
1 small cinnamon stick

for the garnish
1 tbsp crisp-fried shallots (see p.275)
a few fresh flat-leaf parsley leaves
2 tsp chopped fresh chives or
   spring onion
sliced cucumber

Serves 6–8

Put the chicken and all the ingredients for the stock in a heavy saucepan. Pour in 4½ cups cold water. Bring to a boil and cook for 30–40 minutes until the chicken is tender. Strain the stock into a bowl, and keep aside. Discard the solids, and dry each chicken piece with paper towels. Set aside on a plate.

In a clean saucepan, stir-fry the rice with 2 tablespoons of the oil for 5 minutes. Add 2½ cups of the stock to cook the rice; if you find you are short of stock, add water to make up the quantity. Boil the rice until it has absorbed all the liquid – this takes only a few minutes, then steam for 10 minutes.

While the rice is cooking, deep-fry the chicken pieces in the remaining oil. To serve, pile up the rice in the center of a large serving dish, surround with the chicken portions, and sprinkle over the garnishes.

nasi ulam
savory rice with herbs

My first encounter with *nasi ulam* was when we went round Malaysia to research rice. In this section on rice, naturally I must include this recipe – it is, in fact, a variation on kedgeree. The *nasi ulam* I had in Kuala Lumpur looked very green and tasted of herbs all the way; I could hardly taste the rice at all. Now, as I write this while staying in the hill town of Rolle in the Veneto, I recall that the Italians take care not to put too many distracting ingredients in their risotto, so as not to lose the nuttiness of the rice. I like my *nasi ulam* without the fish, and use only three different herbs. It works well as a separate course or appetizer, like a *primo* in Italy, or for breakfast or lunch, as we enjoy it in the East.

2 lb cooked rice
1 lb cold smoked mackerel or haddock
  (optional)
4 tbsp freshly grated coconut, roasted
  (optional)
½ c very thick coconut milk
1 tsp *sambal ulek* (see p.279)
  or 2 fresh green chilies, seeded
  and finely sliced
2 shallots, finely sliced
1 tsp finely chopped fresh ginger
½ tsp salt, plus extra to taste

about 1 tbsp of each of just 3 or 4
  of the following, very finely sliced or
  chopped: turmeric leaves, basil, mint,
  watercress, kaffir lime leaves,
  lemongrass (use only the soft inner
  part), cashew nut leaves, spring
  onions, wild ginger flowers, seeded
  fresh green chilies
juice of 1 lime or lemon

Serves 6–8

Let the rice cool to room temperature. Remove the skin and bones of the fish, if using, and break up the flesh into fine flakes. Put the rice into a large bowl and mix in the fish and the roasted coconut, if using.

Put the coconut milk in a wok or large shallow saucepan. Add the *sambal ulek* or chilies, shallots, ginger, and ½ teaspoon salt. Bring to a boil and let the mixture bubble for 8–10 minutes until it becomes oily. Stir, reduce the heat, and stir in the rice mixture. Toss and stir this for 3 minutes until the rice is hot. Add the sliced and chopped herbs, and continue stirring for 1 minute more. Just before serving, add the lime or lemon juice, and extra salt if needed. Serve hot or warm.

SWEET CORN

nasi jagung
sweet corn cooked as rice with grated coconut

Maize is a staple of the eastern provinces of Indonesia, where the climate is too dry for rice, but it was also our staple during the Japanese occupation between 1942 and 1945. Rice was then hard to find everywhere. To supplement what little rice we had, we bought *beras jagung*, which was dried maize processed to look like yellow grain. The recipe below, however, is for fresh young sweet corn, simply steamed and mixed with freshly grated youngish coconut, a tiny amount of salt, and 2 or 3 teaspoons of sugar. We usually use white cane sugar for this, not the brown palm sugar. For myself, this is one of the breakfasts I used to dream of after I left my grandmother in Padang Panjang. She lavished great care and attention on this heavenly breakfast cereal, and it was enjoyed by all the family.

How was I to make this in London? It turned out to be easier than I had expected. I had no trouble finding young sweet corn, on the cob; for the grated coconut, the old coconut that I bought in the supermarket would just about do. You need to grate the coconut after breaking the shell, then removing the brown outer layer of the coconut flesh so that your grated coconut is white; this is why we use white sugar to mix with it. Nowadays, you can get frozen grated youngish coconut in Chinese or Thai supermarkets, and this, I think, will give the right sweetness to the coconut. Therefore, add less sugar if you are using this young grated coconut from the freezer.

As a breakfast dish, allow 2 corn cobs per person. To cook, either shave the sweet corn off the cob with a sharp knife, then steam it in a steamer or a double saucepan for 5–8 minutes, or boil the corn cobs whole for the same length of time, leave to cool a little, then shave the kernels into a bowl. Mix the corn well with the grated coconut, salt and sugar. The right mix is about three parts corn to one part coconut, with salt and sugar to taste – but very little salt and not too much sugar. I suggest you think of this dish as a kind of porridge, and eat it with a spoon.

tinutuan
menadonese sweet corn, cassava, and pumpkin soup

This is a very substantial soup, or a very good breakfast or lunch dish. For best results all the ingredients used should be fresh. Also, traditionally, in the Minahasa region of Sulawesi, *tinutuan* has to be made with cassava. In the West, cassava is obtainable from Asian grocers.

8 oz cassava, peeled and cut into largish cubes
2 oz white rice, soaked in cold water for 30 minutes, then drained
3 fresh corn cobs, shaved, or 6 oz canned or frozen corn kernels
8–10 oz pumpkin or butternut squash, peeled and cut into cubes the same size as the cassava
4 oz bamboo shoots, sliced (optional)
1 tsp salt, plus extra to taste

to be added just before serving
1 lemongrass stem, outer leaves discarded, finely chopped
1 turmeric leaf, finely shredded (optional)
8 oz young spinach, thoroughly washed
8 oz *kangkung* (water spinach), trimmed and washed (optional)
225 ml/8 fl oz hot water from the kettle
about 20 fresh sweet basil leaves

*Serves 4 as a one-dish meal
or 8 as a soup*

First, put 4½ cups water in a large saucepan and bring to a boil. When boiling, add the cassava and rice, and cook for 8 minutes, stirring occasionally. Next, add the sweet corn, pumpkin, bamboo shoots (if using), and the 1 teaspoon salt. Continue to simmer for 20–25 minutes. The mixture is now ready to become the basis of the soup, and can be prepared and cooked up to this point well in advance. Refrigerate or keep in a cool place until ready to serve.

Just before serving, heat the thick soup. When hot, add the lemongrass, turmeric (if using), spinach, and water spinach (if using). Pour in the hot water from the kettle. Simmer for 5 minutes only. Adjust the seasoning with a litte extra salt if needed, and add the basil leaves. Simmer for one more minute, and serve the soup right away.

jagung bakar
grilled corn on the cob

At any food stall on any street in Indonesia, you will find a man with a brazier, fanning his glowing charcoal and grilling corn cobs by the hundred to sell to passers-by. He calls his wares to attract customers, for he is competing with other vendors, the satay men and many more.

The picture on the opposite page is of one of my young nephews eating freshly roasted sweet corn by a roadside somewhere in West Java. The year was 1987, and I had finally closed my Indonesian delicatessen in Wimbledon and was collecting material for my next book. Roger was still working full-time as a teacher in London, so I was traveling on my own. I stayed for a while in Jakarta with one of my sisters, and borrowed her youngest son to accompany me on a visit to Bandung, where another sister lived. For me, it was a memorable return to Indonesia. My elder son was at university, and the younger was fifteen years old, a couple of years older than my nephew in the picture. I felt I was starting a new chapter in my life.

We went to Bandung by train (and incidentally had a most delicious *nasi goreng* on board), but on our way back we decided to hire a car with a driver. We drove through the hills of West Java, passing tea plantations and rice fields, often shaded from the sun by coconut palms and great forest trees by the roadside. At Puncak, a popular resort on the way to Bogor, we stopped at a big hotel with splendid views of the mountains. The air was almost as cool as in Bandung. I remembered stopping here a few years earlier, with Roger and our two boys, for lunch – I recalled that the food was good, quite sophisticated, well cooked and with first-class ingredients to attract discerning tourists and well-to-do people from Jakarta and other cities. But my nephew, who would later study hotel management, was still very conservative in his eating habits, so we didn't stay for lunch. We drove on until we found this popular food market, where he grinned with delight as he ate his *jagung bakar*.

I took the opportunity to explore the market further, and found all the sweets and snacks that are described in chapter 1 of this book. We had chicken satays with *lontong* for our lunch, then we drove on to Bogor. Just as we were approaching Bogor, we stopped

so that I could photograph sticky rice, just harvested and drying in the sun (see left). We arrived back in Jakarta at my sister's house at supper time, a little before seven o'clock in the evening. The spread of food on the table included *tempe bacem* (p.164), *kering tempe dengan teri* (p.166), *gule kambing* (pp.56–8), and a large fried *gurami* fish, with many other side dishes and sambals. Everything was cooked in the traditional way, for my nephew, like most of his family and many Indonesians still, would eat only cooking that was familiar to him from childhood. The dessert, too, was traditional – fresh fruit. My brother-in-law loved durian as much as I do, and we had durian, rambutan, mangoes, duku, and papaya.

Jagung bakar, roasted sweet corn, is very easy to make at home. Naturally, it tastes best if it is grilled on charcoal. When you are having a barbecue party on a warm summer's day, especially if there are lots of children around, just pop the corn cobs on your barbecue. Turn them several times, and the cooking need only take 5–7 minutes. In Indonesia, we never brush the cobs with melted butter or anything else. They are just so good eaten without embellishment.

Left: By a roadside in West Java, a farmer and his family wait for the day's rice harvest to be taken to the granary.
Right: How to eat fresh-roasted corn on the cob.

SAGO

jilabulo
chicken livers with sago and coconut

This recipe from Sulawesi is an excellent way to cook chicken livers. The result is not entirely unlike a coarse pâté, and although I would not like to push the resemblance too far it did suggest to me that this would be a good first course for a dinner party, perhaps with some toast and a little parsley to garnish it, or simply by itself. The taste and texture are not like pâté at all, but they seem to be acceptable to most palates. At home we would cook *jilabulo* in banana-leaf packets, and just undo and eat them whenever we felt like it.

5 chicken livers	3 tbsp sago flour or sago pearls or
2 shallots	tapioca pearls
2 garlic cloves	1½ c thick coconut milk
½ tsp freshly ground black pepper	salt
1 tsp ground ginger	
	Serves 2

Clean the liver and slice it thinly. Set aside. Peel, slice, and crush the shallots and garlic, or pound them until smooth using a mortar and pestle. Add the pepper, ground ginger, and salt to taste. Mix all these in a saucepan with the sliced liver. Stir the sago into the coconut milk, and add to the liver mixture. Cook slowly for about 5 minutes until the sago becomes thick, stirring occasionally, then get ready to steam the mixture. In Indonesia, we get some good-sized squares of banana leaf, drop a large spoonful from the pan on each square, and fold it over and under to make an oblong packet. The packets are then steamed for 15–20 minutes. Where there are no banana leaves, I use a small soufflé dish or several ramekins to hold the mixture, and steam them in my rice steamer for 20 minutes. Serve hot or cold.

Right: *Gula jawa*, palm sugar, for sale at Padang central market.

gula melaka
sago pudding

I don't know why this pudding, which is really a kind of porridge, is called by the name of the sugar which is one of its ingredients. Anyway, *gula melaka* is the same as *gula kelapa* or *gula jawa* (see p.276); in Malaysia, it is also called by one of its Indian names, "jaggery." This palm sugar is quite hard, and you need to shave or chop it with a sharp knife, or grate it with a hand grater, before putting it into the dish you are cooking.

8 oz sago or semolina
1 cinnamon stick
3 oz *gula melaka* (palm sugar)
3½ c thick coconut milk
pinch of salt

to serve (optional)
1 c *gula melaka* syrup, made from about
  6 oz palm sugar

Serves 6–8

Put the sago or semolina in a saucepan with 1 cup water and the cinnamon stick. Leave to soak while the other ingredients are being prepared.

Chop the *gula melaka*, then dissolve over very low heat with ½ cup water; strain. Cook the sago mixture by bringing to a boil and letting it simmer for about 3 minutes, stirring all the time. Add the coconut milk, pinch of salt, and the dissolved sugar syrup, and continue stirring for 10–15 minutes until the mixture becomes thick. Discard the cinnamon, and pour the porridge into a large bowl or into several small individual bowls. Chill until the mixture is firm. It can be turned out of its mold or served in the small bowls where it has set. Alternatively, spoon the porridge out onto a dish, with the *gula melaka* syrup poured over it.

To make the syrup, boil the *gula melaka* for a few minutes in 1 cup water, stirring continuously. Strain through a fine sieve.

ina avau au
sago and pork rolls from irian jaya

Sago is a staple of the eastern provinces of Indonesia, where rice is not grown. It is cooked on an open fire in containers woven from sago leaves. My recipe is certainly not the original -- I have adapted it in several directions to suit my taste. The rolls can be made with pre-boiled pork or a ground raw lean cut of pork such as tenderloin; the pre-cooked meat gives a drier, firmer result. They make an excellent snack food as well as a popular nibble at parties. Also, cold slices cut from the rolls can be pan-fried at short notice and served, with salad and a piquant dressing, as a first course.

1 lb 10 oz pork loin chops or spare ribs off the bone, or tenderloin of pork, minced or ground
4 oz sago pearls or tapioca pearls
4 oz freshly grated coconut or shredded coconut
3 shallots, finely chopped
2 garlic cloves, finely chopped

2 large fresh red chilies (more if you like it hot), deseeded and finely chopped
2 tsp finely chopped or grated fresh ginger
2 tsp ground coriander
½ tsp ground turmeric

Serves 4–6

If using pork loin chops or spare ribs, put the pieces of pork in a saucepan. Cover with cold water, bring to a boil and keep boiling over high heat for 5 minutes. Drain, cover with fresh water, and add 1 teaspoon salt. Cook for 40–50 minutes until the meat is tender. Keep the liquid for a pork stock, if you like – you may need a little right away, if using shredded coconut. Let the pork cool.

Preheat the oven to 350°F (180°C). Chop the cooled pork finely with a sharp knife, or grind in a blender or food processor to the texture of sausage meat. Mix with the other ingredients in a bowl. If using shredded coconut, add ¼ cup warm water or pork stock. Mix together thoroughly. If using ground pork, just mix well with the other ingredients. Divide the mixture into four portions. Using foil, roll each portion into a long, thick sausage. Cook, wrapped in the foil, in the oven for 45 minutes. Leave to cool a little, then remove the foil and cut the rolls into slices ½–¾ inch thick. Serve warm. If you intend to pan-fry the rolls, chill or even put them in the freezer for 1–2 hours first, then slice and pan-fry until golden.

FISH AND SHELLFISH

ikan kuah asam
tamarind fish from sulawesi

Fish is one of the staple foods of Indonesia. Any town near the sea will have many ways of cooking freshly caught sea fish, and any one recipe is likely to have different names in different places. This dish is popular on the island of Sulawesi, where it may also be served as a fish soup. It is usually made with grouper, but other sea fish can be cooked in this way. I often choose grouper or red snapper (in Indonesian, *kakap merah* or *tambak merah*), or maybe sea bass when it is not too expensive. Whichever fish you choose, it needs to be fileted and skinned, and the head, skin, and bones are used to make the stock.

1 or 2 red snappers, 1½–2 lb in total,
   fileted and skinned
2 tbsp butter or peanut oil
2 shallots, finely sliced
1 or 2 fresh red chilies, seeded and very
   finely sliced
1 tsp finely chopped fresh ginger
1 tsp finely chopped lemongrass, soft
   inner part only
2 kaffir lime leaves, very finely shredded

1 turmeric leaf, very finely shredded
   (optional)
3½ c fish stock
2 or 3 ripe tomatoes, skinned, seeded,
   and chopped
2 tbsp finely shredded fresh basil
4 spring onions, cut into thin rounds
2 tbsp tamarind water (see pp.118–19)
   or freshly squeezed lime juice
salt and freshly ground black pepper

Serves 4–6 as an appetizer or fish course

Cut the fish filets into small pieces, rub with about ½ teaspoon salt and set aside.

Heat the butter or oil in a saucepan, and sauté all the chopped and shredded ingredients, except the basil and spring onions, for about 2 minutes until they are quite soft. Add the fish stock, simmer for 5 minutes, season with salt and pepper, and add the fish slices. Continue to simmer for 2–3 minutes, then add the basil, spring onions, and tamarind water or lime juice. Give everything a stir, adjust the seasoning, and serve hot right away.

palumara ikan
tamarind pickled mackerel

The flavor of this delicious dish is much better if the fish is cooked a day in advance, then skinned and fileted. It is a lovely dish for a picnic, served with a summer salad and some crusty Italian or country-style bread. Here, I use lots of lemongrass stems to line the cooking pan. Always make sure that the water for poaching the fish is sufficient to submerge it completely.

3 or 4 fresh mackerel, about 3½ lb, total
1 tsp salt
½ tsp ground turmeric
2 tbsp freshly squeezed lime juice
1 lb lemongrass stems, washed
10 shallots or 2 large onions, sliced
5–10 large fresh red chilies, seeded and sliced

4 garlic cloves, sliced
2 in piece of fresh ginger, thinly sliced
1 c tamarind water (see pp.118–19)
2½ c (or more) cold water
1½ tbsp coarse sea salt

Serves 6–8

Clean the fish well and rub all over with the salt, turmeric, and lime juice. Leave in a cool place to marinate for 1 hour before cooking.

Line the bottom of the saucepan with the lemongrass, and sprinkle about ½ tablespoon of the sea salt over it. Spread half of the sliced shallots or onions on top of the lemongrass, followed by half of the chilies, garlic, and ginger. Sprinkle on another ½ tablespoon of the sea salt. Lay the fish on top of this in one layer, then spread the rest of the onions, garlic, chilies, and ginger on top. Sprinkle with the remaining sea salt. Pour in the tamarind water, and add 2½ cups water (or more, if necessary) to submerge the fish.

Cover the pan and cook over low heat for 40–50 minutes. The lemongrass may get a little burned, but this will only give a nice smoky taste to the fish. Leave the fish to cool completely in the pan, then transfer to a glass container without the lemongrass. Discard all the solids. Keep in the refrigerator until needed the next day or the day after. Serve cold, skinned, and fileted, as suggested above.

cumi-cumi isi
stuffed squid

I remember only one or two occasions when I ate stuffed squid in Indonesia, though the Javanese are fond of squid *sambal goreng*. Now, buying and experimenting with squid has become quite a passion for me. My attempt to make squid *kalio* was very successful. The *kalio*, my West Sumatran curry, is delicious, and the baby squid, which I cooked whole, were very tender. Naturally, the recipe below has become more Mediterranean, as I'm using local ingredients as well as virgin olive oil and a still Prosecco. I use medium-sized squid, one per person, sliced diagonally into three or four pieces. These would be just right for serving with pasta as a main course. Or you can serve the squid as part of an antipasti platter, and use the tomato sauce to accompany pasta – papardelle, perhaps – served separately as a *primo*, or first course.

6 medium squid, cleaned thoroughly, and ink sacs discarded (or reserve for use in another recipe)
½ c Bisol Molera or other light fresh white wine
3 tbsp virgin olive oil

for the stuffing
12 oz raw shrimp, peeled and deveined
½ of the tentacles from the squid (use the rest in another recipe)
2 oz pork fat or Italian *lardo*, finely chopped
4 shallots, finely chopped
3 garlic cloves, finely chopped
1 tsp ground coriander
½ tsp ground turmeric
½ tsp chili powder

1 tsp grated fresh ginger
1 tbsp finely chopped fresh flat-leaf parsley
1 large egg, lightly beaten

for the tomato sauce
3 tbsp virgin olive oil
6 shallots or 2 large red onions, finely sliced
2 garlic cloves, crushed
1 lb fresh plum tomatoes, peeled and roughly chopped
1 tbsp chopped fresh basil leaves
salt and freshly ground black pepper

Serves 8–10 as an antipasto or appetizer, or 6 as a main course served with pasta or boiled new potatoes

To make the stuffing, chop the shrimp and squid tentacles finely with a cleaver or a large, very sharp knife. Put in a bowl and mix in the rest of the ingredients for the stuffing, including the egg. Divide the mixture into six portions, and use to stuff each squid. Close the opening with a wooden cocktail stick. Keep in a cold place while making the tomato sauce.

Heat the oil in a frying pan, and when hot, gently fry the shallots or onions and the garlic, stirring, for 5–8 minutes until they have wilted and are just about to turn color. Add the tomatoes, and season with salt and pepper. Continue cooking for 3 minutes. Add the basil, cover the pan and turn off the heat.

In another frying pan, heat the remaining 3 tablespoons olive oil. Put in the stuffed squid, and stir for a couple of minutes until they all become opaque. Increase the heat, add the Molera or other white wine, and keep the heat quite high for a minute or so. Stir the squid again with a spatula, cover the pan, reduce the heat and cook for 5–8 minutes. The squid should be tender by now, and the stuffing cooked through. Transfer to a wooden board and slice each squid into three pieces. Arrange the squid on a warmed serving dish, and pour the tomato sauce over the top. Serve hot right away.

udang goreng asam pedas
shrimp in tamarind sauce with chilies and tomatoes

This is a variation of the tamarind sauce that is popular in the port city of Ujung Pandang, formerly Makassar. Tomatoes grow profusely in this area. It is perhaps unusual to peel tomatoes, but for this dish it is worth the trouble of doing so; I sometimes seed them as well. In Indonesia, we would use salam leaves, not kaffir lime, but fresh salam leaves are often hard to find, and dried ones may lack flavor. Fresh kaffir lime leaves are very similar, and easier to find.

12–16 raw jumbo shrimp, peeled
  and deveined
½ tsp chili powder or cayenne pepper

½ tsp ground turmeric
1 tsp salt
3 tbsp peanut oil

for the sauce
2 tbsp peanut oil
3 large red onions, chopped
6 fresh kaffir lime leaves or salam leaves
3 garlic cloves, finely chopped
1 tsp finely chopped fresh ginger
1 tsp finely chopped galangal
1 tsp finely chopped lemongrass
1 tsp finely chopped fresh green chili
1 tsp salt
5 tbsp hot water

2 tsp ground coriander
3 tbsp tamarind water (see pp.118–19)
5 large red tomatoes, peeled
   and chopped

for the garnish
handful of fresh flat-leaf parsley leaves

Serves 3–4 as an appetizer,
or 2 as a main course

Rub the cleaned shrimp with the mixture of chili powder or cayenne, turmeric, and salt. Set the shrimp aside in a cool place for 30 minutes or so, while you prepare and make the sauce.

Heat the 2 tablespoons oil in a shallow saucepan or a sauté pan. When the oil is hot, add the chopped onions, reduce the heat, and sauté the onions, stirring often, for 4–5 minutes. Add the kaffir lime or salam leaves, garlic, ginger, galangal, and green chili. Stir through, add the salt and hot water, cover the pan and cook for 4 minutes.

In a frying pan, heat the 3 tablespoons oil. When hot, fry half the shrimp, stirring all the time, for 2 minutes, until the shrimp start to change color and turn pink. Using a slotted spoon, transfer the shrimp to a colander. Repeat this process with the remaining shrimp.

Uncover the pan containing the onions, stir, and add the ground coriander. Cook, stirring, for a few seconds, then add the tamarind water and tomatoes. Let this sauce cook over high heat, stirring constantly, for a minute or two. Adjust the seasoning with a little salt if necessary. Add the prawns from the colander to this thick sauce. Stir well, cover the pan for 2 minutes, stir again and transfer the shrimp and the sauce to a warmed serving dish. Scatter the parsley over the top, and serve at once, with rice, noodles or pasta.

udang bakar
marinated and grilled shrimp

At home, we used fresh large green shrimp (probably *Penaeus semisulcatus*) for this dish. Similar shrimp are available in Australia, and the jumbo shrimp of North America are equally suitable. Here in England, my fish dealer sells me what he calls Mediterranean shrimp – and very good they are, too. In fact, you may use whatever shrimp are available to make this dish. The real variations in the recipe are in the marinade. My favorite is the real hot one – chopped ripe tomatoes, soy sauce, a little brown sugar, grilled *terasi* (shrimp paste), and plenty of bird's-eye chilies, the very small chili peppers. But here is the simplest recipe for this.

for the marinade
3 tbsp light soy sauce
4 garlic cloves, crushed
1 tsp crumbled shrimp paste (see p.279)
1–3 red bird's-eye chilies (fresh or dried),
    crushed, or a pinch of chili powder

2 tbsp freshly squeezed lime juice
1 tbsp olive oil
1 tsp soft brown sugar

Enough for 12–16 large shrimp

Mix together all the marinade ingredients in a bowl. Clean the shrimp and discard their heads. Partly peel them, leaving the tail (i.e. the fan-shaped piece right at the back end) and the back plates of each one intact. Turn each shrimp over, slice it lengthwise and open it out flat. Marinate the shrimp in the spices etc. for at least 30 minutes, then grill, preferably over charcoal, for 3–4 minutes, turning once or twice and brushing with the marinade. Serve hot. They are delicious when eaten with the fingers, so remember the napkins.

kohu kohu
salad of smoked fish and beansprouts

On my last visit to Ambon, more than ten years ago, I found, as I had done in Menado and the whole Minahasa region, that the local fishermen had a wonderful way of smoking tuna. I have never come across this speciality of smoked tuna anywhere else in my travels. Very expensive smoked tuna used to be available in specialized delicatessens in the West, and it was, of course, perfectly suitable for this salad. Sadly, it seems to be no longer available, so I have to find other alternatives. I found that smoked salmon and smoked eel are excellent substitutes. If the smoked salmon has already been sliced thinly, cut each slice into narrow ribbons, like pasta; the smoked eel is cut into pieces about 1 inch long. The best beansprouts for this dish are soy bean sprouts, which are short; however, the long mung beansprouts will also do very well.

8 oz thin smoked salmon slices, cut into
   ribbons
8 oz smoked eel, cut into 1 in pieces
4 oz beansprouts, blanched
   with hot water for 1 minute only
   and drained
2 oz cos lettuce, finely shredded,
   or arugula

for the dressing
4 tbsp freshly grated coconut or ground
   kenari (see p.278) or ground almond
½–1 tsp *sambal ulek* (see p.279)
1 shallot, finely sliced
1 garlic clove, very finely sliced
1 tbsp chopped fresh chives
2–4 tbsp freshly squeezed lime or
   lemon juice
salt to taste

Serves 6–8 as an appetizer or 4 as a
lunch dish, with some bread

Mix all the ingredients for the dressing in a glass bowl. Add the salmon, eel, beansprouts and lettuce or argula just before serving, and toss through gently.

pais ikan dengan udang
fish and shrimp parcels

Pais in Sundanese, *pepes* in Javanese and Indonesian, *palai* in the Minangkabau area — all are names for this concoction of fish and shrimp, together or separately, wrapped in banana leaves. The spice mixture varies slightly from region to region, as good cooking is a matter of using the freshest ingredients from the garden around your house. My Sumatran grandmother would use *limau*, very similar to limes, that grew on her patch of land, while my West Javanese aunt in Tasikmalaya always used *belimbing wuluh* (see p.274) because she had her own tree. People elsewhere use whatever ingredients are easily available to give sourness to the *pepes*: *kedondong* and their leaves, *asam jawa* (tamarind), or *asam gelugur* (see p.274).

The recipe below is my variation as I make it in Wimbledon. My favorite souring agent is, in fact, *belimbing wuluh* for any *pais* or *pepes* that I make, but this is one ingredient that has not traveled to the West as yet because it does not like a long journey. Banana leaves are now available in the West, but, as I explain on p.176, they are time consuming to prepare as wrappers for cooking. So I usually use a casserole or gratin dish to cook this. Or, of course, you can use wax paper or foil instead of the banana leaf.

4 salmon or cod filets, weighing
  3½–4 oz each, or 4 whole small trout
1 tsp freshly squeezed lime juice
½ tsp salt
8 oz peeled and deveined raw shrimp
1 tbsp thick tamarind water (see
  pp.118–19) or 1 oz rhubarb, finely
  sliced, or 1 oz young vine leaves,
  shredded
2–3 large fresh red chilies, seeded and
  finely sliced
2 in piece of lemongrass stem, tough
  outer leaves discarded, finely chopped

2 kaffir lime leaves, finely shredded
½ oz coconut milk

for the bumbu (paste)
1 tsp *sambal ulek* (see p.279)
3 candlenuts or macadamia nuts,
  chopped
3 shallots, finely chopped
2 garlic cloves, finely chopped
1 tsp chopped fresh ginger
1 tsp crumbled shrimp paste (see p.279)
5 tbsp coconut milk
½ tsp salt

Serves 4

Left to right: *carambola* (starfruit; *belimbing manis*); *belimbing wuluh*, leaves and fruit.

Preheat the oven to 400°F (200°C). Rub the fish filets with the lime juice and salt. Keep to one side.

Put all the ingredients for the *bumbu*, or paste, in a blender, and purée until smooth. Transfer the paste to a wok or frying pan, and fry gently, stirring often, for 4 minutes until aromatic. Now add the rest of the ingredients, except the fish and the shrimp. Simmer until the mixture has no more liquid, but is still moist. Add the shrimp, remove from the heat, and stir to coat the shrimp with the spice mixture.

Now put each fish filet on a square of banana leaf or wax paper or foil, or arrange them side by side in a casserole or a gratin dish. Top the fish with an equal quantity of spiced shrimp. Wrap neatly, or put the cover on the dish, and bake in the oven for 10–12 minutes. Serve right away, either as a first course on some lettuce leaves, or with rice as the main course.

TOFU AND TEMPEH

paria berisi tahu dan udang
bitter melon stuffed with tofu and shrimp

Everyone in Southeast Asia loves bitter melon, or bitter cucumber, balsam pear, karela, ampalaya … it has many names. Botanically, it is *Momordica charantia*. In Indonesia, it is known as *paria*, and we are convinced that, as it is bitter, it must also be good for us. I'm diabetic, and have been told that *paria*, though it won't cure diabetes, can help diabetes sufferers. I eat *paria* because I like it, but I must admit I'm still waiting to see if it will have any effect on my blood sugar. In fact, *paria* is a very healthy vegetable, with plenty of minerals and fiber, and useful vitamins. And the bitterness is good; a bit of an acquired taste, perhaps, but once you acquire it you're hooked.

1 *paria* (bitter melon), 14–16 in long
1 tbsp sea salt

for the stuffing
12 oz tofu, diced
8 oz peeled and deveined shrimp,
   without heads, finely chopped
4 shallots, finely chopped
3 garlic cloves, finely chopped

1 tsp ground coriander
½ tsp ground cumin
½ tsp soft brown sugar
1 kaffir lime leaf, shredded,
   or 1 tbsp chopped fresh mint
1 tsp salt
½ tsp ground white pepper
2 tbsp coconut milk or stock or water

Serves 6 as an appetizer

Preheat the oven to 350°F (180°C). Cut the *paria* across into rounds, about 1¼ inch thick, or a little thicker, to make 12 rounds in all. With a small knife, scrape out the seeds and membranes. Put the rings in a colander, sprinkle with the sea salt, and leave to stand for about 2 hours. Rinse off the salt under cold running water, then rinse each *paria* round (and the colander) in a bowl of cold water. Leave the *paria* in the colander to drain.

Bring about 2 cups water to a boil in a largish saucepan. Add the *paria* and ½ teaspoon salt. Reduce the heat and let the *paria* bubble gently, covered or uncovered, for 2–3 minutes. Drain once again in the colander.

In a bowl, mix together all the stuffing ingredients thoroughly. Arrange the *paria* rounds on the bottom of an ovenproof dish, spoon the stuffing into them, and cook in the oven for 20–25 minutes. (Alternatively, steam for 20 minutes.) Serve hot, warm, or cold as an appetizer, or as a side dish to be eaten with rice.

semur tahu
tofu in soy sauce

1 oz *so-un* (vermicelli made from green bean starch)
vegetable oil or butter
4 pieces of tofu (about 4 oz each), halved
1 small onion, finely sliced

2 garlic cloves, crushed
4 tbsp dark soy sauce
1 tbsp ketchup
crisp-fried shallots (see p.275)
fresh flat-leaf parsley, chopped

Serves 2–4

Soak the *so-un* in warm water for 30 minutes.

Heat 3 tablespoons oil or butter in a frying pan. Fry the tofu pieces for 3 minutes on each side. Keep warm. Put another tablespoonful of oil or butter in the same pan, and fry the onion for about 2 minutes. Add the garlic, soy sauce, and tomato ketchup. Put in the tofu and 1 cup water, and simmer slowly for 4 minutes. Drain the *so-un* and add to the pan. Increase the heat slightly, and cook for another 3 minutes. Serve hot, garnished with crisp-fried shallots and chopped parsley.

tempe bacem
twice-cooked tempeh

For many Indonesians, especially those from Java, tempeh is a staple food. Nowadays, tempeh is available in many other countries because it is considered to be an excellent substitute for meat. When I was at high school, *tempe bacem* was the bestselling food in any school tuck shop. We ate it cold, at any time of the day — as a snack, or to accompany a full meal with rice.

12 oz tempeh (see pp.123–4)
1 small onion, chopped
2 garlic cloves, chopped
1 tsp ground coriander
1 tsp finely chopped fresh ginger
1 salam leaf or bay leaf
1 tsp chopped galangal
1 heaped tsp soft brown sugar (optional)

½ tsp chili powder
1 tbsp *kecap manis* (sweet soy sauce)
1 cup tamarind water (see pp.118–19)
1 tsp salt
peanut oil for frying

Serves 4

Cut the tempeh into thick slices. Put all the ingredients (except, of course, the oil) in a saucepan. Add 1 cup water, cover, and cook for 50–60 minutes until all the liquid has been absorbed by the tempeh. Take care that the contents of the pan do not burn. Leave everything to cool for a few minutes, then deep-fry in hot oil, turning once. When the slices of tempeh are nicely brown, drain on a plate lined with paper towels. Serve hot, warm, or cold. They can be kept in the refrigerator for up to a week, to be served cold, or you can reheat them in a non-stick frying pan, or in a preheated 300°F (150°C) oven for 10 minutes.

tempe rendang
rendang tempeh

If you are vegetarian or vegan, *tempe rendang* makes a most satisfying main-course dish, full of proteins and vitamin B12. On pp.120–4 are instructions for making tempeh at home, but you can also buy it in many good health food shops. Tempeh can be cooked for a long time without becoming soft or disintegrating, so it is perfectly suitable for making *rendang*. (Don't be surprised if it doesn't become as dark in color as beef *rendang* does.) As with beef, you can stop the cooking somewhat earlier, when there is still quite a lot of sauce in the pan; the dish is then *tempe kalio*. *Rendang* and *kalio* can both be frozen very satisfactorily. All the other ingredients are the same as for making Beef Rendang (pp.180–1); the method is also exactly the same. You will need three 1 pound slabs of homemade tempeh (see pp.120–4). If buying your tempeh, you will need about 3 pounds.

kering tempe dengan teri
crisp-fried tempeh with dried anchovies

Here, the word *kering* (meaning "dry") is a short way of saying *sambal goreng kering* (explained on p.170). The recipe below is the simplest of all dishes that can be categorized as a *sambal goreng kering*.

1 lb tempeh (see pp.120–4)
peanut oil for frying
8 oz *ikan teri* (tiny dried anchovies),
  heads discarded
5 shallots, sliced
3 garlic cloves, sliced
1 tsp chopped fresh ginger
1 tsp chili powder or *sambal ulek*
  (see p.279)
½ tsp salt

for the marinade
1 c tamarind water (see pp.118–19)
2 garlic cloves, crushed
1 tsp salt

*Serves 4 as an accompaniment
to a main meal with rice*

Slice the tempeh slab into thin pieces, then cut these into tiny squares. To make the marinade, mix together tamarind water, crushed garlic, and salt. Marinate the tempeh in this for 30 minutes.

Drain the tempeh, and dry the pieces with paper towels. Heat the oil in a wok, and deep-fry the tempeh until crisp and golden brown. Don't try to fry all the tempeh at once: do it little by little, keeping the pieces you have fried warm, wrapped in paper towels. When you have finished frying the tempeh, start frying the *ikan teri*, stirring continuously until crisp. This will take 2–3 minutes. Drain and keep warm.

Discard the oil that you have used for frying the *ikan teri*, and put 2 tablespoons fresh peanut oil into the wok. Fry the sliced shallots and garlic until slightly colored, then add the chopped ginger, chili powder or *sambal ulek*, and ½ teaspoon salt. Stir-fry for a few seconds, then put in the reserved tempeh and *ikan teri*. Continue stirring for a few more seconds. The dish can be served warm or at room temperature, to be eaten with rice. When cool, it can be stored in an airtight jar, where it will keep and remain crisp for several days.

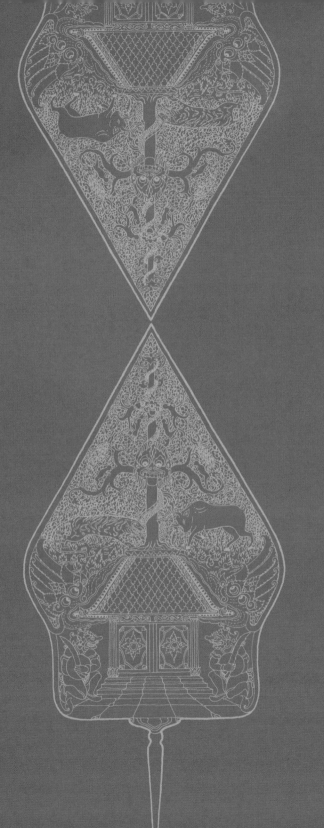

Chapter Five:
Methods and Techniques

SAMBAL and SAMBAL GORENG

Sambal and *sambal goreng* are two terms that are often misunderstood and misapplied by people who are unfamiliar with Indonesian and Malaysian cooking. They know that *sambal* is a spicy chili-hot sauce or relish, and that *goreng* means "fried," and they quite reasonably assume that *sambal goreng* is a fried relish. In fact, the phrase is used to identify a whole class of dishes – or, to put it another way, it is the name given to a kind of general purpose recipe, in which the method remains more or less the same, but the ingredients can be whatever you fancy or whatever you happen to have in the pantry. Cookbooks and restaurant menus often use it, followed by the name of the principal ingredient. *Sambal goreng daging*, for example, is obviously a *sambal goreng* made with *daging* – literally, "meat," but when the word is used by itself it is understood to mean beef. *Sambal goreng daging* is a classic dish, traditionally served as part of the celebrations for Idul Fitri, the end of the fasting month of Ramadan. Beef is far too expensive for anyone to eat every day, so it is reserved for the most special days of the year. But you can make *sambal goreng* any day using a more affordable main ingredient, often something you take from your backyard – a few eggs, a chicken, homegrown vegetables – or a piece of tofu from a street vendor.

Most *sambal goreng* dishes are, in essence, curries – that is, dishes cooked with a lot of sauce. It is the sauce that gives much of the flavor. *Sambal goreng daging* can properly be translated "Indonesian beef curry," but to call it "fried sambal with beef" is really not very helpful. *Sambal goreng* can be made either with or without coconut milk. In this section, I give directions for both, so that either can be used as a curry sauce with meat, fish, seafood, vegetables, or tofu, thus catering for everyone, vegetarians and vegans included. There is also the question of how much liquid the sauce should contain, so we have curries that are very runny, others in which the sauce is much reduced by longer cooking, and still others, *sambal goreng kering*, which are barely moist (*kering* means "dry"). Wet or dry, every *sambal goreng* needs a spice mix. The general Indonesian word for this is *bumbu*, though the Malaysians more often call it *rempah*; it is very similar to what in Indian cooking is called *masala*.

sambal goreng
sambal goreng sauce

Here is my basic recipe for a rich, creamy *sambal goreng* sauce, followed by a description of how to use the sauce with several main ingredients.

for the bumbu (paste)
4 shallots, chopped
2 garlic cloves, chopped
3 large fresh red chilies, seeded and
    chopped, or ½ tsp chili powder and
    1 tsp paprika
1 tsp *terasi* (shrimp paste)
2 candlenuts or macadamia nuts or
    blanched almonds (optional)
1 tsp chopped fresh ginger
1 tsp ground coriander
1 tsp chopped galangal
½ tsp salt

2 tbsp peanut oil
2 tbsp tamarind water (see pp.118–19)
2 tbsp of the coconut milk

other ingredients
3½ c coconut milk
2 in piece of lemongrass stem
2 kaffir lime leaves
2 large red tomatoes, skinned, seeded,
    and chopped
salt to taste

Makes about 2½ cups

Blend all the ingredients for the paste until smooth, and put in a heavy saucepan. Fry gently, stirring often, for 5 minutes. Add the coconut milk, lemongrass, and kaffir lime leaves. Bring everything to a boil again, then reduce the heat and simmer for 50 minutes, stirring occasionally. Add the chopped tomatoes and some more salt. Continue simmering for another 10 minutes. Adjust the seasoning, and serve hot. Alternatively, let the sauce cool and refrigerate until needed. It will keep in the refrigerator for 3–4 days. To serve, reheat the sauce gently almost to boiling point, then simmer for 15 minutes, stirring frequently.

sambal goreng ikan
fish sambal goreng

Any white fish, such as cod, halibut, or monkfish, is good for this *sambal goreng*. Salmon or trout are equally delicious. For 4 people, as an appetizer, or for 2 as a main course, you need 4 filets (4–6 oz each) of whichever fish you choose.

Clean and prepare the fish, ready to be arranged on a large non-stick frying pan, side by side. Heat the *sambal goreng* (p.172), reducing it to the thickness you prefer. Adjust the seasoning as desired, adding a little salt and freshly ground black pepper, or a squeeze of lemon juice. Bring the sauce to a rolling boil, stirring all the time, and pour over the fish in the frying pan. Continue cooking over medium heat for 5–6 minutes until the fish is just cooked. Serve hot right away.

Making *sambal goreng* with meat or poultry demands a slightly different approach: the meat must be cooked until tender before the coconut milk is added.

Sambals

Sambal (Javanese, *sambel*; West Sumatran, *sambal lado*) is a hot relish that is treated and used rather as one might use chutney with Indian food, or redcurrant jelly or horseradish sauce with an English roast. The usual purpose of a *sambal* is to add more chili heat to dishes that are probably quite hot already, but if you make your own, or choose carefully among commercially made *sambals*, you can go for less chili and less heat. Many of the *sambals* that you can buy in jars are made in the Netherlands, and there are of course lots of chili sauces made in Thailand, Malaysia, Hong Kong, and elsewhere which are sold in Asian food stores and Thai or Chinese supermarkets. Conimex and Lucullus are the best-known Dutch brands outside the Netherlands, and their products include *sambal badjak* and *sambal brandal*, *sambal manis* (literally, "sweet sambal") and *sambal oelek*. This last word, pronounced something like "Ooh, look!" is the old Dutch spelling of the modern Indonesian word *ulek*, meaning the pestle which is used to pound the ingredients into a paste. *Sambal nasi goreng* is intended for use as a *bumbu* (spice mix) in making *nasi goreng*, Indonesian fried rice. This brings us back to the notion of *sambal* as an ingredient in a cooked dish; if you have a stock of ready-made *sambal*, it can often be used as a shortcut or at any rate a labor-saver in your cooking. All your *sambals* should, ideally, be homemade, although I admit that I buy some of mine because I know they are trustworthy. One that I always make myself is *sambal kacang*. *Kacang* (pronounced, and in the old days spelled, *katjang*) are peanuts, and this is the *sambal* traditionally served with satay and with *gado-gado*; it often appears on menus as peanut sauce or satay sauce. It goes well with any grilled meat or most savory snacks, and makes a good dip for *lalab* (uncooked vegetables, or crudités).

sambal kacang
peanut sauce

½ c canola or peanut oil	½ tsp chili powder
8 oz raw peanuts (with their skins)	½ tsp soft brown sugar
2 garlic cloves, chopped	1 tbsp dark soy sauce
4 shallots, chopped	2 c water
1 thin slice *terasi* (shrimp paste)	1 tbsp tamarind water (see pp.118–19)
(optional)	or juice of 1 lemon
salt, to taste	

Makes about 1 ¼ cups

Heat the oil in a wok or frying pan, and stir-fry the peanuts for 4 minutes. Remove with a slotted spoon to drain in a colander; leave to cool. Once the peanuts have cooled, pound or grind into a fine powder using a blender, coffee grinder or a mortar and pestle. Discard the oil, reserving 1 tablespoon for cooking the paste.

Crush the garlic, shallots, and shrimp paste, if using, in a mortar with a little salt. Fry in the reserved oil for 1 minute. Add the chili powder, sugar, soy sauce, and 2 cups water. Bring to a boil, then add the ground peanuts. Simmer, stirring occasionally, for 8–10 minutes until the sauce becomes thick. Add the tamarind water or lemon juice, and more salt if needed. Remove from the heat.

Once cool, keep in an airtight jar in the refrigerator. Reheat as required for use. The sauce will keep in the refrigerator for up to a week.

Another *sambal* that needs to be made fresh is *sambal kelapa*, or coconut *sambal*. There are two equally good ways to make this: one with freshly grated coconut; the other with shredded coconut. Either can be used to dress a cooked vegetable salad. Such a salad is generally called *urap*, but there are regional variations. In Central Java, for instance, and some parts of Sulawesi, it is more often called *gudangan* (pp.194–5).

sambal kelapa

coconut relish for a cooked salad

flesh of ½ fresh coconut or about
   4 oz shredded coconut
1 tsp crumbled grilled shrimp paste
   (see p.279)
½–1 tsp chili powder

1 garlic clove, finely chopped
½ tsp soft brown sugar
1 tbsp thick tamarind water (see
   pp.118–19) or juice of ½ lime
salt to taste

If you are starting with a fresh coconut

Break open the coconut and remove the flesh. Peel the brown rind from it, using a potato peeler or a sharp knife, so that you have pure white coconut only. Grate the coconut flesh with a hand grater, or put it, a little at a time, in a food processor, and blend so that you get fine coconut granules. Put the shrimp paste in a large bowl, and crush it further using the back of a spoon or a pestle. Add the grated coconut and the rest of the ingredients, and mix well. Adjust the seasoning.

If you are using shredded coconut

Put the shrimp paste in a large bowl, and crush it further using the back of a spoon or a pestle. Add the shredded coconut and the rest of the ingredients, plus 1 cup water, and mix well. Bring the mixture to a boil in a heavy saucepan, and continue boiling for 5 minutes, stirring continuously. Adjust the seasoning with a little salt. If using the dressing for a cold salad, let it cool before use. For a warm salad, you may need to reheat the vegetables before serving.

sambal terasi

sambal with shrimp paste

This is the *sambal* loved by all Javanese. It is usually made with fresh bird's-eye chilies, and the shrimp paste must be either fried in a little oil or grilled first before it is mixed into the chilies that have been crushed using a mortar and pestle. In Java, of course, we use the *cobek* and *ulek-ulek*, which are traditionally made of stone. But I always use my wooden mortar and pestle for making *sambal terasi*. Bird's-eye chilies make the *sambal* very hot indeed; if you like your *sambal terasi* less fiery, then use commercially produced *sambal ulek* (see p.279). All you need to add then is just the *terasi*, crushed in the mortar, ½ teaspoon soft brown sugar, and 1 teaspoon freshly squeezed lime or lemon juice. This mixture is now ready to use as a dip or as a condiment to add piquancy to *gule kambing* (pp.56–8), or other dishes such as *urap* (cooked vegetable salad), or even *soto* (spicy soup). If you make a lot of *sambal terasi* in one go, it will keep in an airtight jar in the refrigerator for 2 or 3 days.

WRAPS and BANANA LEAVES

Most of the wrapped dishes in this book are wrapped either in wonton skins or spring roll skins, with filo pastry as a substitute. Others are contained in banana leaves. Banana leaves are easily torn, so, before we use them for wrapping, several things need to be considered. To start with, the banana leaves that are sold in Thai and Chinese supermarkets abroad, for instance, usually come from Thailand. They are brought in by air, so they are expensive. They also take time and trouble to prepare. First, they must be thoroughly washed and, while still wet, wiped clean with a dry towel. You'll see immediately that your towels are black, mainly because banana leaves in the tropics are exposed to a lot of dust. The next step is to soften the leaves, so that they will be pliable and not torn to shreds while you are trying to wrap the food. The most practical way to do this is to heat them, such as over a gas flame turned up quite high, or over an electric hotplate. Pass the piece of banana leaf over the flame or the hot metal, but not too near, until the whole piece is wilted. When all the leaves are wilted, you may need to wipe them again with a dry cloth or paper towels. Use as appropriate: see the picture on p.199, for example.

Preparing real banana leaves definitely demands both time and trouble, if you are able to find a good source of them. For greater convenience, I recommend wrapping the food in foil for cooking, or placing it in ramekins, as appropriate.

Right: Folded banana leaves, for use as food wrappers.

KALIO and RENDANG

I have included recipes for *kalio* and *rendang* in several of my other books: the ingredients are the same for both. *Kalio* is simply *rendang* before all the coconut milk has been absorbed by the meat. The final stage, when the meat has absorbed almost all the sauce and has become dark brown in color and very succulent, is *rendang*.

My grandmother used to cook 5–10 kg (11–22 lb) buffalo meat in a large steel wok. Even as a five-year-old child, I watched this process with fascination, and listened to my grandmother's story about how *rendang* was taken as essential provisions by people making the *haj*, the pilgrimage to Mecca. *Rendang* is not only very nourishing, but also can be kept without refrigeration for a month or longer. In a cool place, inside an airtight container, it doesn't even need to be reheated frequently. It can be heated once a week, enough to soften the congealed coconut milk, which also makes an excellent sandwich filling. Traditionally, in West Sumatra, *rendang* is eaten at a *selamatan* or at the end of Ramadan with *lemang* (see p.234), sticky rice cooked in coconut milk inside segments of bamboo.

I have cooked *rendang* many times, and I always use the recipe that I got from my mother, who wrote down what her mother-in-law, my grandmother, told her. The spicing is very simple, and, as it has always given me good results, I never think of changing it. If you travel around Malaysia, however, you will find local variations, with extra ingredients added to the spice mix. I must also mention that *rendang* can be made with other meat besides the traditional buffalo or beef. I made it with kangaroo in one of my cooking classes in Australia, and I've made it also with pork and with lamb. In Indonesia, you can find *rendang nangka*, made with jackfruit, and *rendang jengkol* (see *jengkol* in the glossary, p.277). And while in the Veneto, I have cooked my baby squid from the Rialto fish market in just the same way, stopping, of course, at the *kalio* stage because the squid need plenty of sauce. They were delicious, and I have no hesitation in recommending them to you as *kalio cumi-cumi* (pronounced, don't forget, "chew-me chew-me," though in fact they are beautifully tender). During the Japanese occupation of Java, my mother used to make *rendang* with very little beef, making up for it with potatoes or red beans

Right: Making *rendang*: the sauce is not yet fully absorbed by the meat, but the dish is ready to eat as *kalio*.

(kidney beans). Big supermarkets and many small delicatessens are now selling ready-made *rendang* sauce or *rendang* marinade in vacuum packs or in jars. I have tried these instant *rendang* preparations, and I have to say that the flavor they give to the finished dish is far from the real thing. Making *rendang* from scratch, though time-consuming, is easy (see pp.180–1), and doesn't require constant attention except in the final stages; if you are spending a lot of time in the kitchen preparing and cooking other things, your own delicious *rendang* is worth the time you spend on it.

If you stop cooking *rendang* about 40 minutes before the sauce becomes really thick – in other words, when it has reached the *kalio* stage – the slow-cooked meat has become so succulent, soft and flavorful already that you can afford to use the sauce that is still in the pan for other purposes. For instance, it is an excellent and tasty gravy for medium-rare roast beef or any other roast or grilled meat. To test this, I cooked a large piece of brisket, weighing about 4½ pounds, in a large square shallow saucepan (or casserole), with the same amount of coconut milk that I use for making *rendang* the traditional way, and the same spice mix (see the *rendang* recipe on pp.180–1). I boiled the brisket in the spiced coconut milk for 20–30 minutes, then put the pan, uncovered, in a preheated oven at 325°F (160°C). After 20 minutes, I reduced the heat to 150°F (75°C) or less, and continued the slow cooking for another 4 hours, turning the meat once only after 2 hours. What started me off on this experiment was an Italian recipe for *stuffato*, for which a large piece of beef is covered with red wine and slowly cooked for up to 3 hours. This method of cooking leaves you with beef that, when thinly sliced, really tastes of beef. I have often heard European and American friends, who like *rendang* very much, comment that the meat has become somewhat overcooked and the taste has become very rich, too rich certainly for people who are thinking of reducing their weight. If you feel the same way, a good alternative to brisket of beef cooked in a slow oven is a nice piece of not-too-fatty shoulder of lamb, again about 4½ pounds. Lamb cooked this way, then allowed to cool and thinly sliced, is really delicious with a green salad. The sauce can be kept in the refrigerator for a week or more, and used to marinate any meat that you are going to grill, either on skewers on the barbecue or indoors under the grill.

rendang daging
beef slow-cooked in coconut milk with spices

Rendang is a traditional dish of West Sumatra. It was probably developed out of the need to preserve the meat from a newly killed buffalo for as long as possible in a tropical climate with no refrigerators. The meat was cut into chunky cubes, then boiled in large pots, not in water, but in spiced coconut milk, which slowly penetrated the meat and incidentally gave it a delicious flavor. My recipe was dictated to my mother by my paternal grandmother, who used to cook buffalo *rendang* for large family gatherings. *Rendang* is traditionally eaten with sticky rice cooked in coconut milk, or with *lemang* (p.234), the same sticky rice, but cooked in a bamboo segment. It is just as good, however, with plain boiled rice.

6 shallots, finely sliced
4 garlic cloves, sliced
1 in piece of fresh ginger, peeled and
   roughly chopped
1 in piece of turmeric root, peeled and
   roughly chopped, or 1 tsp ground
   turmeric
6–10 fresh red chilies, seeded,
   or 3 tsp chili powder
1 tsp chopped galangal or ½ tsp laos
   powder (ground galangal)

10 c coconut milk
1 salam leaf or bay leaf
1 fresh turmeric leaf or
   1 lemongrass stem
2 tsp salt
3 lb buffalo meat or beef (preferably
   brisket; otherwise chuck steak or
   silverside), cut into cubes of about ¾ in

Serves 8–10

Put the shallots, garlic, ginger, turmeric root or ground turmeric, chilies, and galangal or laos powder in a blender with 4 tablespoons of the coconut milk, and purée until smooth. Put this paste and the coconut milk in a large wok or saucepan. (It is generally more convenient to start in a pan, and transfer to a wok later.) Add the meat and the rest of the ingredients to the pan, making sure that there is enough coconut milk to cover.

Stir the contents of the pan, and cook, uncovered, over medium heat. Let the pan bubble gently for 1½–2 hours, stirring from time to time. The coconut milk will by then be quite thick and, of course, much reduced.

Right: *Rendang*: the spiced coconut milk sauce has now been completely absorbed by the beef.

If you started in a large saucepan, transfer everything to a wok and continue cooking in the same way for another 30 minutes, stirring occasionally. By now the coconut milk is beginning to reduce to oil, and the meat, which has so far been boiling, will soon be frying. From now on, the *rendang* needs to be stirred frequently. Taste, and add salt if necessary. When the coconut oil becomes thick and brown, stir continuously for about 15 minutes until the oil has been more or less completely absorbed by the meat. Take out and discard the salam or bay leaf, turmeric leaf or lemongrass. Serve hot with lots of rice.

BOILING AND SLOW COOKING

terik daging
spiced beef boiled in coconut milk

At home in Central Java, we loved making dishes with a cut of beef we called *sindang lamur*, which is marbled with fat. I make this *terik* with rib of beef, if I want it to be as rich and fatty as the original; for a leaner cut, I choose silverside or topside. You need to use thin coconut milk to start the boiling, until the meat is tender. Only then do you add the thick coconut milk to enrich and thicken the sauce.

4–6 slices of beef from a roll of topside
    or silverside, each slice about 6 oz
2½ c thin coconut milk
2½ c thick coconut milk

for the bumbu (paste)
5 candlenuts or macadamia nuts,
    chopped
5 shallots, finely chopped
3 garlic cloves, chopped
3–6 large fresh red chilies, seeded and
    chopped, or 1 tsp chili powder

1 tsp chopped galangal
2 tsp ground coriander
1 tsp ground cumin
2 salam or bay leaves
1 tsp salt
2 tbsp tamarind water (see pp.118–19)
3 tbsp coconut milk (taken from the
    coconut milk already prepared – see
    above)
2 tbsp peanut oil

Serves 4–6 as a main course

Put all the ingredients for the *bumbu*, or paste, in a blender and purée until smooth. Transfer to a heavy saucepan, and heat, stirring often, for 3–4 minutes. Add the pieces of beef and cook, turning them several times, for 3 minutes, then add the thin coconut milk. Increase the heat, and let the beef simmer in the bubbling coconut milk for 45–50 minutes. Turn the slices of beef over several times, and stir to coat them with the sauce. After 50 minutes or so, the sauce will be getting thicker and the meat quite tender. Now add the thick coconut milk, then reduce the heat a little and continue cooking over medium heat, uncovered, for another 10–15 minutes. (It can be longer, if you want the sauce to be thicker.) Taste, and add more salt if necessary. Serve hot right away, with rice or pasta.

pindang daging dengan kol
boiled and braised beef with cabbage

Pindang is another Javanese dish that is boiled without coconut milk, and it's a good way to cook several different meats together in one saucepan. In Central Java, lots of people, especially large families, will cook a *pindang* with *daging sapi* (beef), *daging ayam* (chicken), and hard-boiled duck eggs. In fact, this is really a mixed stew, with the vegetables put in during the final minutes of cooking. For reasons I have never been able to discover, these almost always include cabbage. The sauce is usually dark brown because the main ingredients for it are (as a rule) *terasi* (shrimp paste), thick tamarind water, ground coriander, ground cumin, and dark soy sauce. I like a cold *pindang*, especially if it has hard-boiled duck eggs in it; however, another good thing about *pindang* is that you can heat it up as many times as you like, if you have made a lot of it in one go, and all the family will be happy to see it come back again and again because the more times you heat up the leftovers, the tastier they become. I must admit that it takes some imagination to make this stew look festive or even appetizing. But if you follow my recipe here, I'll show you how to present it to guests outside your immediate family circle (or even to those within it).

1½ lb beef brisket or silverside,
   in one piece
1 tsp salt
4 skinless chicken breast filets
1 white cabbage or savoy cabbage,
   (about 1½ lb in weight)
4–6 hard-boiled duck or hen eggs
1–1½ lb new potatoes (optional; if used,
   scrub or peel them, then parboil for
   about 8 minutes, depending on their
   size)

for the spice mixture
3 tbsp peanut or olive oil
4 shallots, finely sliced
2 garlic cloves
2 large fresh red chilies, seeded and cut
   into three
2 large fresh green chilies, seeded and
   cut into three
¾ in piece of galangal
2 pieces of tamarind pulp, each about
   the size of a walnut, grilled on a
   cast-iron ridged grill pan
1 in square piece of *terasi* (shrimp
   paste), grilled on a ridged grill pan,
   then crushed in a mortar
3 tbsp dark soy sauce

Serves 6–8 as a one-bowl meal

First, boil the beef in 5–7 cups water with the salt for 1 hour, skimming from time to time. After an hour, add the chicken breasts, and continue poaching the meat for another 15–20 minutes. Take the meat out and let it cool on a chopping board. Reserve the stock.

Prepare the cabbage by separating the leaves and discarding the hard leaf ribs. Keep to one side. Slice the beef and chicken breasts into neat diagonal slices about nearly ¾ inch thick. Now, heat the peanut or olive oil in a saucepan. When hot, put in the shallots, garlic, chilies, and galangal. Stir for 2–3 minutes, then add the tamarind pulp and crushed shrimp paste. Continue stirring, and add about ¾ cup of the reserved stock and the soy sauce, followed by the cabbage leaves, and the parboiled potatoes, if using. Simmer for 10 minutes. Using a slotted spoon, take out the cabbage leaves and the potatoes, and keep them in a bowl. Now put the slices of meat into the sauce. Continue simmering for 5–6 minutes while you roughly shred the leaves.

To serve, divide the slices of beef and chicken among six or eight soup plates or bowls, then pile the shredded cabbage on top, top this with the potatoes (if using) and slices of egg. Divide the sauce as equally as possible among the plates or bowls. For a family lunch or supper, just put everything from the pan in a large serving bowl, and either serve the meal at table or let the members of the family help themselves.

babat bacem
hot and sour tripe

I love tripe and, to people who share my passion, I highly recommend this recipe. Long experience has taught me that tripe is sold in different forms in different countries. In Indonesia, I remember that the tripe my grandmother cooked still had a graying layer of thin skin over the outside of its "honeycomb" surface. If your tripe is like this, boiling it will take a long time. You can, of course, boil the grayish tripe in water, with just a little salt, for perhaps 45 minutes. Discard the water and, when the tripe is cool enough to handle, scrape off the grayish skin with a small knife while holding the tripe under cold running water. When I buy tripe (from those butchers that still sell it), it's already cleaned and boiled, so it looks already white and tender. But for making this *babat bacem*, you will still need to boil it for at least 40 minutes, so that it has time to soak up the flavor of the spices.

1 lb 5 oz prepared tripe,
  in one piece

for the bumbu (paste)
4 shallots, finely sliced
6 garlic cloves, crushed
½ c thick tamarind water
  (see pp.118–19)
1–2 tsp *sambal ulek* (see p.279)
  or chili powder
1 tsp crumbled shrimp paste (see p.279)
2 tsp ground coriander

1 tsp ground cumin
2 tsp chopped fresh ginger
¾ inch piece of galangal
1 lemongrass stem, cut into three
2 salam leaves or bay leaves

to serve
2 or 3 large red onions, finely sliced, fried
  in 3 tbsp olive oil, with ½ tsp salt and
  ½ tsp sugar added, until caramelized

Serves 4–6 as an appetizer or antipasto

Lay the tripe in a saucepan. Mix all the *bumbu* (paste) ingredients in a bowl, add 2½ cups cold water, then pour the mixture over the tripe. Put the saucepan over a medium heat and bring to a boil. Cover the pan and boil the tripe slowly for 40–45 minutes until the liquid has become quite thick. Transfer the tripe to a chopping board, and pass the cooking liquid through a sieve into a smaller saucepan. Keep aside.

Slice or cut the tripe into any shapes you like, perhaps diamonds, or diagonally into long strips. Prepare the caramelized onions in a non-stick frying pan (see "to serve" above) at the same time heating the thick sauce in a different pan. As soon as you are ready to serve, stir-fry the tripe pieces briefly in the caramelized onions, just for a minute or two. Pour in the thick sauce, stir once, and serve hot right away.

gang asam
braised rib of beef from samarinda

The best cut of beef for this recipe is short ribs, which in Indonesia is called *tulang iga*. This recipe is for an everyday dish, loved by children and adults, who would usually eat the ribs by hand with plenty of boiled rice. If your butcher or supermarket can supply you with short ribs, use these; otherwise I suggest using back rib or thin rib, in one piece. *Daun kedondong* are used to add some sourness to the dish; as a substitute, I suggest rhubarb or young grape leaves, or, better still, tamarind water (see pp.118–19) or *asam gelugur* (see p.274).

2¼ lb or a little more of short rib, back rib, or rib of beef	6 shallots or 1 large onion, finely sliced
1 lemongrass stem, crushed at the thick end, and cut across into three	4 garlic cloves, finely sliced
	1 tsp crumbled shrimp paste (see p.279)
2 salam leaves or bay leaves	1 tsp salt or a little more, to taste
¾ in piece of galangal	2 oz *daun kedondong* (see p.278) or
4 fresh red chilies, seeded and each cut into 4 pieces	4 in rhubarb stalk, chopped, or 10–15 young grape leaves, shredded, or 3
3 fresh green chilies, seeded and each cut into 4 pieces	tbsp tamarind water (see pp.118–19) or 2 slices *asam gelugur* (see p.274)

Serves 6–8

Trim away some of the excess fat from the beef. Put the meat in a large saucepan. Add 5–7 cups cold water and the lemongrass, salam or bay leaves, and galangal. Bring to a boil, then reduce the heat slightly and simmer for 50 minutes, skimming often. By now the water has reduced a little; add the chilies, shallots or onion, garlic, shrimp paste, and salt. Continue to simmer for 25–30 minutes, turning the meat several times.

Adjust the seasoning of the liquid with a little more salt if needed, then add the *kedondong* or whichever other souring agent you choose. Continue cooking, turning the meat more often now, for about 10 minutes. Discard the salam and kaffir lime leaves, galangal, lemongrass (and *asam gelugur* if using). If one-bone rib or thin rib are used, cut the joint into thick slices. Serve hot with the thick sauce.

kambing bacem
spiced tamarind lamb

Bacem is a cooking term I became familiar with when I was a high school student in Yogya. We could get *tempe bacem* and *tahu bacem* at our school, but this way of cooking was also used for meat, poultry, and offal (variety meats). Such dishes were then sold all over Central Java, as street food, in food shops, and in the public markets of every small town and big city. This recipe is a lovely way of cooking either a largish joint of lamb or a lean rack of lamb. Lamb cooked in the way I describe below should really be served hot right from the pan. You can, of course, reheat leftover meat by pan-frying it, but I find this toughens it a little, and serving it cold is preferable.

3 lb leg or shoulder of lamb, trimmed of
    fat, or 1 rack of lamb,
    cut into 2 cutlets per person
2½ c tamarind water (see pp.118–19)
3 shallots, finely sliced
3 garlic cloves, finely sliced
3 tsp ground coriander
3 tsp ground cumin
3 large fresh red chilies, seeded and
    finely sliced

1 tsp chopped fresh ginger
1 tsp chopped lemongrass, soft inner
    part only
1 tsp chopped galangal
1 tsp soft brown sugar
1 tsp salt
1 tbsp dark soy sauce
2 kaffir lime leaves or bay leaves

Serves 4–6 as a main course

Put the lamb in a saucepan that will accommodate the leg or shoulder lying flat, or the cutlets in a single layer. Mix the rest of the ingredients in a bowl, add 2½ cups water, and pour over the lamb. Put the pan over medium heat, and bring to a boil. Reduce the heat slightly and continue boiling the meat – not on a rolling boil, but just bubbling gently. Cover the pan, and cook for 50–60 minutes if using leg or shoulder, but only 20–25 minutes if using rack of lamb.

Transfer the meat to a warmed serving plate. Slice the joint thinly and discard the bone; the rack can stay as it is, without further cutting. Boil the cooking liquid until reduced to a nice thick sauce. Adjust the seasoning with salt and freshly ground black pepper if needed, and pour the hot sauce over the meat. Serve right away, with potatoes, rice, or pasta.

STEAMED DISHES

Steaming is, after boiling, the most frequent way of cooking in Indonesia, as well as in other Southeast Asian countries. In Java, the earliest rice steamer I noticed, from the time I moved to live in Yogyakarta in 1952, was a *dandang* and *kukusan*. This is not only for steaming rice, but also for steaming vegetables, and any food that is wrapped in banana leaves. The traditional *dandang* used to be made of high-grade copper, although nowadays it is made of something cheaper, usually aluminum. The *kukusan* is always made of woven bamboo strips (see image on p.128). People who did not cook their rice in one saucepan by the absorption method would steam it in a more modern-looking rice steamer. I own one such rice steamer, finished in enamel, which I bought in the Netherlands soon after I came to live in London (see p.7). There are now many different steamers, single- or double-decker, most of them variations on this model. The materials used are now generally much better, most steamers being made of stainless steel. My Thai double-decker steamer is quite large, so I can steam in it anything that I put in ramekins, or even a good-sized fish. In Chinese supermarkets, as well as in most Thai shops, you can now get basket steamers made from bamboo, in different sizes. These are very useful for steaming fish, and anything in ramekins or wrapped in banana leaves, as well as molded vegetables and little ramekins containing rice cakes and similar small items. They are inexpensive, and can be re-used many times after they have been washed in warm water. They can simply be thrown away when they start to look shabby and blackened, but, as they are so inexpensive, I find them an easy way of steaming my cooking. You need a saucepan or a wok to put these bamboo baskets in; note that the water level in the pan or wok must not come above the bottom edge of the basket. You can line a small part of this basket with banana leaf or a piece of foil, and put, say, your filet of fish on it, so it won't stick to the bamboo. Just make sure that most of the bottom of the basket is left uncovered so that the steam can get in to cook the food. Also remember that steaming is quicker than boiling because steam has much more latent heat (or, in effect, is hotter) than boiling water.

siu mai kukus
steamed stuffed wontons

In chapter 2, I talked about *pangsit goreng* (see pp.40 and 60–1), a popular Chinese restaurant snack in Yogya. Wonton skins, called *kulit pangsit* in Indonesia, are used in Chinese recipes for wrapping different fillings in almost the same way that we use banana leaves. These steamed *siu mai* (the name is Chinese, but is well known in Indonesia and in the West) are also delicious served as wonton soup, or deep-fried; the filling is the same in each case. At private parties, the three different types of *siu mai* – the soup, the steamed, and the deep-fried – are usually served as appetizers, followed perhaps by a barbecue, or by a buffet lunch or dinner, for which the hostess can put on the table as many dishes as she wants. In Yogya, Chinese restaurants would be more than happy to cater for your party, but in North America now I see leading supermarket chains acting as caterers and offering their customers satays and spring rolls. I'm sure it won't be long before *siu mai*, with assorted fillings, are on their menus. This is my version of *siu mai* filled with shrimp. Note that you can deep-fry them from raw, but for soup they need to be partly cooked by steaming. Much the best container for steaming is a bamboo basket with a lid; these are easily available, not just in Chinese supermarkets, but in many department stores that have good kitchenware sections. Obviously, check before starting that your plate full of *siu mai* will fit inside your steaming basket, and the basket inside your wok or saucepan.

For a party with plenty of other food, allow three *siu mai* per person to get things going. Three or four more per person will be ample for serving with your favorite stock or broth, as a soup course at the beginning of the meal itself.

To fill 16 to 24 *siu mai*, using a packet of 24 wonton skins, you will need:

16–20 raw shrimp, peeled and deveined
2 oz shiitake or brown mushrooms, finely diced
1 tsp chopped fresh ginger
1 tbsp finely chopped spring onions or
fresh chives
1 tbsp finely chopped fresh flat-leaf parsley
large pinch each of salt and freshly ground black pepper
1 tbsp light soy sauce
1 egg, plus 1 egg yolk, lightly beaten together (keep the egg white of the extra egg for sealing the wonton skins)

Mince or chop the shrimp, and mix these in a bowl with all the other ingredients, except the egg, unless you are ready to fill and cook the wonton skins almost right away. Add the beaten egg to the mixture only when you are ready to cook.

When you are ready to fill and cook the wontons, cover a plate with cling wrap to stop them sticking to its surface. To fill each wonton skin, lay it flat on a clean work surface, and put a heaping teaspoonful of the well-mixed filling in the center of it. Brush some egg white on the skin around the filling. Gather up the skin like a purse around the filling, leaving the "purse" a little open at the top. You can leave it as it is, though usually the four corners of the skin are trimmed off with scissors. Repeat this process until all the skins are filled (you will probably need to do them in several batches). Arrange on the plate lined with cling wrap, keeping them apart from each other to prevent sticking. As soon as the batch is complete, put the lid on the bamboo steamer and cook them straight away.

To steam, arrange strips of banana leaf or parchment paper in the bottom of the steamer, leaving gaps for the steam to escape. Place the *siu mai* on the strips. Put water into a saucepan, taking care that it is not too deep – when you put the steamer in the pan, the water must not come into contact with the *siu mai*. Bring to a boil, and put the steamer in the pan. Leave uncovered. Steam for 3–4 minutes. The *siu mai* can now be served. If you have several batches to do, keep the already-cooked ones warm. For putting in soup, the *siu mai* need only be steamed for 2 minutes, then put in the hot soup for another minute immediately before serving.

To deep-fry, heat peanut oil in a wok or deep-fryer. Cooking in batches, deep-fry the *siu mai* for 2–3 minutes from each batch. Remove and drain on paper towels. Serve hot or warm, with or without a dipping sauce.

Left: *Siu mai kukus* (steamed stuffed wontons).

gudangan
mixed vegetables with coconut dressing

This is the basis of all cooked vegetables with coconut dressing. All the others are regional variants. The usual name for such a dish is *urap*, but in some parts of Sulawesi people call it *gudangan*, and people in Central and East Java also called it *gudangan* or *kuluban*. *Gudangan* can be made with almost any combination of vegetables that appeals to you, and these may be either steamed or boiled. So my recipe here is divided into two parts: first, a section on how to steam or boil the vegetables, and, secondly, the ingredients for the *bumbu*, or dressing, and the instructions which apply to it.

Whether you steam or boil the vegetables, it is advisable to use fresh coconut, freshly grated. (See the section on coconut on pp.112–17 and the note that follows the recipe on using shredded coconut.)

for the cooked vegetables
4 oz of each of the following:
cabbage or spring greens, shredded but
    not too finely
French or runner beans, cut into pieces
    ½ in long

carrots, peeled and cut into sticks,
    the same length as the beans
cauliflower florets
beansprouts, rinsed and drained

Serves 4–6

Boil each vegetable separately (except, of course, the beansprouts) for not more than 5 minutes. Alternatively, you can steam the vegetables, putting them on top of each other in the following order: carrots at the bottom, then cabbage, then beans, then cauliflower on top (and the beansprouts for one minute only). Serve hot or warm, as explained in the final part of the recipe.

for the bumbu (dressing)
½ coconut (see the section on coconut
    on pp.112–17 and the note below*
    on using shredded coconut)
1 tsp crumbled grilled shrimp paste (see
    p.279) (optional)

½–1 tsp chili powder
1 garlic clove, finely chopped
½ tsp soft brown sugar
juice of ½ lime or 1 tbsp thick tamarind
    water (see pp.118–19)
salt, to taste

Break open the coconut and remove the flesh. Peel the brown rind from it with a potato peeler, so that you have pure white coconut. Grate the coconut flesh with a hand grater, or put a little at a time in a food processor and blend until you get fine coconut granules. Put the shrimp paste, if using, in a large bowl, and crush it further using the back of a spoon or a pestle. Add the grated coconut and the rest of the ingredients for the dressing, and mix well. Adjust the seasoning.

Just before serving, mix all the vegetables in a large bowl, and mix in the dressing, tossing the vegetables well. Serve as an accompaniment to a main course of rice and meat. As far as I know, when *urap* is called *gudangan*, the vegetables that have been mixed with the coconut dressing are steamed for 2–3 minutes before being served, either hot or cold. The steamed coconut dressing has, obviously, a longer shelf life.

* NOTE ON USING SHREDDED COCONUT

Shredded coconut can be used for the *bumbu*, or dressing, although it does not taste quite as good as fresh coconut. If you do use shredded, then you will need to boil the coconut and the remaining dressing ingredients in 1 cup water for 5 minutes. Stir continuously while it boils. Your cooked vegetables are then mixed in with this *bumbu* in the pan. You can either steam the already dressed vegetables again for 2 minutes or simply serve right away.

pepes tahu berbumbu
spicy steamed tofu

In Java and a few other islands in Indonesia, this is just another example of food cooked in banana-leaf wraps. The varying lists of ingredients will be just a matter of regional preference (see the recipe for *boboto* on p. 201). The *pepes tahu* here is my adaptation of a *pepes jamur*, a banana-leaf parcel of straw mushrooms which I often enjoyed when I was at university. There was a vendor who used to sell this mushroom *pepes* near Bulak Sumur, the complex which housed many Gajah Mada professors, lecturers and foreign teaching staff; it was where Roger and I lived after we were married. Years later, I introduced Madhur Jaffrey to this same vendor when I happened to be in Yogya at the same time as she was making her Far Eastern cooking series for the BBC. Anyway, I can't use straw mushrooms, as they are only available in cans at the Chinese supermarket. Like *belimbing wuluh* (see pp.204 and 274), straw mushrooms don't travel well when they are fresh. I use fresh shiitake mushrooms for this recipe, or fresh porcini when I'm in Italy, and I add some tofu. When I first cooked this, I was creating the recipe for a vegetarian friend of mine, and I served it as a main course; it works very well. I cook it in a small bread pan or terrine.

2–3 tbsp peanut oil
1 block Chinese-style tofu, about 15–16 oz, cut into quarters, then each piece cut into 4 pieces, to make a total of 16 cubes
2–3 tbsp peanut or rapeseed or olive oil
3 shallots, finely sliced
3 garlic cloves, finely sliced
1 tsp ground coriander
1 tsp *sambal ulek* (see p.279) or ½ tsp chili powder
8 oz fresh shiitake mushrooms, thinly sliced

1 tbsp rice flour
6 tbsp very thick coconut milk
1 tsp salt
4–6 spring onions, trimmed and cut into thin rounds
2 tbsp finely chopped fresh flat-leaf parsley or coriander leaves
1 egg, plus 1 egg yolk, lightly beaten
freshly ground black pepper (optional)

Serves 4 as an appetizer or 2 as a main course

Preheat the oven to 325°F (170°C). Lightly oil a small bread pan or terrine, and sprinkle some fine breadcrumbs or flour in it.

Heat the 2–3 tablespoons peanut oil in a non-stick frying pan, and pan-fry the pieces of tofu for about 4 minutes only, turning them once. This process is to firm the tofu a little and to give it a slight color. Keep to one side.

In another pan or a wok, heat the other 2–3 tablespoons oil. Stir-fry the shallots and garlic for 3 minutes, then add the ground coriander, *sambal ulek* or chili powder, and shiitake mushrooms. Continue stir-frying for another 3 minutes. Now add the rice flour and coconut milk, stir and simmer for 3 minutes. Add the salt. Taste, if necessary adding some more salt and perhaps also some freshly ground

Right: Porcini mushrooms on sale in the Rialto market in Venice.

black pepper. Remove from the heat, and leave to cool. When cold, add the spring onions and beaten egg. Using a spoon, mix these well into the other ingredients.

Arrange a layer of tofu on the bottom of the bread pan or terrine. Spread half of the mushroom mixture on top of this. Add another layer of tofu, followed by the rest of the mushroom mixture. Tap the whole thing all over with the back of a spoon to fill any hidden gaps, and bake in the oven for 40–45 minutes. When cooked, turn the terrine over on to a serving dish. Cut it into four or two pieces. Serve hot or warm, as an appetizer with salad or with pasta (or potatoes) and salad as a main course.

pisang raja kukus dengan urap teri
steamed plantain with crisp-fried dried anchovies in coconut sambal

In Central Java, the plantain is steamed after each individual portion has been wrapped in banana leaf. The *sambal kelapa* (Coconut Sambal, p.175) can be made well ahead of time. You will need one heaping tablespoonful of it for each portion. The dried anchovies can also be made a few days in advance – they will stay crisp if they are stored in an airtight container.

for the crisp-fried dried anchovies
3½ oz dried anchovies
½ c rapeseed or peanut oil

Serves 6 as an appetizer or 3–4 as a main course, with rice and a vegetable dish or salad

Heat the oil, preferably in a wok or a deep frying pan, until quite hot. Put in the dried anchovies, which should sizzle right away, and stir them almost continuously for 4–5 minutes. Remove the anchovies with a slotted spoon and spread on a tray lined with paper towels. Do not throw away the oil until you have made sure that the anchovies are crisp; if they are not, heat the oil again, fry them for just one more minute, and drain again on kitchen paper. Now you can discard the oil. Leave the anchovies until cold, then store them in an airtight container until needed.

for the steamed plantains
½ c coconut milk
2 shallots, finely sliced
1 garlic clove, finely sliced
1 tsp chopped fresh ginger
pinch of cayenne pepper
1 tsp ground coriander

4 ripe plantains, peeled and cut into
 rounds ½ in thick
½ tsp salt or to taste

to serve
1 quantity *sambal kelapa* (Coconut
 Sambal, p.175)

Put 2 tablespoons of the coconut milk in a saucepan to heat for 2–3 minutes. Add the shallots, garlic, and ginger, and stir-fry for 2 minutes. Add the cayenne and

ground coriander, and continue stir-frying for another minute, before adding the rest of the coconut milk. Reduce the heat and simmer for 2 minutes. Now add the slices of plantain and the salt. Simmer for 3–4 minutes until the coconut milk has all been absorbed by the plantain.

Divide this mixture among six banana-leaf squares or six ramekins. Steam for 8–10 minutes. Put the crisp-fried anchovies and *sambal kelapa* in a bowl, and toss through. Serve the plantains hot or warm, topped with the crisp-fried anchovies dressed with the *sambal kelapa*.

boboto
parcel of minced chicken with kenari
from nusa tenggara

In Nusa Tenggara, the south eastern islands of the Indonesia archipelago, kenari trees grow in abundance. The kenari nut tastes similar to an almond, although the outer shell looks more like a walnut. In fact, the taste is also quite similar to that of the Philippines' pili-pili nut. Its uses in cooking are various: it thickens sauces, and provides a rich, nutty taste. The kenari is also as expensive as almonds, but I use almonds for this recipe, rather than the candlenuts (kemiri) preferred by Indonesians in the western part of the country. But of course the Javanese, and the Sundanese (who have a similar dish), will use kemiri nuts. In Java, the preparation for this dish involves simply mixing whatever ingredients you have, or whichever ones you like: vegetables, fish, offal, tempeh, or tofu, mixed with either young grated coconut or thick coconut milk. This is wrapped in banana leaves, then steamed. But this sort of banana parcel is also familiar in Bali and Lombok. It will be filled with chicken in Lombok; pork in Bali. The Balinese call it tom, pronounced "toom," a very spicy ground pork dish, made with the liver and blood also. The Javanese call it botok. The recipe below is my version of boboto, made with kenari nuts and cooked in ramekins.

12–16 oz chicken meat from the breast
  and thigh, minced or sliced thinly
4 oz young coconut, grated, or 1 c
  very thick coconut milk
2 shallots, finely sliced
1 tsp finely chopped galangal or lesser
  galangal (*kencur*, see p.278)
2 oz ground or slivered *kenari* nuts
  or almonds

½ tsp ground cloves
½ tsp freshly grated nutmeg
2–4 fresh green chilies, seeded
  and very thinly sliced diagonally
1–1½ tsp salt, plus a few turns of a black
  pepper mill if you wish

Serves 4–6 as an appetizer

Mix all the ingredients well in a bowl, and divide the mixture among four or six ramekins. Steam in a large steamer, or a steam oven, for 12–15 minutes. Serve hot or cold. Alternatively, the ramekins of boboto can be baked in a preheated oven at 325°F (170°C), on a tray half-filled with hot water, for 20–25 minutes.

Left to right: Macadamia nuts and *kemiri* (candlenuts).

GRILLED, BAKED, AND ROASTED DISHES

"Grilling" and "roasting" translate into Indonesian as *membakar* and *memanggang*, formed from *bakar* and *panggang*. And these methods are usually not applied in the oven or under a grill because, until very recently, hardly anyone in Indonesia had an oven or an electric or gas grill in their kitchen. *Ikan bakar*, therefore, means fish grilled on charcoal.

gurami bakar
grilled gurami

Gurami is a freshwater fish cultivated in artificial ponds in many parts of Indonesia. The last time Roger and I had a large grilled *gurami* was when we revisited my home country of West Sumatra, collecting material for my *Indonesian Regional* book. We stayed in Bukittinggi and went on a scenic drive to Lake Maninjau, one of the two largest and most beautiful lakes in that part of Sumatra. It is not as big as the famous Lake Toba in North Sumatra, and does not attract as many tourists, but, like Toba, it occupies the crater of a former volcano and is therefore surrounded by steep hills. It is an extraordinarily beautiful spot, and on a bright sunny February day we had an exquisitely grilled *gurami* in a little restaurant near the water's edge. The fish was not from the lake itself, but was "farmed" in a special enclosure nearby. *Gurami* can grow as big as 11 pounds, but we were advised to take one half that size, as it would taste better. Several deep scores were made on both sides of it, and the cook then covered the fish in the paste usually used to make *pangek ikan* (pp.17–18), before grilling it in the embers of what must shortly before have been a blazing wood fire. He put the fish on a simple contraption made of wires, and turned it several times with special tools made of bamboo. We ate it on plates lined with banana leaf, accompanied, naturally, by steaming white rice, and with more of the same sauce on the side.

As I write this, it occurs to me that, in other parts of Indonesia, this fish would be deep-fried – if anyone had a big enough wok. My grandmother could have done it easily, in the big steel wok she used when she made buffalo meat *rendang*. But, as I have said elsewhere in this book, she rarely deep-fried anything. I am thinking also about what alternative fish I would recommend in places where there are no *gurami*. I would use turbot, large red snapper, or John Dory; for anyone who can get sea perch easily, this would be an excellent way of cooking it.

Now for the paste or marinade that can be used for the *gurami* or a similar fish. My Maninjau version had the *bumbu pangek* for the rub and marinade. My aunt in West Java would have used her simple marinade of chili, with a little salt and sugar, and lots of crushed garlic. For the souring agent, she would use *belimbing wuluh*, a small fruit of the carambola (starfruit) family that I have not yet been able to find in the West, apart from some I came across in a Thai shop; but they were in such bad condition that the shopkeeper realized that they were too delicate to withstand the long flight from Bangkok. *Sambal terasi* (pp.175–6) could be a good marinade for this, and also the Thai *nam pla prik*, which is just chopped-up bird's-eye chilies in fish sauce (*nam pla*). If you use this *nam pla prik*, you'll find that the hotness of the chilies won't penetrate too strongly into the taste of the fish, which will be pleasantly hot or piquant.

pecel lele
grilled catfish with shrimp paste sambal

This is not a recipe, simply an account of how you can cook a wide variety of fish very simply, but with very tasty results. If you can get hold of catfish, try this, if only for the sake of trying a street-food favorite of the 1980s in West Java. On the right is a picture I took of a friend of mine in 1987, when I was traveling round Indonesia to research my next book. We were sitting at a typical open-sided *warung*, a small eating house, on the outskirts of Jakarta, where we had gone for their *pecel lele*. There was a basket full of rice

on the table, and we were expected to eat the fish by hand and help ourselves to as much rice as we wanted. The chef asked us whether we liked our *sambal terasi* (see pp.175–6) very hot or not too hot. I was surprised that our catfish was not to be accompanied by *sambal pecel*, which is, in fact peanut sauce, the same as we eat with *gado-gado* (pp.61–4). My friend explained that *pecel* in this case did not mean the West Javanese mixed vegetable salad with its peanut dressing. The word *pecel* here was derived from *pecak*, which means "to beat gently," in this case with a pestle. When our catfish arrived, after being beautifully grilled by the cook over a charcoal fire, the waitress brought us two shallow wooden mortars, each containing a good quantity of *sambal terasi*. She explained how we should apply our *sambal terasi* to the fish, using the wooden pestles that were also provided. We each dipped a pestle into the *sambal*, and with it we gently beat the fish so as to break the surface of its flesh and let the *sambal* penetrate.

The accompaniment to our simple lunch of fish and rice was a large plate of *lalab*, a selection of raw vegetables that the French, would called crudités. The West Javanese, or Sundanese as they are named by Indonesians outside West Java, love their raw vegetables — they have their own equivalent of *gado-gado*, a collection of uncooked, beautifully sliced and shredded vegetables, dressed with peanut sauce — they call this *karedok*. Simple dishes such as this can be made anywhere, using whatever materials are to hand — this is street food, brought into the home, inspired by whatever is fashionable for a light lunch or a substantial snack.

ayam panggang kecap
chicken roasted and grilled in soy sauce

My grandmother, and even my mother, never cooked in an oven — there were very few ovens in Indonesia in those days, except in professional bakeries. That is now changing: my sisters, who live in large cities, have electric or gas ovens. The nearest thing to an oven that my mother used was a roughly made metal cabinet into which two trays of glowing charcoal could be placed, above and below the cake tin in which she baked her *lapis legit* (spiced layer cake). When people of her generation talked about roast chicken, therefore,

Left: Sri's best friend eating at a fish restaurant in Jakarta.
Above: To eat *pecel lele*, coat an *ulek-ulek* in *sambal terasi* and use it to gently beat the fish and make it spicy.

they meant *ayam panggang*, which is also called *ayam bakar*: chicken roasted or grilled over charcoal. The charcoal could be in a shallow trench or on a brazier, or what nowadays would be called a barbecue. The original recipe specified that the chicken, or the chicken halves or pieces, should be marinated with soy sauce and chili, then grilled over charcoal. My recipe below has the chicken roasted in the oven first, then the marinade is rubbed all over the chicken and under the skin. The idea is that a number of chickens can be prepared well in advance, then kept in the freezer, ready for when you have a large party or barbecue. The marinade here is enough for 2 chickens, and the chilies can be replaced with 1 red pepper plus a pinch of chili powder.

2 x 2¼–4½ lb chickens
freshly squeezed lemon juice
a little salt
butter or olive oil

for the marinade
3 large fresh red chilies
2 in piece of fresh ginger

2 tsp crumbled shrimp paste (see p.279)
4 garlic cloves
3 tbsp light soy sauce
1 tsp soft brown sugar
1 tbsp freshly squeezed lime or
　lemon juice

Serves 4–6

Preheat the oven to 325°F (170°C). Rub the chickens, outside and inside, with lemon juice, salt, and butter or olive oil. Roast in the oven for 55–60 minutes. While the chickens are in the oven, prepare the marinade.

In a mortar, pound the chilies, ginger, shrimp paste, and garlic. Add the soy sauce, brown sugar, and lime or lemon juice.

When the chickens are cooked, leave to cool a little, then cut each one in half. Discard the large and inconvenient bones, and any skin that is not covering the breasts, thighs, and legs. Lay the four halves of the chickens on a flat surface, and rub them with the marinade, under the skin of the breasts, thighs, and legs, then all over. Leave to get cold, wrap them individually in foil, and freeze until needed.

When you are ready to serve the chickens, thaw them completely, and grill or barbecue over charcoal until they are hot and a little charred. (This can also be done under an electric grill in the oven.)

Right: Bali: roasting pigs in a village that specializes in this art.

DEEP-FRIED DISHES

Deep-frying is not as unhealthy as you may think or as people may tell you. Deep-frying, in whatever kind of pan you use, requires whatever you are cooking to be submerged in very hot oil. The temperature must be right; as a general rule it needs to reach 350°F (150°C) before the food to be fried is put into it. If the temperature is too low, the food will absorb oil and be less crisp than it should be. If the oil is too hot, whatever you are frying will brown on the outside too quickly, leaving the inside still raw.

How to know that the oil is the right temperature: if you drop a small cube of bread into it, the oil should sizzle right away and the bread should brown gradually. If the cube of bread turns brown right away and, in a few seconds, becomes burned, then the oil is too hot. Turn off the heat, wait a few seconds until the smoke from the oil has disappeared, and drop in another cube of bread – this will probably sizzle right away. Now that you have the right temperature, turn on the heat again and start deep-frying whatever you are going to fry. If you are deep-frying a large number of small items – for instance, lots of *lumpia* (pp.215–16) in quick succession – you will need to control the heat by turning it down and up again several times.

rempeyek teri
savory rice flour crisps with dried anchovies

Rempeyek, more often shortened to *peyek* by the Javanese, is one of the most popular snacks in Java and has now spread everywhere else in Indonesia. In the Netherlands, I think one can now find *rempeyek kacang*, or the peanut version of this crisp, in most "Indische winkels," or Indonesian-style food shops. I don't think, however, it has reached the vending machines yet, alongside the *lumpia* (pp.215–16). After watching a number of teenagers in the Hague many years ago, I was tempted, for research purposes of course, to try a large *lumpia* from a vending machine. I don't think I ate even half of it — it was just too large and rather oily, and the filling was mostly long beansprouts. It was totally different from my recipe for fried spring rolls.

I mentioned *rempeyek kacang* above, and in this recipe I'll talk about other ingredients that you can use to make *rempeyek*. The batter will be exactly the same as for *rempeyek kacang* on pp.28–33.

For making *rempeyek teri*, you should be able to buy dried anchovies without heads; if you can't, discard the heads before putting the *teri* in the batter. You can also make *rempeyek kacang hijau* (mung bean *rempeyek*), using dried mung beans, which need to be soaked in cold water overnight. The next day, the beans will be quite plump. Drain, and dry with paper towels before putting them in the batter, and fry them as for frying the *rempeyek kacang* on pp.28–33. Cashew nuts are also good for *rempeyek*; split each one in two down the middle before putting them in the batter. Another nice *rempeyek* is made with fresh spinach leaves. Each leaf for this must be individually washed and dried, and the batter needs to be a little thicker. Spinach *rempeyek* do not have a long shelf life; they should be eaten as soon as possible after frying.

Right: *Tampah* filled with dried anchovies on a market stall.

goreng teri dan kacang tanah
deep-fried dried anchovies and peanuts

I don't remember having this very addicting snack, either during my childhood in Sumatra or in my student days in Yogyakarta. As well as boiled soy beans, we also had boiled peanuts in their shells when I was a toddler. It occurs to me now that my Sumatran grandmother was very health-conscious. She always gave us healthy and fresh food. She hardly bought any food items from the market — almost everything came from her own land. Although she did have fried cassava and fried plantain in her cooking repertoire, I didn't see fried peanuts until, I think, I went to Yogya. I remember, during the celebrations at the end of Ramadan, among the glass jars of biscuits, and any delicacies that needed to be kept in airtight containers, there were different kinds of fried peanuts in some of the jars. We call these jars by the Dutch name for them, *stopfles*, which Indonesians pronounce "stopless". These jars have airtight stoppers, necessary for keeping their contents crisp. These *goreng teri dan kacang tanah* are nowadays produced commercially, and you will see this anchovy-and-peanut combination served in bowls in bars frequented by tourists in Indonesia and Malaysia. They are also served by families who are in the habit of having a drink and nibbles (*makanan kecil* — "small eats") before their evening meal.

The dried anchovies and peanuts are always deep-fried in separate woks or frying pans. They are then drained separately, and only when they have cooled a little can they be mixed in a bowl. Quite often a teaspoonful or so of chili flakes or chili powder is mixed in, and perhaps some crisp-fried shallots (see p.275). I don't like to share a bowl of these, especially the ones coated with chili, with anyone else. So, put a spoon in the bowl, and give each guest a little bowl or plate, and let them spoon some of the *goreng teri* and *kacang* onto it. Of course, you will need to provide the guests with napkins, too.

ikan pesmol (kakap goreng berkuah)
jakarta-style fried fish (fried red snapper served with a sauce)

This is a very good example of a deep-fried dish, which also shows that we like to eat something that is crisp on the outside, but moist and tender inside. It helps us to eat with our fingers (of the right hand only) much more neatly. However, the feel of this delicious fried fish, both in your hand and also in your mouth, when you eat it with fluffy white rice, makes you think that it would be better still with a little sauce. I have never found out why it is called *ikan pesmol*, but I know that whenever I go to Jakarta I will be offered this dish, either in a restaurant or at a friend's home. I cook it with red snapper because red snapper is easier to find than the *kakap putih* usually favored by Jakarta cooks. *Kakap putih* is sea perch, which I think is easier to get in Australia than anywhere else outside Indonesia.

1 large or 4 small red snapper
2 tbsp freshly squeezed lime juice or
   tamarind water (see pp.118–19)
½ tsp salt
½ tsp ground turmeric
½ tsp chili powder
peanut or rapeseed oil,
   for deep-frying

for the sauce
10 or more shallots
5 candlenuts or macadamia nuts
2 tsp chopped fresh ginger

1 tsp chopped galangal or (if you have it)
   lesser galangal (*kencur*, see p.278)
3 tbsp peanut oil
3 large fresh red chilies, seeded and
   thinly sliced diagonally
3 large fresh green chilies, seeded and
   thinly sliced diagonally
2 lemongrass stems, soft inner
   layers only, thinly sliced diagonally
1½ c hot water
a little sugar

Serves 4

Keep the fish whole. Clean them, and cut two deep scores on each side of the fish. In a bowl, mix the lime juice or tamarind water with the salt, turmeric, and chili powder. Rub the mixture as evenly as possible over the outside of each fish. Keep the fish in a cool place while you prepare the sauce.

   Pound or blend the shallots, candlenuts or macadamia nuts, ginger, and galangal or lesser galangal into a paste. Heat the oil in a wok or saucepan, and stir-fry the paste for 4–5 minutes until aromatic. Be careful not to let it burn. Add the red and green chilies and the lemongrass, and stir-fry for a minute or so. Pour in the hot water, bring to a boil, and cook until the sauce is the right consistency – it should not be too thick or too thin. Season with salt and a little sugar to taste. You can keep this sauce simmering in the pan while you deep-fry the fish.

Half-fill a deep-fryer or a wok with peanut or canola oil. Heat to about 320°F (160°C), or until you can see smoke rising above the oil. Put the fish in carefully. If you are using the small red snapper, start by cooking two at a time. The fish must be fully submerged in the oil. After 3 minutes, turn the fish over, and let it (or them) fry in the hot oil for another 3–4 minutes. Repeat the process with the other snapper. Serve piping hot with the hot sauce poured over each portion of fish.

tempe kemul
fried tempeh in spiced batter

This is a variation on plain fried tempeh. As tempeh is quite bland, apart, of course, from the nutty flavor of the soy bean it's made from, it needs to be marinated before frying. If you like your simple fried tempeh to be hot and spicy, add some chilies to the marinade. Spicing the batter helps the tempeh to retain its softness, while the batter makes it crisp outside. Unfortunately, as tempeh has nowadays become very expensive in Indonesia (you might not think this from looking at the quantity of tempeh sold in the market), simple fried tempeh is better value there because the sellers of *tempe kemul* are likely to put a very small piece of tempeh inside a thick coating of cheap batter. Here's how to make your own.

1 lb tempeh (see pp.123–4), cut neatly, slantwise, into pieces about ¾ in on a side (see p.121)
rapeseed or peanut oil for deep-frying

for the marinade
2 shallots, finely sliced

2 garlic cloves, chopped
1 tsp chili powder
1 tsp ground coriander
1 tsp salt
1 tsp soft brown sugar

Serves 8–10 as snacks with drinks

Put all the ingredients for the marinade in a bowl, then pour 2½ cups boiling water from the kettle into the bowl. Add the tempeh, and stir the pieces around with a spoon. Leave the tempeh to marinate for an hour or so until it has absorbed all the water. The tempeh will, of course, be moist at this stage. The pieces can be deep-fried right away if you are making simple fried tempeh.

For *tempe kemul*, you need to put the marinated tempeh pieces into the following batter before deep-frying them until crisp.

for the batter

5 garlic cloves, chopped
1 in piece of peeled turmeric root
2 candlenuts or macadamia nuts,
   finely chopped
4 oz rice flour

1 c coconut milk
2 tbsp finely chopped fresh
   Chinese chives
1 tsp ground coriander
1 tsp salt, or more to taste

Using a mortar and pestle, crush the garlic, turmeric, and candlenuts or macadamia nuts until quite smooth. Mix together in a large bowl with all the other ingredients for the batter. Stir thoroughly, then put the moist marinated tempeh pieces into the bowl. Turn them around by hand so that all the tempeh slices are coated with batter. Heat the oil in a wok or deep-fryer, and deep-fry 5 or 6 slices of battered tempeh, turning them over with a slotted spoon from time to time, until lightly browned and crisp. Remove with a slotted spoon, and drain on a plate lined with paper towels. Repeat the process until you have fried all the tempeh.

lumpia goreng
fried spring rolls

Spring rolls of many different shapes and fillings have been popular snacks throughout Southeast Asia for centuries. Like so many deep-fried dishes, this one originated in China. It started as a pancake filled with the new season's spring vegetables, a welcome change from the preserved food of the long winter months. Today's spring roll wrappers are thin sheets of pastry, not pancakes, and they are commercially made. They are quite reasonably priced and can be found, in various sizes, in the freezers of all Chinese supermarkets. This recipe uses cooked vegetables in mid-sized wrappers. If you like, add some ground beef, chicken or shrimp to the vegetables.

1 packet of 20 spring roll wrappers,
   8–10 in square, defrosted
1 egg white, lightly beaten
peanut oil for deep-frying

for the filling
2 tbsp peanut or rapeseed oil
1 lb carrots, cut into matchsticks
4 oz white cabbage, shredded
5 oz fresh shiitake or porcini mushrooms,
   thinly sliced
 8 oz button mushrooms, thinly sliced

7 oz snow peas, sliced into
   diagonal strips
2 tsp finely chopped or grated
   fresh ginger
3 tbsp light soy sauce
3 oz cellophane vermicelli, soaked in hot
   water for 5 minutes, drained
   and cut into about 2 in lengths with
   scissors
5 or 6 spring onions, cut into thin rounds
pinch or more of chili powder, or a few
   turns of a pepper mill

Makes 20 rolls

To make the filling, heat the oil in a wok or frying pan, then stir-fry the carrots, cabbage, and two kinds of mushrooms for 3–4 minutes. Add the snow peas, stir-fry for another minute, then add the ginger, soy sauce, and vermicelli. Continue stir-frying, over high heat now, for 2 more minutes. Add the spring onions and chili powder or pepper. Stir-fry for another minute. By now, there should be no more liquid in the mixture, but the vegetable filling should still be moist, not dry.

Put a spring roll wrapper on a flat work surface, so that one corner is pointing towards you. Put 2 tablespoons of the filling on this corner. Press the filling down a little, and roll the corner of the wrapper over it, away from you and towards the center. Fold in the two corners that lie to your left and right. Brush the far corner of the wrapper with a little egg white, and roll it up to make a neat, well-sealed cylindrical parcel. Repeat with the rest of the filling and the wrappers, making sure that your spring rolls are as even in weight and shape as possible.

Heat the oil in a wok or a deep-fryer, or a deep saucepan with a frying basket, to 350°F (180°C). Put 4 or 5 spring rolls at a time into the hot oil, reduce the heat a little and deep-fry for 6–8 minutes, turning them several times, until golden brown. Remove with a slotted spoon and drain on paper towels. Serve hot.

Right: *Lumpia goreng* (fried spring rolls).

SHALLOW-FRIED, PAN-FRIED, AND STIR-FRIED DISHES

daging masak habang
pan-fried steak from samarinda

I first had this beef dish in Samarinda's open-air evening food market. It was so good that I've made it many times since. The Samarinda version was made with local beef and was a slow-cooked dish. They would never cook the steak rare or even medium, as Indonesians believe that meat should be cooked right through. My recipe has more or less the same sauce, but I cook the steak to suit the Western taste for lightly done meat. *Habang* means red, and the redness of the sauce comes from lots of red chilies; for those who don't like their food chili-hot, I replace them with red peppers.

4 slices rump steak, 6–8 oz per piece

for the marinade
2 tbsp thick tamarind water (pp.118–19)
   or freshly squeezed lime juice
3–4 garlic cloves, crushed
1 tsp salt
large pinch of chili powder
large pinch of ground turmeric
1 tsp peanut or olive oil

for the sauce
1 large fresh red chili, seeded
   and chopped

1–2 red peppers (bell peppers or
   Romano), seeded and chopped
3 shallots, chopped
1–2 tbsp peanut or olive oil
½ in piece of fresh ginger, chopped
2 lemongrass stems, inner part only,
   sliced into thin rounds
2 oz chopped fresh flat-leaf parsley
½ c hot water
½ tsp salt
2 tbsp freshly squeezed lime
   or lemon juice

Serves 4

Mix all the ingredients for the marinade in a glass bowl, then put in the steaks. Rub well with the marinade, and leave in a cool place for 2 hours. Alternatively, leave the steaks to marinate in the refrigerator overnight.

    The sauce can be made an hour or so before you intend to serve the meal. To start with, purée the chili, peppers, shallots, and ginger in a blender until smooth.

Heat the oil in a saucepan, add the paste, and stir-fry for 2–3 minutes. Add the lemongrass, parsley, hot water, and salt. Simmer for 3–5 minutes, taste and adjust the seasoning with a little sauce if needed. If you have to reheat the sauce later on, add the lime or lemon juice only just before you are about to serve the steaks.

Cook the steaks in a non-stick frying pan or ridged grill pan, or on a charcoal barbecue. Oil the frying pan or grill pan lightly, heat until very hot, put in the steaks and cook for 2–3 minutes on one side, then turn over. Reduce the heat a little, and cook for 4–6 minutes, depending how rare you like your steak. Reheat the sauce, add the lime or lemon juice, pour the sauce over the steaks and serve at once.

oseng oseng sayuran
stir-fried vegetables

Although Indonesians use woks for stir-frying, their stir-fried dishes are quite different from the Chinese. After eating a dish of sautéed ham with zucchinis in Italy, I think my *oseng-oseng* is closer to Italy than to China, although in Indonesia we do sometimes mix our vegetable *oseng-oseng* with chicken or a dozen or so small shrimp.

2–3 tbsp peanut or olive oil
3 shallots or 1 white or red onion,
    finely sliced
2 garlic cloves, crushed
1 tsp ground coriander
½ tsp chili powder
1 tbsp light soy sauce
2 tsp tomato purée
½ c hot water

the vegetables
3 carrots, peeled
5 small long green or yellow zucchinis

2 red peppers, cut in half and seeded
1 yellow pepper, cut in half
    and seeded
6 runner beans, or similar flat green
    beans, topped and tailed
2 waxy potatoes, peeled

*Serves 4–6 as a side dish with the
main course, or for 2 as a vegetarian
dish with pasta*

To prepare the vegetables, using a potato peeler, slice the carrots and zucchinis to make strands like pasta. Slice the peppers into long strips. Cut the beans in half, then slice each half into three or four long strips. Cut the potatoes into strips like the peppers, and keep in a bowl of cold water until ready to cook, then drain the potato strips into a colander. Discard the soaking water.

When ready to cook, heat the oil in a wok or in a sauté pan, and add the shallots or onions and the garlic. Stir-fry (or, as we say in Indonesian, *oseng-oseng*) for 2–3 minutes. Add the ground coriander, chili powder, soy sauce, tomato purée, and hot water. Stir and simmer for 2 minutes. Add beans and drained potatoes, stir and cover the pan for 3 minutes. Uncover and add the rest of the vegetables. Continue stir-frying the vegetables for another 3 minutes. Taste and add some more salt if necessary, and perhaps a few turns of the pepper mill. Serve hot.

lapis ikan tongkol berbumbu
pan-fried tuna with red chili sauce

Tongkol, or tuna, which the people of Minahasa in North Sulawesi call *ambu-ambu*, is one of the fish that in that region are often cooked as *rica-rica*. This simply means "with lots of chilies." I daresay this is another recipe that I have adapted rather freely from the original. My excuse is that you get different kinds of tuna in the West from the *tongkol* that you get in Meñado, and they are cut up quite differently, too.

4 tuna steaks, weighing about
  6 oz each
1 tsp salt
1 tsp peanut oil,
  plus 3 tbsp extra
1 tsp freshly squeezed lime or
  lemon juice
2 large white or red onions, finely sliced

for the bumbu (paste)
5–8 large fresh red chilies, or 1 large
  chili plus 1 large red pepper, seeded
  and chopped
3 shallots, chopped
3 garlic cloves, chopped

2 tsp chopped fresh ginger
1 candlenut or macadamia nut, chopped
  (optional)
2 tbsp freshly squeezed lime or
  lemon juice
1 tsp salt
2 tbsp peanut oil

for the garnish
2 tbsp, or more, fried ginger strips
  (see recipe, right)
handful of picked fresh *kemangi*
  (see p.278) or Thai basil

Serves 4

fried ginger strips

This is a good way to preserve ginger, and to have it ready in an airtight container to use as a garnish instead of crisp-fried shallots. Any leftovers that have become less crisp can be used instead of chopped ginger in cooking, or added to a paste with other ingredients for *sambal goreng*.

1 lb fresh ginger, peeled
½ c rapeseed oil, for deep frying

Makes 1 cup

With a sharp knife, slice the ginger very thinly, lengthwise or at an angle. Pile these thin slices on top of one another, a few at a time, and cut them into very tiny matchsticks.

Blanch the ginger in boiling water for 30 seconds. Refresh in cold water, drain, and pat dry with paper towels.

Heat the oil in a small pan or a wok. Fry the ginger, stirring all the time, for about 2 minutes or until crisp. Drain on paper towels. When cool, keep in an airtight container until needed.

Right: *Lapis ikan tongkol berbumbu* (pan-fried tuna with red chili sauce and crisp-fried ginger).

Rub the tuna steaks with the salt, 1 teaspoon peanut oil, and lime or lemon juice. Set aside. Heat the extra 3 tablespoons oil in a frying pan, and gently fry the onions until soft and almost caramelized.

Meanwhile, blend all the ingredients for the paste until smooth. Gently fry the paste in a small pan, stirring all the time, for 3–4 minutes. Add to the caramelized onions, and fry, stirring often, for 3 minutes. Remove from the heat, and set aside.

Heat a large non-stick frying pan until hot, and carefully lay the tuna steaks in it in one layer. Cook for 2 minutes, then turn over and continue cooking for another 2 minutes. Reduce the heat, and spread the mixture of chili paste and onions on top of each tuna steak. Cover the pan just for 1 minute longer, and serve hot right away, with the garnishes strewn on top. This tuna dish is good for eating with Chinese Fried Noodles (p.67) or pasta, or just with a mixed salad.

* **NOTE** As I've mentioned, Indonesians dislike fish to be served "just right" – they think it's still undercooked. My tuna, therefore, is not quite as rare as the trend nowadays for serving pan-fried or seared tuna. In my experience, cooking tuna steaks for exactly 2 minutes on each side should make them acceptable to almost anyone, Indonesians included. The fish is then neither under- nor overcooked.

Below: Bali: tuna fisherman returning to a port on the north coast.

pergedel udang
shrimp cakes

In the Indonesian food vocabulary, *pergedel* is a transcription of the Dutch word *frikadel*. Indonesian *pergedel* are usually fritters, almost always deep-fried in a lot of hot oil in a wok until they are golden brown, regardless what the ingredients are. After long experience in cooking, I realized that shrimp must not be cooked for too long a time, otherwise they become tough and rubbery. So here is a recipe for shrimp cakes using lots of herbs, shallow-fried in clarified butter or olive oil.

1 lb peeled and deveined raw shrimp (if frozen, thaw completely first), chopped finely with a cleaver or a large sharp knife
4–6 shallots or 1 large red onion, finely sliced
3 garlic cloves, crushed
1 tsp finely chopped or grated fresh ginger
1 tbsp chopped fresh chives
1 tbsp chopped fresh flat-leaf parsley or coriander leaves

1 tsp chili powder or *sambal ulek* (see p.279)
1 tbsp rice or all purpose flour or 1 tbsp fresh breadcrumbs
1 tsp corn flour
salt and freshly ground black pepper
1 egg, plus 1 egg yolk, lightly beaten
¼ c peanut or olive oil for shallow-frying

Serves 4 as an appetizer with a salad

In a glass bowl, mix together all the ingredients for the shrimp cakes (except the oil). Divide the mixture into four, shape into balls, then, on a floured work surface, flatten to make round, quite thick cakes. Chill for an hour or so before frying.

Heat the oil in a large frying pan that can take the shrimp cakes side by side. Put them straight from the refrigerator carefully into the pan. Cook over high heat for 2 minutes only on one side. Turn them over, reduce the heat a little and continue cooking for 3–4 more minutes. Serve hot right away.

oseng-oseng paria, cumi-cumi dan petai
sliced bitter melon stir-fried with squid and petai beans

Squid here is used as an alternative to the *ikan teri* (dried anchovies, see p.277) that no Javanese would care to miss in his everyday menu. Although *ikan teri* are now much more easily available in Chinese or Thai supermakets in the West, they are rather expensive, especially from an Indonesian point of view. I use squid instead, not because it is a near equivalent – in fact, it is the opposite of *ikan teri*, in texture, taste and everything else – but because, for my taste, squid goes so well together with petai beans: the softness of the slices of bitter melon is different in texture from the softness of the well-cooked squid, and the bitterness of the melon is again different from the slight bitterness of the beans. So there is a balance here of contrasting textures and tastes, a quality considered important in Asian cooking.

1 *paria* (bitter melon), halved lengthwise,
   seeds and membranes removed
1½ tsp salt
8 baby squid, or 3 medium ones,
   thoroughly cleaned
pinch of chili powder
pinch of ground turmeric
2–4 oz petai beans (see p.278), left
   whole or halved lengthwise

for the oseng-oseng
2 tbsp peanut or olive oil
4 shallots or 1 large onion, finely sliced
3 garlic cloves, crushed
2 tsp finely chopped or grated
   fresh ginger
2–3 fresh green chilies, seeded and
   cut into thin diagonal slices
4–6 anchovy filets, chopped
3–4 spring onions, cleaned and cut
   as the green chilies

Serves 6–8 as a side dish

Prepare the *paria* well in advance. Cut the two halves into thin semicircular slices. Put these in a colander, sprinkle with 1 teaspoon of the salt, and turn gently with your fingers to coat them evenly. Leave to stand over a bowl for at least 30 minutes. Rinse to get rid of the salt, then set aside in a clean bowl.

    If using baby squid, just cut their bodies into thin rings, and chop the tentacles finely, as not everybody likes the look of tentacles in their food. In any case, rub the squid rings and tentacles with the remaining ½ teaspoon salt, chili powder, and ground turmeric. Keep aside in a cool place until ready to cook. If using medium-sized squid, boil them whole in about 2¼ cups water, seasoned with the salt, chili powder, and ground turmeric, for 50–60 minutes. They will then be very tender. Cut them up when cool, as for the baby squid, and keep aside.

When you are ready to finish and serve the dish, heat the peanut or olive oil in a wok or large frying pan. Stir-fry the shallots or onion, garlic, ginger, and green chilies for 3–4 minutes. Add the bitter melon slices, stir, and cover the pan for 3–4 minutes. Uncover, add the squid and petai beans, and continue stirring almost continuously for 3 minutes. Next, add the anchovies and spring onions. Cook and stir again for just another 2 minutes. Serve hot right away.

Below: Nightfishing for squid off the north coast of Sulawesi.

serundeng
dry-roasted spiced grated coconut

I'm including this recipe as an example of a dish that can be shallow-fried or pan-fried, although in fact it is more accurate to describe it as dry-roasted. Another reason for including it is that this is a most versatile recipe: it can be used to make a kind of relish, or a side dish with peanuts. It is also useful, assuming that you have a lot of *serundeng* made in advance and stored in airtight container, for use as a dressing for *anyang sayuran* (Cooked Vegetables with Spiced Roasted Coconut, p.21).

5 shallots, chopped
3 garlic, chopped
2 tbsp rapeseed or peanut oil
1 tsp ground coriander
1 tsp crumbled shrimp paste (see p.279)
½ tsp ground cumin
½ tsp chopped galangal

1 tbsp tamarind water (see pp.118–19)
½ tsp soft brown sugar
3 kaffir lime leaves or 1 bay leaf
1 tsp salt
6 oz freshly grated coconut or
   shredded coconut*
3 oz fried peanuts (optional)

Using a mortar and pestle, pound the shallots and garlic in a mortar with a pestle until smooth. Heat the oil in a wok, and fry the shallots and garlic for 30 seconds before adding all the other ingredients, except the coconut and the fried peanuts (if using). Stir-fry for 1 minute, then add the coconut (and 1 cup water if using shredded coconut; see note). Mix well. Continue cooking, stirring from time to time, until the coconut starts to color. When this happens, stir continuously until the coconut is golden brown. Add the fried peanuts, if using. Stir for 1 more minute, and serve.

   Serundeng will keep in an airtight jar for several months. It is usually served cold, as described in the introduction above.

* **NOTE** If, and only if, you use shredded coconut, when you add it to the mixture you must also add 1 cup water. Let it simmer until the coconut has soaked up all the water, then start stir-frying.

SLOW-COOKED DISHES
(2–3 hours or longer)

bebek betutu
traditional slow-cooked balinese duck

It looks as if this traditional way of cooking duck has long ago disappeared from any restaurant menu in Bali. My first taste of it was back in 1987, when I had Bebek Betutu at the Bali Beach Hotel, brought in by the general manager and his wife; it had been specially made for me by his mother in Bangli, in the traditional manner, the duck stuffed with cassava leaves and spiced with the full Balinese spice mixture. The wrapping, which consisted of layers of banana leaves and *seludang mayang* (the hard outer sheath of the coconut flower), opened to reveal a mass of black and tender meat. The color of the stuffing had become black as well. Not very appetizing to look at, maybe, but the taste was exquisite.

Here is the recipe for preparing and cooking the duck in the oven.

6–8 oz curly kale, or grape or zucchini
    leaves, or spinach, blanched,
    squeezed dry, and shredded
1 duck, 3½–4 lb, cleaned and ready
    for roasting

for the bumbu (paste)
5 shallots or 2 onions, chopped
4 garlic cloves, chopped
5 fresh red chilies, seeded and
    chopped, or 1 tsp chili powder
2 candlenuts or macadamia nuts
    (optional)
2 tsp coriander seeds
1 tsp cumin seeds
2 cloves

2 green cardamom pods
1 in piece of cinnamon stick
½ tsp ground or grated nutmeg
½ tsp ground turmeric
1 tsp chopped galangal
½ tsp ground white pepper
2 in piece of lemongrass stem, tough
    outer layer discarded, chopped
1 tsp *terasi* (shrimp paste)
3 tbsp tamarind water (see pp.118–19)
    or freshly squeezed lime juice
2 tbsp peanut oil
2 tbsp water
1 tsp salt

Serves 4–6

Blend all the ingredients for the paste together until smooth. Transfer the mixture to a saucepan and simmer for 6–8 minutes, stirring often. Transfer to a bowl and leave to cool completely. Adjust the seasoning with a little salt if necessary.

When the paste is cold, mix half of it in a bowl with the shredded leaves. Rub the remaining paste on the duck, inside as well as outside. Stuff the shredded leaves into the duck. Wrap the duck, first with some banana leaves, then with two or three layers of foil, quite loosely, but sealing the top well. Everything up to this point can be done the day before, and the parcel can be left in the refrigerator overnight so that the duck marinates thoroughly.

To cook, preheat the oven to 325°F (160°C), and put the parcel on a baking tray in the middle of the oven. Cook for 2 hours, then reduce the heat to 250°F (120°C) and continue cooking for another 3–4 hours.

To serve, unwrap the parcel and transfer the duck to a large dish. Separate and discard the oil from the cooking juices. Put the cooking juices in a small saucepan, add to this all the stuffing, which has now become a dark-colored purée (but tastes delicious), heat and serve as a thick sauce. The duck should have become very tender, and the meat will come off the bones very easily. With a fork, transfer the meat to a well-heated serving plate. Serve right away with plenty of hot boiled white rice, with the sauce poured over the duck meat or in a sauce boat for everybody to help themselves.

bebek dengan bumbu betutu
breasts of duck cooked in balinese spices

This is a variation of the traditional *bebek betutu* (above). When I demonstrated it at one of my Indonesian evenings at the Gas Cooking School in Sydney in 1991, everyone in the audience liked it; one of them, Genevieve Harris, was inspired to go to Bali, where she became the founding executive chef of the Amankila Resort. She duly placed this on her menu, accompanied by *urap*, or *gudangan* (pp.194–5), a Javanese vegetable salad with coconut dressing.

Here, I use the same marinade or spice mixture as for the traditional *bebek betutu* on pp.228–9. You can either slow-cook the duck breasts, or cook them for a short time so that they are rare or medium-rare. They can then be served with the *gudangan* or some other salad, such as a combination of watercress, celery, oranges, and fresh garden peas dressed in your favorite vinaigrette. In my home in Wimbledon, I often serve this as a first course at my dinner parties. As a main course, the duck can be served with a spinach sauce, and accompanied by rice, potatoes, or pasta.

6 or 8 duck breasts
1 lb spinach, stalks removed,
  well rinsed and finely shredded
1¾ c coconut milk or chicken stock or
  water

for the marinade and sauce
see *bebek betutu* (Traditional Slow-
  cooked Balinese Duck, pp.228–9)

Serves 6–8

Make two deep scores through the skin of each duck breast. Put the breasts in the cold marinade, and turn each one once or twice to make sure that it is well coated on all sides. Put in the refrigerator to marinate overnight.

To slow-cook the duck breasts, wrap them with half of the marinade, in three layers of foil, and cook in a preheated oven at 325°F (160°C) for 3 hours, reducing the temperature to 250°F (120°C) after the first hour.

To cook the duck breasts quickly, take them out of the marinade, and with a knife or the side of a fork scrape off all the marinade from the skin side of the breasts. Put the duck breasts on a wire rack, and roast in a preheated oven at 400°F (200°C) for 20–30 minutes.

Meanwhile, put 2–4 tablespoons of the marinade, or the remaining half (depending on how strong you like it), in a saucepan. Add the coconut milk, stock or water. Bring to a boil, then simmer for 10 minutes. Add the spinach and continue to cook for 4–5 minutes. Adjust the seasoning. Keep to one side until ready to use; it can be reheated. (If you slow-cooked the breasts, separate and discard the oil from the cooking juices, and mix the cooking juices into the sauce.)

Cut each duck breast diagonally into several slices, and serve hot as suggested above. The spinach sauce can be served separately.

Right: *Bebek betutu* (traditional slow-cooked Balinese duck).

gulai bagar
chunky mutton curry

Not all Sumatran-style *gulai* can be called curry, but this is very much like one because it uses almost all the curry spices: cloves, cumin, cardamom, coriander seeds. This is also one dish that I prefer served in the original way, on top of a mountain of white rice, or in a large earthenware bowl with the gleaming rice on the side in a woven bamboo tray or basket, lined with banana leaves. It is the appropriate food for a family gathering or *selamatan*, as it was served during my grandmother's time – for instance, on the day one of my boy cousins was circumcised. She would have made this with several whole young goats, specially slaughtered for the occasion. I replace the goat meat with mutton, if I can get good mutton; otherwise a shoulder or a leg of lamb will do very well. Better still, if you don't want the trouble of cutting the shoulder or leg meat into large chunks, buy some chump chops or a mini shoulder joint, usually weighing around 14 ounces.

6½ lb good-quality mutton, or shoulder
   or leg of lamb, or chump chops, or
   5–6 mini shoulder joints
2 tbsp peanut oil or coconut oil
3 kaffir lime leaves
3 cloves
1 cinnamon stick
4 green cardamom pods
1 lemongrass stem, cut across into three
2½ c thin coconut milk
   (the second extraction, see p.115)
2½ c thick coconut milk
   (the first extraction, see p.115)
10 small round white eggplants
   or 2 large purple ones
salt

to be roasted first
6–8 tbsp freshly grated or
   shredded coconut
3 tsp coriander seed
1 tsp cumin seed
5 candlenuts or macadamia nuts,
   roughly chopped

for the bumbu (paste)
8 shallots or 2 large onions, chopped
6 garlic cloves, chopped
4–8 large fresh red chilies, seeded and
   chopped
2 tsp chopped fresh ginger
1 tsp ground turmeric
large pinch of grated or ground nutmeg
4 tbsp thick coconut milk
3 tbsp tamarind water (see pp.118–19)

Serves 8–10

Cut the shoulder or leg of lamb into large chunks still on the bone. If using mutton, chops or mini shoulder joints, just trim off and discard some of the fat.

Put all the ingredients to be roasted in a wok or a heavy frying pan over low heat. Stir almost all the time with a wooden spoon until the coconut is golden brown. Transfer the roasted ingredients to a bowl to cool.

Put all the ingredients for the *bumbu*, or paste, in a blender or food processor. Add to it all the roasted ingredients from the bowl. Purée until a smooth paste forms. You may need to do this in two batches. Transfer all the paste to a large saucepan and simmer, stirring often, for 8 minutes. Add the 2 tablespoons peanut or coconut oil, and keep on stirring for another 2 minutes. Now add the kaffir lime leaves, cloves, cinnamon stick, cardamom pods, lemongrass, and chunks of meat, and stir so that all the chunks are well coated with the paste. Add the thin coconut milk, reduce the heat a little, and simmer, uncovered, for 30 minutes. Now add the thick coconut milk, and bring almost to a boil, then simmer for 20 minutes.

If you are using the small round eggplants, cut them in half. The large purple eggplants need to be cut into several thick round slices. Add the eggplants to the pan, and continue to cook the *gulai* for another 15–20 minutes. Check and adjust the seasoning with a little salt if needed.

To serve, take out the chunks of meat and cut them into largish pieces. If using mini joints, carve these into thick or thin slices as preferred. Arrange the meat on a large flame- and ovenproof dish, and the eggplants on top of the meat. Extract from the sauce all the unwanted solids and discard: cloves, cardamom pods, cinnamon stick, and leaves. Pour away the excess oil, which will be floating on the top of the sauce, and pour the sauce over the meat. Keep the dish hot in the oven at about 210°F (100°C) until you are ready to serve the *gulai bagar*, piping hot, with plenty of boiled rice or boiled potatoes.

lemang
sticky rice cooked in bamboo

This is a Sumatran equivalent of *lontong* or *ketupat*; like them, it is associated with a major feast of the Islamic year -- in this case, Maulud Nabi, or the Prophet's birthday. We eat it then with *rendang* (pp.180–1), and neighbors send little packets of *lemang* to each other rather as some people might exchange Christmas cards. The Javanese do the same with *ketupat* at Lebaran. Throughout the rest of the year, *lemang* is seen as a sweet dish and eaten with *kolak*, which is thickened coconut milk sweetened with *gula jawa* (palm sugar) and with bananas added to it, or with durian in season.

It is made from sticky rice, cooked with thick coconut milk in segments of bamboo: not just any bamboo, but specifically *Schizostachyum zollingeri*, which we call *telang*. This variety has very thin walls, allowing heat to penetrate, and unusually long internodes. Cooks may prepare 15 or 20 or more of these cylinders, 20 inches long and 2 inches across, open at the top and lined with banana leaf. The rice is usually white, but red and black sticky rice are also used. It is first soaked for several hours, then dried. Each length of bamboo is filled about one-third full of rice, and topped up with thick, slightly salted coconut milk. A banana-leaf lid is tied down firmly over the mouth of the tube. A wooden crossbar is rigged over a low fire and the bamboos are placed so that they lean against it, even numbers on one side and odd numbers on the other, like the rafters of a little house. Cooking takes up to 2 hours, with the rice swelling to absorb the coconut milk to make a soft, firm mass. When it is cooked, the *lemang* is shaken and slid from the tubes, unwrapped from its banana-leaf coverings and sliced into good chunky rounds.

ikan bakar dalam bambu
fish cooked in bamboo segments

In one of our research trips to Indonesia, Roger and I went to Menado and stayed in a small town in the hills a few miles to the south, at a most desirable and welcoming homestay in Tomohon. It is run by Ibu Bernadeth Ratulangi, the wife of Dr Ratulangi, who is related to the late Dr. Sam Ratulangi, a leader of the nationalist movement in this province of North Sulawesi. After independence, he became the first governor of the province and every Indonesian town has a street named after him. Ibu Bernadeth is a good cook, and she showed me that many Minahasa dishes have been influenced by the Spanish and Portuguese, either directly or through the neighboring Philippines. Traditional local cooking, however, has also survived. An example of it is this fish cooked in bamboo. Its local name is *ikan dibuluh*. Pak Dokter, as we respectfully addressed Ibu Bernadeth's husband (*pak* is father; *ibu* is mother), took us one late afternoon to a small eating house, about 2 miles from his home, to taste this local delicacy. As happens in small and remote places, you can't make a restaurant reservation, but when you arrive they tell you the dish you want must be ordered 24 hours in advance. So instead we had *ikan bakar*, literally "grilled fish," which was flat, quite large, and not unlike a *gurami* (see p.202). It had been marinated in what looked to me like a runny curry paste. The chef-proprietor grilled it in front of us on a makeshift brazier until it was quite charred. Pak Dokter explained that *ikan dibuluh* would have the same marinade, but the whole fish, bones and all, would be chopped very finely, so that it could be wrapped and put inside the bamboo segment to cook. Before that happened, however, extra seasoning would be added: crushed garlic, chilies, leaves of the *kedondong* tree to make the dish sour, and *kemangi*, a kind of mint, to give it extra fragrance. There would also be chopped galangal and perhaps more chopped chilies. I recalled that some years before, at the home of one of my sisters in Pontianak (West Kalimantan), a Dayak friend of my sister had chopped up and cooked all the meat, innards included, of an entire piglet, in bamboo segments, at my special request (see picture opposite). He had used exactly the same spicing. I have experimented with both recipes, using pork filet and pork liver for one, and a whole fish for the other, all chopped up and wrapped in banana leaves. I confess I didn't have suitable bamboo segments, nor in Wimbledon are we allowed to light fires out of doors, so I wrapped these banana-leaf rolls in foil, then baked them in the oven at 210°F (100°C) for 3 hours. They both tasted reasonably good, but I thought they were scarcely worth those long hours of cooking.

Top: *Lemang* (sticky rice cooked in bamboo segments) on sale in Padang central market.
Left: Cooking in bamboo: a small-scale demonstration in the garden of my sister's house in Pontianak, West Kalimantan.

Chapter Six: Food for Celebrations and Special Occasions

I'm starting this chapter with my story of *sate* (or satay), followed by the recipes. For Indonesians, *sate* has always been a usual part of any *selamatan* and any communal eating: it is a festive treat, it marks an occasion as special and it is easy to prepare in large quantities. After the section on *sate*, you will find a discussion of the *selamatan* itself, followed by further recipes for typical celebration dishes.

SATAY

My survey of Indonesian satays begins in Bali and its sister island, Lombok. Roger and I spent our honeymoon in East Java, with a side trip to Bali; he had been there twice already; I had never even thought of going. It was very different then from what it is now: no tourists; therefore few and mostly bad hotels. We explored the night market in Denpasar, crowded with local people besieging the satay vendors and other food stalls so that it was difficult to get near them. I felt I was in a foreign country; in Java, the crowds were just as dense, but there I knew how to make my way through and get what I wanted. The next time we came, almost twenty years later, the atmosphere was quite different – more relaxed, prosperous, sophisticated even. The food on sale in the streets and markets had improved; in hotel restaurants, it had been transformed. Meanwhile, off the tourist track, the Balinese maintain the food habits and food rituals of past generations. To paraphrase a well-known Western resident on the island: "Visitors almost never see real Balinese food and wouldn't want to eat if they saw it." But there are points of contact with the West, and satay is one. For the Balinese, it is an important part of many domestic and temple rituals; for Westerners, it reminds them of barbecues, and the flavors quickly become familiar.

We first went to Lombok in the late 1980s, when a tourist boom was threatening over-rapid development of what seemed a very fragile island, its community lacking the tough cultural and commercial bargaining sense of the Balinese. I was working on a series of radio programs about modern Indonesian food, and one of my interviews was with the chef of the Senggigi Beach Hotel. A lot of hotels were importing their meat from Australia and New Zealand, but he assured me that all his ingredients were locally produced and bought in the town market. The *sate pusut* that I ate in the hotel restaurant was so good that, when I make it now, I cannot use anything less than a good piece of rump steak, which I grind myself. If you do not have an electric grinder, cut the steak into very small dice with a large knife, then chop these smaller still with a sharp cleaver. Most of the population of Lombok are Muslims, so they make their satay with beef, whereas the Hindu Balinese prefer pork.

Pusut and *pentul* mean much the same thing. Both indicate that meat has been marinated in spices, finely chopped and molded onto satay sticks. Strictly speaking, *sate pusut* (also called *sate lilit*) means that the meat mix is in one chunk, molded into a sausage shape, whereas *sate pentul* means it has been formed into walnut-sized balls that are pushed onto the sharpened stick.

NOTE: Both recipes call for oil to be brushed onto the hot meat during cooking. Doing this with a nylon brush can result in sticky melted nylon. I suggest you use a lemongrass brush – simply a brush made from a lemongrass stem.

Page 236: *Sarad* offering at a Balinese wedding.
Left: Preparing *sate lilit* for a feast in Bali.
Right: Grilling *sate* on a market stall in Bukittinggi.

ground beef satay

1 lb 2 oz rump steak, ground
1 tsp salt
2 tsp freshly squeezed lime juice

for the bumbu (spice mixture)
1–2 tsp coriander seeds, roasted
2 tbsp freshly grated or shredded
　coconut, roasted (optional)
1–2 tsp *sambal ulek* (see p.279)
　or ½ tsp chili powder
2 shallots, very finely chopped
2 garlic cloves, very finely chopped

1 tsp finely chopped fresh ginger
1 tsp soft brown sugar
1 tbsp light soy sauce or 1 tsp crumbled
　grilled shrimp paste (see p.279)
6 tbsp thick coconut milk or
　Greek-style yogurt

sufficient soaked split-bamboo or steel
　satay sticks or skewers

*Serves 4–6 (enough for
18–20 satay sticks)*

In a bowl, rub the salt and lime juice into the ground beef. Keep to one side. Put the roasted coriander seeds and shredded coconut in a mortar, and crush them with a pestle. Mix these with the other ingredients for the spice mixture, then mix this well into the meat. Knead for a while with your hand so that all the ingredients are well distributed. You can prepare the mixture up to 24 hours in advance and keep it in the refrigerator until needed, but don't mold it or put it onto skewers until the last possible moment; if you do, it will tend to split and fall off.

At least an hour before you are ready to grill, divide the meat mixture equally among the satay sticks or skewers that you intend to use. Either mold each share directly onto a stick, making a sausage shape, or shape it into small balls, each about the size of a walnut, and put three or four balls onto each stick. Put the sticks in a bowl, cover the bowl with cling wrap and chill for at least an hour.

Grill slowly, turning carefully from time to time. After 4 or 5 minutes, when the satays should be half-cooked and pretty firm, brush the sausages or balls with some oil, and continue cooking for 2–3 minutes longer. If necessary, keep them warm in the oven until ready to serve. Serve hot, as finger food with drinks, as a separate course, or with rice and salad.

sate pentul
balinese ground pork satay

1 lb 2 oz tenderloin of pork, ground

for the bumbu (paste)
3 shallots, chopped
2 garlic cloves, chopped
1 tsp *sambal ulek* (see p.279)
   or ½ tsp chili powder
1 tsp chopped fresh ginger
1 tsp chopped galangal
1 lemongrass stem, tough outer leaves
   discarded, chopped
1 tsp coriander seeds
½ tsp cumin seeds
2 green cardamon pods

½ tsp ground cinnamon
pinch of grated nutmeg
1 tbsp tamarind water (see pp.118–19)
   or freshly squeezed lime juice
1 tsp salt
½ tsp soft brown sugar
1 tbsp peanut oil

sufficient soaked split-bamboo or steel
   satay sticks or skewers

*Serves 4–6 (enough for
18–20 satay sticks)*

Put all the ingredients for the paste in a blender, and purée until smooth. In a bowl, mix this paste by hand thoroughly with the ground pork, kneading it a little until everything is well blended. You can prepare the mix up to 24 hours in advance and keep it in the refrigerator, but don't mold it on skewers or satay sticks until the last possible moment.

From this point on, follow the method described in the second and third paragraphs of the recipe for *sate pusut* (opposite).

You will have noticed that the list of Balinese spices is a little longer than the one for Lombok. I think this is because the Balinese are very particular about both the taste and the ritual correctness of their satay, especially if it is being prepared for a temple festival. All the six tastes – salt, chili-hot, sweet, sour, bitter, and "green banana" (i.e. astringent, which I don't use in my recipe here) – should be present in their correct proportions. They therefore have a number of prescribed spice mixes, each in effect a recipe with a name. (No doubt there are local variations.) This has a practical aspect when very large quantities of food have to be cooked for a big temple festival or even a wedding *selamatan*: the man in charge of the cooking knows how many people his team has to feed, and which dishes are required. He knows exactly the quantities of everything he requires. Such people are found in every Balinese village, and the whole operation of preparing, cooking and serving the feast is carried out with great efficiency and on time. In addition, a big temple festival attracts street vendors from far and wide; if you join the crowd to climb the hill to the temple, you will walk along an avenue of food stalls – satays always being the biggest attraction.

In Java, too, people often find they are expected to entertain on a large scale. Well-off middle-class families in the big cities, or individuals and groups in small towns and villages, all want or need to give a *selamatan* from time to time – quite possibly as often as once or twice a month. Satay, either meat or seafood, is usually among the dishes offered to guests; in Java, as in Bali, this is often regarded as a necessary component of a ritual meal. It will be served, of course, with the appropriate accompaniments: steamed rice, *lontong* (see p.132), and several vegetable dishes and salads. I still find myself subconsciously thinking along these lines when I give parties in Wimbledon; the concept of the varied but quite simple marinades for large quantities of meat works just as well for a dozen or so friends as it did in Yogya when I was helping to prepare food for perhaps a couple of hundred guests.

Above: Bali: pushing *sate pusut* into a fragment of banana stem so that a number of sticks can be handled at once.

I'll start with chicken, lamb, and beef satays. I use one simple marinade for these three meats. Do not be tempted to add more spices, such as nutmeg, cinnamon, and mace, which are sometimes included in commercially mixed satay marinades. I can tell you from experience that these just mask the taste of the good meat that you are using.

Whenever I am teaching or demonstrating, I am invariably asked how large the pieces of meat should be. The satays that the street vendors sold when I was living in Yogya always had the meat cut very small, whether it was chicken, beef, or lamb. (In fact, there was no lamb in Indonesia until it began to be imported from Australia and New Zealand; even now, *kambing* is more often understood to be goat meat.) There were several reasons for this. First, the vendors usually preferred to sell their satays in bundles of ten sticks at a time: that way, they increased their turnover. Secondly, they believed the smaller the cuts were, the better cooked the meat would be and the more tender. Finally, they believed that each piece of meat should just be a nice mouthful. People in Indonesia may eat by hand, or with spoon and fork, but they very rarely need to use a knife at table. It is only recently that middle-class restaurant-goers have learned to feel comfortable using knives and forks.

In response to my students' questions, however, I would say that, provided your meat is suitable for cooking quickly at a high temperature, you need to cut the meat across the grain to make pieces about ¼ inch across, but only half that in thickness. I use rump steak for the beef satay, shoulder or leg for the lamb, and a combination of breast and thigh meat, without the skin, for the chicken. I marinate each kind of meat separately, in the refrigerator, for at least 2 hours or overnight.

The marinade is as follows. For 1 pound of meat, you need:

3 small shallots, finely chopped	1 tbsp peanut oil
2 garlic cloves, finely chopped	1 tsp ground coriander
1 tsp chopped fresh ginger	½ tsp ground cumin
½ tsp *sambal ulek* (see p.279) or chili powder	2 tbsp light soy sauce
	1 tsp soft brown sugar (optional)
1–2 tbsp distilled white vinegar or freshly squeezed lemon juice or tamarind water (see pp.118–19)	½ tsp salt
	Serves 3–4

In a glass bowl, mix all the marinade ingredients together well, add the cut-up meat and mix again so that every piece of meat is coated on all sides by the marinade.

Only after the meat has been marinated can you start putting it on skewers. I suggest metal skewers if you are cooking your satays on the barbecue. If using bamboo skewers, soak them first in cold water overnight. Barbecuing satays on glowing charcoal, and turning them often, will take only about 5 minutes. I also find that cooking satays indoors on or under a grill is less satisfactory than simply cooking them in a hot oven at 350°F (180°C) for 10–12 minutes. But don't put them in the oven to keep warm. Take them out after the 10–12 minutes of cooking, and keep on a plate, covered with a towel or paper towels. Keep the oven on, even increasing the temperature to 400°F (200°C). Just before you are ready to serve, pop the satays in the oven for 2 minutes. Serve right away with your choice of sauce – see pp.174 and 248.

sate udang
shrimp satay

The best shrimp for this are jumbo or colossal shrimp. Use the largest you can find, with their shells on, but no heads. Allow three shrimp per stick.

18 large raw unpeeled jumbo or colossal
   shrimp, heads removed

for the marinade
2 tbsp tamarind water (see pp.118–19)
   or freshly squeezed lemon juice

4 garlic cloves, crushed
pinch of ground turmeric
1 tsp coarse sea salt
½ tsp chili flakes

Makes 6 skewers

If the shrimp you purchased still have their heads on, remove these, then remove all the legs. Cut each shrimp lengthwise on the underside, not piercing the shell. Turn each one over and press its back so that it lies straight and flat. Turn it over again and remove the black "vein" (i.e. the intestine). Wash the shrimp under cold running water, dry with paper towels and put in a glass bowl.

Mix all the ingredients for the marinade, and pour this into the bowl with the shrimp. Carefully turn them over by hand or with a spoon, so that all the shrimp are coated with the marinade. Leave to marinate in a cold place or in the refrigerator for at least 3 hours.

When ready to grill, put three shrimp onto each skewer, piercing them either from side to side or from the tail forward. Grill over hot charcoal for 2 minutes on the shell sides, then turn them over to be grilled for another minute. Serve right away, with or without a dipping sauce. They can be served as an appetizer with green salad, or as a main course with the vegetable satay (opposite) and a salad.

Previous spread: *Sate pusut* (on lemon grass stems), *sate daging* and *sate udang* grilling on earthenware and metal *anglo* (charcoal stoves). **Right:** Sweet potato and vegetable satay.

sate ubi jalar dan sayuran
sweet potato and vegetable satay

2 or 3 sweet potatoes, peeled
2 or 3 carrots, peeled
4 or 5 baby turnips, peeled
1 white radish (*mooli*), peeled
1 red pepper, halved and seeded
1 yellow pepper, halved and seeded
2 red onions, peeled

for the marinade
3 ripe tomatoes, peeled and seeded,
   then roughly chopped
½ tsp chili flakes
1 tbsp light soy sauce
½ tsp brown sugar
1 tbsp peanut oil

Makes 4–6 skewers

If using bamboo skewers, soak them overnight in cold water. Preheat the oven to 350°F (180°C).

Cut the vegetables into chunks, about ¾ inch across. Cut each half of the red and yellow peppers into four, and cut the onions into six. Mix the marinade in a bowl. Put all the vegetables with the marinade in a self-seal plastic bag. Seal the bag, and carefully roll it on the kitchen table several times so that the marinade will coat all the vegetables. Transfer the vegetables to a baking dish, and bake in the oven for 25–30 minutes. Leave to cool.

When the vegetables are cool enough to handle, spear them onto long metal or bamboo skewers. Make sure that each skewer has its fair share of each vegetable. Grill on a barbecue for 3–4 minutes just before you are ready to serve. Or roast them in a preheated 400°F (200°C) oven for 4–5 minutes. Serve hot with the shrimp satays (opposite) or any other meat or seafood satays.

For all these satays, the peanut sauce described on p.174 is the usual accompaniment on all occasions. If you want a change, however, or if someone is allergic to nuts, here are a couple of other sauces which can be prepared in a short time and which go very well with any satay.

sambal kecap dengan lombok rawit
soy sauce with chilies

Mix the ingredients below in a small glass jar with a screw top. Seal tightly, and shake the jar well to mix the contents. The sauce keeps in the refrigerator for up to a week.

4 tbsp light soy sauce
1 tbsp dark soy sauce or *kecap manis*
  (see p.277)
1 tbsp freshly squeezed lemon juice

2 tbsp warm water from the kettle
3–6 fresh bird's-eye chilies, seeded and
  finely chopped

sambal tomat
tomato sambal

6 large ripe red tomatoes, peeled,
  seeded and chopped
2 shallots, finely chopped
2 garlic cloves, crushed in a mortar with
  1 tsp crumbled grilled shrimp paste
  (see p.279), a pinch of coarse sea salt
  and ½ tsp soft brown sugar

1 tsp chopped fresh chives
1 tsp light soy sauce
½ tsp *sambal ulek* (see p.279)
  or chili powder
½ tsp fine salt

Mix all these together, and serve as a dipping sauce, or just spoon it over the satays. Add more chilies and/or sugar as preferred.

Having started this section with satay in Bali, then moved back to my kitchen in Wimbledon, I would like to continue with some satay recipes from Java. I'm not too familiar with East Javanese preferences in satay marinades, but I guess they won't be very different from those of Central and West Java. I remember that for *sate pusut* or *sate pentul*, the Javanese add a small quantity of thick coconut milk to the marinade. Some cooks prefer grated coconut -- naturally from not-too-old or "middle-aged" nuts, the *kelapa setengah tua* (see p.114). Their methods of putting the ground meat onto the skewers, and of grilling them, are exactly the same as for other satays.

It is worth noting here that the Balinese have never seen fit to make shrimp satay, though for any big *selamatan*, in villages on the south coast, they make satay with the meat of sea turtles. As far as I recall, the Javanese make fish satay, but not from fish cut up into small pieces. Instead they use ground white fish, molded onto a square stick cut from bamboo; this they call *sate lilit*. I follow the current fashion among renowned restaurant chefs, especially those who specialize in fusion cooking, and mold my ground fish satay onto the upper, pointed part of lemongrass stems, rather than on bamboo skewers.

In Java, however, there has long been a way of cooking a milkfish, or *bandeng*, which for some reason is called *sate bandeng* even though the technique and the result are quite unlike conventional satay. For an unmarried girl to be able to perform this rather tricky operation is one of the more practical ways to impress a potential mother-in-law. The *bandeng* is usually wrapped in banana leaves and grilled, so don't look for *sate bandeng* on skewers; it is just not done that way. Recipes for *sate bandeng* and *sate lilit ikan* follow immediately.

sate bandeng
stuffed, roasted, and grilled milkfish

In Java, mothers make, or used to make, a point of teaching their daughters how to get all the bones, the flesh, and everything else from inside the fish without cutting it. The trick is to clean the inside part of the head of the fish completely first, then beat the fish all over with the blunt side of a large knife, carefully, so as not to damage the skin. You have to break up the meat and detach it from the skin, making it possible to scoop out the meat, bones and all, from the head. I've made several attempts to do this, but always failed, so for me there is no alternative but to cut the belly of the fish lengthwise, after beating the fish all over to loosen the flesh from the skin. Take everything out carefully, starting with the inedible parts – internal organs, bones – and discarding these. Using a small knife or spoon, scrape out all the flesh, chop it finely, and keep it to one side in a bowl.

Next, clean the skin and the head of the fish thoroughly, and remove the scales. Clean the whole fish again under cold running water. Dry with paper towels, and, if you have time and patience, rub the skin and head inside and out with no more than ½ teaspoon fine sea salt. Keep to one side while preparing the stuffing.

for the stuffing
2 tbsp peanut oil
4 shallots, finely chopped
3 garlic cloves, finely chopped
½ tsp *sambal ulek* (see p.279)
　or chili powder
1 tsp ground coriander
1 tsp crumbled shrimp paste (see p.279)

½ c very thick coconut milk
1 tbsp tamarind water (see pp.118–19)
　or freshly squeezed lime juice
1 tsp salt, and more to taste
1 egg, lightly beaten

Serves 4–6

Heat the oil in a non-stick frying pan. When hot, add the shallots and garlic. Stir for about 3 minutes, then add the *sambal ulek* or chili powder, coriander, and shrimp paste. Give this another stir, and add the coconut milk, tamarind water or lime juice, and salt. Stir around for 2 minutes or until the coconut milk has thickened, and add the chopped-up flesh of the fish. Cook over medium heat for just another minute or until the coconut milk has been absorbed by the fish. Transfer the fish from the pan to a bowl. Using the back of a large spoon, mash the fish to a smooth paste. When this is cold, add the beaten egg and mix well. Spoon this paste into the fish-skin, remembering also to fill the head. At this stage, the Javanese would put the fish on a square of banana leaf and wrap it tightly, so there would be no need to sew the opening. The wrapped fish would then be grilled over charcoal for 5–6 minutes on each side, and turned over only once.

If you are not going to wrap the fish at all, sew the opening or secure with cocktail sticks, then rub the fish all over the outside with some oil. Put in a baking tray and cook in a preheated oven at 350°F (180°C) for just 15 minutes. Finish the

Notes: Up to the time of writing, *ikan bandeng* (milkfish) has been available in the West only from the freezers of large Chinese supermarkets. They usually weigh about 2¼ pounds, which I think is an ideal size and enough to serve 4 people. If I can't get one, I replace the milkfish with a sea bass of the same size. Another good alternative would be a red snapper.

cooking over charcoal or on a barbecue for 2–3 minutes on one side, turning the fish. If you don't intend to grill the fish, continue cooking it in the oven for another 15–20 minutes. Remove from the oven and leave to cool a little, perhaps as long as 2 minutes, before cutting into large chunks. Serve this as you would other satays, with peanut sauce or soy sauce with chilies.

sate lilit ikan
ground fish satay

The Balinese, who like making their satays with ground meat, are also fond of the ground fish variations. This is one of the many different recipes that I like making at home, with either monkfish or cod, or with sea perch when I can get it.

1 lb monkfish, cod, or sea perch filets
¼ c thick coconut milk
3 shallots, finely chopped
2 garlic cloves, finely chopped
1 tsp finely chopped fresh ginger
½ tsp freshly ground white pepper
1 tbsp freshly squeezed lime juice

1 tsp sea salt or more to taste
1 egg white, beaten

Makes 8 sticks (use soaked flat bamboo satay sticks or the sharp upper halves of lemongrass stems)

Finely chop the fish filets with a large sharp knife, or put in a blender and pulse until chopped. Mix the fish and all the remaining ingredients, except the egg white, in a bowl, working by hand and kneading the paste a little, until everything is thoroughly mixed. Add the egg white, and, using a fork, stir the mixture in one direction only, until it becomes difficult to move the fork. Form the mixture into eight balls, and chill these in the refrigerator for 30 minutes

When ready to grill, whether on a charcoal fire or under a grill or a salamander, take out the fish balls from the refrigerator, and form each of them into a sausage shape around a bamboo or lemongrass stick. Grill, turning them several times, for 4–5 minutes. Brushing them while grilling, with a brush made from a lemongrass stem and dipped in oil mixed with soy sauce, will improve the taste considerably. Serve hot, with a mixed salad and with the satay sauce of your choice.

The Javanese will make satay out of whatever ingredients are at hand provided they can easily be put on skewers. If there are only a few satays, they may be grilled on an earthenware or cast-iron anglo (see picture on pp. 244–5). They make *sate tempe*, of course, but not tofu satay, as tofu is just too soft to put on skewers.

Now we leave Bali and Java and go back to the town where I was born, Padang Panjang in the province of West Sumatra. The modern capital of West Sumatra is Padang, a city and seaport. The old capital was Bukittinggi, which means "High Hill," and Bukittinggi is indeed high up on the mountain range that runs parallel to Sumatra's west coast. One typical and renowned satay of West Sumatra is *sate Padang*, which is very different from any of the satays I've talked about in this section so far. Many people from outside West Sumatra, not to mention visitors from the West, look askance at *sate Padang* when they first encounter it, although some quite quickly acquire a taste for it. On my first return visit to Padang Panjang, more than fifty years after I left it in 1942, I wanted to take Roger to see my birthplace. Naturally we had to eat first, so we went to the *warung* that I had seen recommended as the place to find the best *sate Padang*. I knew about it only from a tourists' guidebook, as I had had no contact with our family in Sumatra since 1942. If I remember correctly, it was called Warung Sate Syukur and was run by a man called Pak Djafar. From the outside, it didn't look very attractive, but, once we were inside, the glow of the open fire where the satays were grilled cheered up the room considerably.

I had eaten *sate Padang* often, in Java, because Padang restaurants can be found all over Java nowadays; they cater for the young Minang men who come there during their time of *merantau*, the journey they are supposed to make to the outside world before they return to their homeland and marry. Many find there are better careers in Java and decide to stay there. Some of them open Padang restaurants, and, as Padang food is well liked by most Indonesians, these "Rumah Makan Padang" do good business; you will see the signs over the shopfronts in many towns and cities.

I was looking forward to sampling *sate Padang* in its home town, but I was quite concerned that Roger might not like it — indeed, might refuse point-blank to touch it. *Sate Padang* is different from other satays because it is made almost entirely from offal (variety meats), with the occasional piece of meat among the liver, intestines, tongue, tripe, lungs etc. These are, as far as I know, always from cow or buffalo. They are not simply cut up, put on sticks, and grilled from raw; they are first boiled in spices, sometimes in meat stock, sometimes in coconut milk. The usual accompaniment to *sate Padang* is compressed rice, either *lontong* (see p.132) or *ketupat*. The sauce looks like curry sauce that has been thickened with "rice cooking water" (see p.279) or, in restaurants, usually with rice flour. I enjoyed the *sate Padang* in this *warung* very much, as the offal had been boiled in stock, not in coconut milk, which would have made the spice mixture congeal and taste too rich. Roger looked a little startled when his plate was put in front of him, but he went ahead and ate it all without demur, even saying that he liked it. Afterwards, we drove all round town looking for the site of my grandmother's old house and the Mahameru Instituut, but Padang Panjang had been so completely rebuilt, probably more than once, that I could not find a single street or building that I remembered. I have since made this satay several times at home, and I recommend it to everyone who likes offal; *sate Padang* is easy to grill over charcoal or under a really hot salamander. Here is my version of the recipe.

sate padang
offal satay with a special padang sauce

1 fresh ox tongue, soaked in cold water
  for 2–3 hours
1 tsp salt
1 lb honeycomb tripe, soaked in cold
  water for 10 minutes
1 ox heart
1 c hot water
1 turmeric leaf (optional)
½ c rice cooking water (p.279) or 2 tbsp
  rice flour diluted in 4 tbsp water,
  plus ½ c hot water

for the bumbu (paste)
4 shallots, chopped
4 garlic cloves
2 tsp ground coriander

½ tsp ground cumin
1 tsp chopped ginger
½ tsp chopped galangal or laos powder
1 tsp chopped lemongrass, soft inner
  part only
2–6 fresh red chilies, seeded
  and chopped
½ tsp ground turmeric
1 tsp salt
2 tbsp peanut oil
2 tbsp tamarind water (see pp.118–19)

metal or soaked wooden or bamboo
  satay skewers

Makes 48 skewers, or more if smaller

Drain the ox tongue, then put in a large saucepan. Cover with cold water, add the salt, and bring to a boil. Simmer for 2 hours, then leave to cool in the water. When cold, peel the tongue, and slice it into six or seven slices. Drain the tripe and cut it into six pieces. With a very sharp knife, trim off the fat around the heart, and also cut away the arteries and fibrous tissue. Cut the heart in half.

Blend all the ingredients for the paste until smooth. Transfer the paste to a saucepan, and gently fry, stirring often, for 4–5 minutes until aromatic. Transfer half of the paste to another saucepan. Put all the offal in the first saucepan, cover the saucepan tightly, and simmer for 15 minutes to allow the offal to cook in its own juices. Uncover, and give the contents a stir. If they are already too dry, add about 5–8 tablespoons of hot water from the kettle (or use the rice cooking water), and continue cooking, again covered with a tight lid, for 10 minutes. Remove from the heat, adjust the seasoning with a little salt if necessary, and keep to one side while you finish cooking the sauce.

Add the 1 cup hot water to the pan with the other half of the paste and the turmeric leaf, if using (here's where you can put in coconut milk instead of water, if you wish). Bring the whole thing to a boil, and continue cooking until the sauce has reduced by half. Taste, add more salt if necessary, and keep to one side.

Cut the offal into cubes, ready to be put onto skewers. Just before serving, grill the skewers over a charcoal fire, in a salamander or under a grill for a few minutes to brown them. Reheat the sauce, and serve the satay while the sauce is piping hot, with boiled rice or *lontong* (see p.132).

Left: Roger tackles *sate padang* at Warung Sate Sjukur in Padang Panjang.
Right: East Kalimantan: grilling satays in a new food center in Samarinda.

SELAMATAN

A *selamatan*, of one sort or another, is a frequent event in the life of pretty well every Indonesian. The word *selamatan* means a blessing, or a celebration of an achievement, great or small. In some areas, the word *kenduri* is used instead, but the meaning is the same. The first *selamatan* I remember was for the circumcision of one of my cousins, a boy of eight or nine who greatly enjoyed being the center of attention and receiving lots of presents. This, obviously, was a specifically religious occasion, but the tradition of these big love feasts goes back long before Islam was brought to the islands and drove out, or at least drove underground, the old animistic beliefs and practices of the people. At most *selamatan* today there will be a prayer, perhaps a reading from the Koran, and the men will wear the *peci*, the plain black cap. But there is always food. Sharing a meal is part of the tradition of every religion. The party may be large and quite noisy, or very small and quiet. The food likewise can be lavish, the most important item on the agenda, or so simple as to be almost an afterthought. You give a *selamatan* when a baby is expected, when it is born and at regular intervals thereafter; and every birthday party is a *selamatan*. My childhood birthdays, from the age of seven, were not marked by any great celebration, as the family was forced to move from place to place, and there were long periods when my parents had no work and no income. On my twenty-first birthday, I was living in my students' boarding house in Yogya, run by the kind mother and daughter who I called *eyang* and *ibu*, my surrogate grandmother and mother throughout my student days. I had a dozen or so high school friends in, and we ate *gado-gado* and satays provided by *ibu*. No birthday cake, as I could not afford to order one from Toko Oen, the top Chinese food shop in town, and it did not cross my mind to hire their large and handsome assembly room.

When Roger and I were married in August 1962, however, we had one of our two wedding receptions at Toko Oen. There was nothing traditional about it, but it was still a *selamatan*. The food was Chinese banquet food, and for non-Muslims, i.e. foreigners, there was a crate or two of Bir Bintang, good beer locally made under licence from Heineken. We had about 150 guests, mostly our colleagues from the English Department,

Left: North Sumatra: a wedding feast, with bride and bridegroom, in Banda Aceh, shortly after the tsunami of December 2004.

a few professors from the Faculty of Letters, and a great many of our students, plus, of course, my parents and five sisters. The other reception, attended by at least as many guests and entertained by a small gamelan orchestra, had taken place some hours earlier in the family home in Magelang. Although my parents were not Central Javanese, most of the guests were, and the wedding feast broadly followed local tradition. We ate *terik daging* (p.182), *gule kambing* (pp.56–8), *ayam goreng jawa* (pp.270–2), and other appropriate dishes such as *gado-gado* (pp.61–4) and *soto ayam* (pp.53–4). For all of these, the ingredients are cut up small before cooking, so that guests can eat comfortably with their fingers or with a spoon.

There were also several of the dishes that people in West Sumatra call *lauk gadang*. These consist of joints of meat, usually beef, or chickens cooked whole or in halves, such as the *singgang ayam* on pp.269–70. Or, if the *lauk gadang* is fish, then a large fish is dressed with what is, in effect, a curry sauce, and is put on the grandest available plate as the centerpiece of the buffet table. Ordinary guests can help themselves to whatever they want from the other dishes, but the *lauk gadang* must be carved by the person responsible for the food, plated along with choice parts of other dishes, and delivered to the important guests, who are not standing in line but are already seated in their appointed chairs or on beautiful rugs or mats. This is the custom not only at weddings, but also at every significant *selamatan*, such as for the completion of a new house or a successful rice harvest.

Harvest time has always been celebrated everywhere with a big meal for everyone who has worked in the fields. I remember vividly the last rice harvest that I saw in my grandmother's fields in Sumatra, and the feast that followed it. In the late afternoon, my grandmother led me and many of the women and girls of the family, laden with food, into the last field. There, men were cutting the rice with sickles for the women to gather up, thresh

Below: West Sumatra: the complete traditional Minangkabau bride's headdress, of gold and precious stones, weighing several pounds.

by hand, and winnow by tossing it on circular woven trays called *tampah*, so that the chaff would fly away on the evening breeze. The sun was almost down when work stopped and everyone settled down to eat. In the tropics, there is no long period of dusk; when the sun sets, night comes quickly, although a fine night is luminous with moon and stars and fireflies. Then I saw the young men and women jump up and begin to dance on a floor of beaten earth, the couples forming and re-forming, never touching each other, but moving limbs and bodies gracefully, to the sound of singing from us who were watching. Next, every girl picked up, in each hand, a saucer with a burning candle on it, and as they danced they turned their wrists so that the flames turned and rose and fell, illuminating faces and bodies, outlining them as shadows. This *tari lilin*, or candle dance, is performed again and again every night in tourist hotels all over Indonesia, and it is beautiful everywhere; however, in the rice fields among the Sumatra hills, it was the continuation of an ancient courtship ritual. My grandmother told me that this was a proper way for young people to find partners and show who they fancied, with a view to starting serious courtship if their elders approved. But, as arranged marriages were still the custom, any who fell in love during these moonlit dances among the rice stalks would still have to get permission from their respective *ninik mamak*, their family heads. Marriage-arranging was a serious matter, based on matching pedigrees rather than sentiments, and no doubt a few hearts were broken after every harvest.

The second harvest I took part in, only a year or so later, was in Beran, the village south of Cirebon in West Java where my other grandmother, my mother's mother, lived. She was, in effect, the lady of the manor. At harvest time, unlike my Sumatran grandmother, she didn't even supervise the food for the reapers, let alone sit with them in the field to eat it. It was all cooked by the wives of the men who came to dry and bring in the new rice, which was cut and gathered by the women. Each used an *ani-ani*, a small sharp blade held between the fingers, to cut each rice stalk individually, before adding it to the bundle she carried in her left hand. When the bundle was as big as she could hold, she tied it with rice straw and left it at the side of the field. The men collected and carried these bundles to a place where they were weighed, then dried in the sun. Careful weighing was important because each reaper was given as payment one-tenth of what she cut. My grandmother entrusted me, aged eight, to one of her neighbors, who taught me how to use the *ani-ani*. I think I managed to cut quite a bunch of paddy, about 2 pounds as far as I remember, so I got about 3½ ounces of *padi*, or unhusked rice, to bring back and show to my grandmother, who was very proud of me for using the *ani-ani* without cutting my fingers. My bundle of *padi* was then given to the man who was responsible for drying all of it and sending it to the miller. A month or so afterwards, the man came to visit my grandmother, presumably with a full account of the harvest, and he also brought a basket full of gleaming white rice for me. I was a specially honored person, of course, being the granddaughter of the lady who was the principal landowner of the village. I gave "my" rice to my mother, and for several days we had beautifully fresh steamed rice to eat with my father's cooking of catfish and shrimps from the river in front of the house, and duck eggs, and some duck meat from the small duck farm he had started on my grandmother's land. For me and my four younger sisters, it was an idyllic life.

Unfortunately, my father never got on with his mother-in-law, and it became clear that we would have to leave. Also, I think my parents were longing to get back to teaching. After Beran, we led an unsettled life, moving from one place to another, living with distant relations of my mother or with old school friends of my parents, until eventually my father got a job as teacher in Tanggerang, a small town that is now part of south Jakarta. From this time on, I don't recall any *selamatan* that I actually attended, apart from a small birthday *selamatan*, or a wedding that was attended by too many people.

For Muslims, Hari Raya, the "big day," is the first of the new year, immediately following the fasting month of Ramadan. We also call it Eid, or Idul Fitri (which is Arabic, more or less) or Lebaran (which is Javanese). Not that Ramadan itself is a joyless time; we are allowed to eat between sunset and sunrise, and these midnight feasts can be very jolly. Still, the long day without any food or water, in a tropical climate, is a severe test, and one of the things that keeps people going is the thought that the biggest *selamatan* of all is approaching. I don't remember exactly what my Sumatran grandmother cooked for

Lebaran, apart from the traditional *rendang* (pp.180–2) and *lemang* (p.234), beef with sticky rice. But in Java, in our new family home, once we were settled in Magelang, we followed the Central Javanese tradition of eating *lontong* (p.132) or *ketupat* with *sambal goreng daging* (p.170) as our main meal, starting at noon. There is also a tradition of sending gifts of homemade food, biscuits, or other sweet cakes, and cooked meat or poultry (other than *sambal goreng daging*), to close friends and neighbors, and of course they generally return the compliment. Good friends and neighbors naturally send each other the treats that they are known to be good at making. If a household has a reputation for its excellent *lapis legit*, no other family will send *lapis legit* to them. You send people the best things you can make, and expect them to send their best in return.

On the morning of Lebaran day, after morning prayer in the mosque, junior members of the family visit senior members, and employees visit their bosses, to pay their respects and to ask forgiveness for wrongs they have done in the past year. These visits continue on the second day. A large and well-to-do family would, in the past, arrange for all their members to assemble for a big *selamatan* lunch immediately after

Above: Bali: village women carrying offerings to a temple festival; most of the edible items will be offered, in essence, to the gods, then taken home and eaten by the families who made them.

morning prayer on the first day of Lebaran. Nowadays, however, according to my sisters who live in Jakarta, in big cities these gatherings have become rare. There's a tradition that city dwellers' domestic helpers, who come from small villages, must have at least a week off work, so that they can go home to visit their families. Two significant changes arise from this. One is that the middle-class family will themselves go somewhere to visit family or friends, instead of celebrating at home. The second is that catering businesses now flourish, to cater for rich families who must have parties, but don't have the staff to do the hard work. Lebaran nowadays has become a bit like Christmas in the West (although Christmas, too, has become a time for present-giving and hospitality even in non-Christian countries). In Indonesia, all prices for rice and other food items are at least doubled. Traveling, whether by road, rail, air or inter-island ferries, has become a major problem, as everybody tries to return to their native village and their parents' home.

A SELAMATAN IN BALI

Bali, as everyone knows, is unlike the rest of Indonesia and unlike anywhere else in the world. It never seems to have played much part in the island-hopping ocean-voyaging trade that linked Southeast Asia to China, Japan, and India a thousand or more years ago. Its isolation probably increased when, in the early sixteenth century, Islam completed its takeover of the Javanese kingdoms, and the last Hindu rulers of Java removed their court and all its ceremony across the narrow channel that separates the two islands. Javanese Hinduism was already very different from that of India. In the cultural hothouse of Bali, it continued to change, so that what today we too easily think of as a timeless society of priests and artists is, in some of its aspects, a rapidly changing one, and has developed in all sorts of directions since Roger and I first encountered it on our honeymoon, forty-five years ago.

I am not going to try here to sort out the new from the old, and the old from the ancient, in modern Bali. But I have seen for myself the extent to which daily life there is influenced by festivals and ceremonies, and the wholehearted way everyone in the family and the village, as soon as one celebration is over, starts preparing for the next. There is so much to be done: music and dances to be rehearsed, temples and yards to be elaborately decorated, hundreds or thousands of offerings to be cut from palm leaf, colored paper, cloth, and bamboo, elaborate set-pieces

of fried and painted rice flour to be constructed, streamers and banners to be painted. There will be the familiar processions of elegant ladies, carrying on their heads (as a mark of extreme respect) high-piled baskets of fruit and cakes to the appropriate temple. A lot of this is public and visible to every tourist, but there is a lot going on behind the scenes as well. Of particular interest to me, on a visit some years ago, were the preparations for a feast to celebrate and seek the blessing of the gods for the newly renovated family home of a Balinese fellow student. It was a wealthy family, and though the event was purely domestic, with only a dozen or so people present, everything was done properly. My friend's mother cooked the festival lunch. I knew from earlier meetings that she was a first-rate cook (my recipe for *bebek betutu* on pp.228–9 is closely based on hers) and I was eager to taste her food, but we had to wait while a small procession of women relatives made their way to the temple, and to give them time to place food offerings where the gods could see and smell them, before it was seemly for us to tuck in.

A wedding, or a cremation or a tooth filing (a Balinese rite of passage), is an even more serious affair. Even a fairly quiet wedding is likely to entertain a hundred or more guests. This is partly because it is the most important single event in the lives of groom and bride, partly because it affects the whole community and must be witnessed by as many people as possible, and partly – perhaps mainly – because you have been invited to all the weddings in your village for year after year, and now it is your turn to pay back every one of those invitations. Cremations, too, must be carried out with the most scrupulous attention to detail, and at even greater expense, because only a properly cremated body can release its soul, which in due course will be reborn – usually in the same family, and only four generations later, so there is not very much time to lose. Families therefore group together and wait until they can collectively raise enough money to pay not just for the elaborate funeral towers and sarcophagi, the priests and tower-carriers, but also for the massive amounts of food that will be needed to feed everyone. The resulting feast is called an *ebat*, a word that imitates the sound of many knives chopping up complete animals (usually pigs, but on the south coast they favor sea turtles) to make *sate lembat*, satays of spiced meat finely chopped to a paste, molded onto flat

Left: Bali: offerings being carried up the temple steps on a ceremonial day, of which there are many in the complex Balinese calendar.

bamboo sticks, and briefly cooked over charcoal. Only the best of the meat is used for this, but none at all is wasted: blood, guts, and other organs are combined with grated coconut and more spices into *lawar*, a dish that is always served because its red color makes it sacred to the creator, Brahma. The usual vegetable is boiled banana stem. According to Fred Eiseman, whose book *Sekala dan Niskala* and other enquiries into Balinese culture have informed so many visitors, a big wedding may require 4500 sticks of satay and a prodigious quantity of steamed white rice, the latter prepared overnight by a squad of housewives laboring in their home kitchens. Serving the gods is not a task to be undertaken lightly.

TUMPENG

A typical *selamatan* food in Central Java is *tumpeng*, a mound of cooked rice shaped like an upside-down *kukusan*, the woven bamboo basket for steaming rice on the traditional *dandang* – in other words, like a cone. The *tumpeng* may be large or small, depending on the purpose of the *selamatan*. For example, the Javanese hold a *selamatan* called *miton* or *mitoni* when a woman is in the seventh month of pregnancy. The name is derived from *pitu*, the Javanese word for seven, and the centerpiece of the feast will be a large *tumpeng* surrounded by six smaller ones. In Javanese tradition, seven is a magic number, and it is also believed that in the seventh month the baby can be born, premature but sufficiently grown to continue life as would a normal baby carried in the womb for the full nine months.

The rice for this *selamatan* may be either white or yellow, and cooked in coconut milk, as *nasi gurih* or *nasi kuning* (p.131). The accompaniments are those traditional for *tumpeng*, and include *urap* (which is also called *kuluban*), with a number of prescribed vegetables, among which must be *kacang panjang* (yard-long beans) and *kangkung* (water spinach), along with other vegetables that are either seasonal or easily available, or homegrown. There should be two other *tampah* (round trays of woven bamboo): one with different fruits from the market, and some sweets, such as *rujak*, a fruit salad with sweet, chili-hot *sambal rujak*, and *air kelapa muda*, young coconut water. Either on this *tampah* or the other there should be rice flour porridge, made with palm sugar, so that it is brown in color. On top of this porridge is laid one perfect banana, as a sign that the birth will be smooth and without a hitch. I read an article in a magazine called *Selera* – a food magazine started in the late 1980s in Jakarta – that for people in the city of Solo, sometimes called Surakarta, about 35 miles east of Yogyakarta, a *mitoni selamatan* should also have a *tampah* with a young green coconut on it, and on the coconut shell should be painted two figures, one of Janaka, or Arjuna, and the other of Arjuna's wife, Sembadra, or as many call her, Draupadi, the sister of Lord Krishna. If the baby is a boy, the parents' wish is that he may be as handsome as Arjuna, and if a girl, she will be as beautiful as Sembadra.

A very simple *tumpeng*, suitable for a birthday party, usually consists of white or yellow rice, with the traditional accompaniments of *urap* (*gudangan*) and *kering tempe dengan ikan teri* (these two recipes are in this book, on pp.194–5 and p.166, respectively), with a chicken dish, either fried or grilled. Different people follow different traditions for the accompaniments. Nowadays, each guest may be served with

Below: *Tumpeng* prepared for a Javanese *selamatan*.

a miniature *tumpeng* as a complete feast on a plate. But the original purpose of the cone-shaped "rice mountain" was to wish the birthday person success in aspiring to high achievements. Instead of several small *tumpeng*, the rice is piled high and set on a *tampah* lined with banana leaves, with the *gudangan* arranged around its base, together with the *tempe dengan ikan teri* (p.166) and the pieces of fried or grilled chicken. Everybody is then invited to help themselves from this one great *tumpeng*. Of course, there are other dishes, too, but the point is that the feast brings people together: the greetings and good wishes to the birthday person are communal.

Following are some more recipes that are customary for a *selamatan*.

gulai gajebo
brisket of beef cooked in west sumatra style

This dish is typical of the chili-hot cooking found throughout the Padang area, a style that is popular all over Indonesia. Traditionally, it is made with cuts of beef that have plenty of fat on them. It is made richer still by being cooked for a long time with a lot of coconut milk. The large quantity of chilies used makes the sauce quite red, while the tamarind imparts a pleasant sourness. My version is an improved recipe, to cut out most of the fat.

2 lb brisket, in one piece
1 tsp salt
1 lemongrass stem, cut across into two,
 then bruised
3 kaffir lime leaves
small piece of fresh galangal
2 salam leaves (optional)
4½ c very thick coconut milk

for the bumbu (paste)
4 shallots, chopped
4 garlic cloves, chopped

4–6 fresh red chilies, seeded
 and chopped
1 tsp paprika
1 tsp chopped fresh ginger
2 tsp chopped fresh turmeric
 or 1 tsp ground turmeric
2 tbsp tamarind water (see pp.118–19)
2 tbsp coconut milk
2 tbsp peanut (groundnut) oil

Serves 6–8

Put the brisket and 4½ cups cold water in a large saucepan and bring to a boil. Add the salt, and simmer, skimming often, for 1 hour. This can be done a day ahead. Keep the meat and stock separately in the refrigerator. The next day, discard all the fat from the stock, and measure out 3½ cups of stock for cooking the meat. Trim all the fat from the meat, but leave the meat in one piece.

Put all the ingredients for the paste in a blender, and purée until smooth. Gently fry the paste in a saucepan, stirring often, until you get a good aroma, then add the stock. Simmer for 5 minutes, then add the whole piece of meat, lemongrass, kaffir lime leaves, galangal, and salam leaves, if using. Continue to cook slowly for a further 50–60 minutes, then adjust the seasoning with a little salt if necessary. Now add the coconut milk, and continue cooking over medium heat for 30 minutes. Reduce the heat, cover the pan, and simmer for another 30 minutes.

Transfer the meat to a wooden board, and the sauce to a smaller saucepan. Cut the meat into thin slices, and reheat the sauce and put in a sauce boat for everybody to help themselves. Serve hot, with boiled rice or boiled new potatoes.

singgang ayam
boiled and grilled spatchcock chicken

This is an everyday method of preparing and cooking chicken in West Sumatra, and a customary way to cook chicken for a party, whether small or large — even for a wedding. It is equally good for a barbecue or for roasting in the oven. I would allow half a chicken per person, and you will not need much else to accompany it. It's fun to have this with baked potatoes or roasted sweet corn (*jagung bakar*, p.145), and salad.

2 free-range chickens, each weighing
    about 3¼ lb, cut in half lengthways,
    all the fat trimmed off
    and some of the bones removed
2½ c very thick coconut milk
2½ c chicken stock
1 lemongrass stem, cut into 3 lengths
2 kaffir lime leaves
salt

for the bumbu (paste)
4 shallots or 1 onion, chopped
3 garlic cloves, chopped
1–3 large fresh red chilies
2 tsp chopped fresh ginger
1 tsp chopped fresh galangal
1 tsp ground turmeric
2 tbsp peanut oil

Serves 4

Put all the ingredients for the paste in a blender, add 1 tablespoon water, and purée until smooth. Transfer the paste to a largish saucepan, bring to a boil, reduce the heat slightly, and simmer for 4 minutes, stirring constantly. Add the chicken halves and 4 tablespoons of the thick coconut milk, and stir the chicken to coat all the pieces with the paste. Now add the stock, lemongrass, and kaffir lime leaves. Season with salt. Bring everything back to a boil, then reduce the heat slightly. Cover the pan and simmer for 25 minutes.

    Uncover the pan and add the remaining coconut milk. Give the whole thing a little stir, and continue simmering for 20 minutes, stirring occasionally. Adjust the seasoning. Up to this point, the chicken can be prepared up to 24 hours in advance. If you are doing this, remove the chicken halves from the sauce and allow to cool. Keep the sauce in a bowl, and refrigerate both when cold.

When you are ready to serve, grill the chicken on the barbecue for about 6 minutes on each side, or roast in a preheated oven at 350°F (180°C) for 15–20 minutes. Transfer the sauce to a pan and heat until it is hot but not boiling. To serve, either pour the sauce equally on top of each half-chicken, or put in a bowl and ask your guests to help themselves.

ayam goreng jawa
central java special fried chicken

This is a favorite way to fry chicken in Java. Children love it, and so do grown-ups because they remember how fond of it they were when they were children. It is excellent food for a *selamatan*, being quick and easy to bring to table. I admit that real Javanese country chickens have a big advantage over their remote Western cousins: they are truly free-range, to the extent that only the fit survive to become big enough for the table. These *ayam kampung* spend much of their time dodging cars and motorcycles, in the narrow lanes that lead from city streets. The exercise keeps them fit, but makes them rather tough, which is why we boil them first in spiced coconut milk to tenderize them. The chickens I buy are usually tender anyway, but boiling like this improves their flavor enormously. Also, it can be done in advance, so the chickens are ready to fry quickly just before serving. This in turn gives the skin that savory crispness that brings out the child in all of us.

1 chicken, about 3¼ lb,
   cut into 8 pieces
rapeseed or peanut oil for deep-frying

for the bumbu (paste)
1¾ c coconut milk
6 shallots
1½ tsp ground coriander

3 candlenuts or macadamia nuts,
   chopped
1 tsp chopped fresh turmeric root
1 tsp chopped fresh galangal
1 tsp finely chopped lemongrass
1 tsp sea salt and more to taste

Serves 4–6

Using just 3 tablespoons of the coconut milk, blend all the other ingredients for the *bumbu* to make a not-too-smooth paste. Put the rest of the coconut milk in a saucepan, and add the paste. Mix thoroughly, add the pieces of chicken, and boil for 45–50 minutes until all the sauce has been absorbed by the meat. Allow to cool, then deep-fry the chicken four pieces at a time until golden brown.

ikan besar
whole stuffed fish

This is one of the recipes for what is often known as *lauk gadang*, although *lauk gadang* is not always fish. I explain on p.258 how *lauk gadang* is usually served.

Ikan means fish and *besar* means large — so the recipe here is for my special big fish, to be cooked whole after I have stuffed it with a stuffing that may be different every time I cook this dish. I don't recall that there were many variations in stuffings for fish or poultry in Indonesia during my childhood. The recipe here is for a dish that is suitable for a *selamatan*, or any special occasion, but the choice of fish and the stuffing will depend on what is available at the time of cooking. In Indonesia, this dish is usually made with *gurami*. For an alternative, try John Dory or turbot: one weighing about 4½ pounds is just the right size. Other alternatives are sea bass or wild salmon. These are all rather expensive, so I think I'm right in saying that they are appropriate for a special occasion. At home, in Indonesia, *gurami* has always been affordable, so perhaps a farmed salmon from a reputable fish farm will be my best choice. Ask the fish dealer to clean the fish thoroughly, which includes emptying and cleaning the inside of the fish head. And better still, ask him to take out the entire backbone. Any stray small bones need to be picked out just before you put the stuffing into the fish.

1 whole fish as described above   *Serves 8–10*
1 tsp fine sea salt
½ tsp chili powder
½ tsp ground turmeric

Rub the fish well inside and outside with the mixture of salt, chili powder and turmeric. Keep in a cool place, covered with cling film, while preparing the stuffing.

for the stuffing

8 oz raw shrimp, peeled, deveined and rinsed
4 oz filet of cod or monkfish tail, roughly chopped
4 oz fresh shiitake, ceps, or porcini mushrooms, roughly chopped
4 tbsp chopped spring onions
1 tsp chopped fresh ginger
3 garlic cloves, crushed
1 tbsp light soy sauce
1 tbsp lime or lemon juice
½ tsp finely chopped fresh red chili or ½ tsp *sambal ulek* (see p.279)
1 tbsp chopped fresh flat-leaf parsley
½ tsp sea salt
1 egg plus 1 egg white

Preheat the oven to 350°F (180°C). Chop the shrimp with a sharp cleaver on a wooden chopping board, and mix with the other ingredients for the stuffing, except the egg and egg white. Put the mixture in a food processor, and pulse for 10 seconds or so. Transfer to a glass bowl. Add the egg and egg white, and mix and stir them with a large fork, working in only one direction, until the mixture becomes harder to stir. Now knead the mix with your hand until it becomes pliable and soft.

Remove the cling wrap from the fish, and fill the fish with the already quite soft stuffing mixture. Spread the stuffing evenly inside the fish, and either sew the opening or wrap the fish tightly in a sheet of parchment paper. Put the fish on top of a double layer of foil, and close the foil loosely. Cook in the oven for 20 minutes. This process, in effect, steams the fish and makes the stuffing firm, but leaves it not quite cooked. Remove the fish from the foil and from the parchment paper (if using). Rub the fish with some olive oil on both sides, put on a rack in a baking dish and return to the oven at the same temperature. Cook for another 20–30 minutes.

Transfer to a warmed serving dish. Leave the fish to rest for 3–5 minutes, then slice it into as many slices as you need. If you put the stuffing into the head also, serve the head, with another slice, to your most honored guest, as is customary during the *selamatan* meal. I like eating this fish with rice and some vegetables or salad, and no sauce. But it can be served with any sauce – hot chili sauce, or your favorite white or butter sauce, or mayonnaise if you are serving it cold.

GLOSSARY

This is a two-way Indonesian-English-Indonesian glossary. Some Indonesian words which are explained in the text are not included here but will be found in the index. Explanatory notes, if any, usually accompany the English headword; but if the Indonesian has no English equivalent, the notes go with the Indonesian word (e.g. *asam gelugur*, below). Scientific names, if given, usually go with the Indonesian headword; their main purpose is to assist readers who want to find out more from learned sources. Rough pronunciation guides are given for Indonesian words where readers may be uncertain how the words should sound. The symbol *∂* is pronounced like the "e" in "often."

asam gelugur *Garcinia atroviridis*. This fruit, thinly sliced, then dried in the sun, is used as a souring agent. It is marketed as "tamarind slices," although the plant is completely different from tamarind. Added to a sauce while cooking, *asam gelugur* gives the dish a delicate tamarind-like sourness, but it must be removed before serving.

ayam chicken.

babi pig, pork.

bakar grilled or barbecued. *See* recipe for *ikan besar* on pp.272–3.

bakmie, bami noodles with pork; *see* p.67.

banana *pisang*.

bandeng *Chanos chanos*; milkfish. See pp,249–50 for recipe for *sate bandeng*.

basil *kemangi*, *selasih*. Different kinds of basil are easily confused, and these two Indonesian words seem to be used indifferently, both for *Ocimum basilicum* and *O. gratissimum*. The former, sweet or Thai basil, has purple stems, green leaves, smells of aniseed, and tastes of licorice. The latter, called tree basil, smells and tastes pungently of cloves. Several other species are used in cooking, and all have local varieties and names; botanists disagree and reclassify them. The cook is usually constrained by what is available in local markets.

bawang

    bawang goreng *See* crisp-fried shallots.

    bawang merah onion. Note that our *bawang merah* is small, like a shallot. For this reason, I usually specify shallots for most recipes in this book, but you can use an ordinary onion instead.

    bawang putih garlic. *Putih* means "white"; *merah* is "red."

bean generally, *kacang* ['ka-tchang] – this word is also used for nuts.

    mung bean *kacang hijau*. In this book, this refers to mung bean sprouts only. In Indonesian, "beansprout" is *tauge* ['tau-gé].

    soy bean *kacang kedele* [k∂-d∂-'lé]

    yard-long bean *kacang panjang*. The pods really can grow to about 3 feet long, although if they are to be eaten as a vegetable the beans inside them are not allowed to ripen fully. This is much the best bean for eating raw. When I was a young girl in Bogor, we used to slice *kacang panjang* very thin and mix them with plenty of hot *sambal terasi*. The young leaves can also be eaten, lightly boiled or steamed, and mixed with other vegetables in *urap* or *gudangan* (pp,194–5).

beansprouts *tauge* ['tau-gé]. A loan word from Chinese. If the type of bean is not specified, we assume that mung beansprouts are meant; soy beansprouts, which are shorter, are also commonly used, e.g. in *kohu kohu* (*see* p.158).

bebek duck.

belimbing [b∂'lim-bing] the name given to two closely related fruits:

    manis *Averrhoa carambola*, carambola.

    wuluh *Averrhoa bilimbi*, "sour belimbing," is my favorite souring agent for fish dishes. Unfortunately, it doesn't travel well, so is still not available in the West.

bengkuang [b∂ng-kwang] *Pachyrrhizus erosus*, yam bean.

bumbu A mixture of spices and other aromatic ingredients ground to a paste using a mortar and pestle, or, if the quantity is quite large, processed in a food processor or blender. When used as the cooking medium for meat or vegetables, it then becomes the sauce.

cabe, cabai [tcha-bé] *Capsicum annuum* and *C. frutescens*, chili peppers, sweet peppers.

candlenut Indonesian: *kemiri* [k∂'mee-ri]; Malaysian: *buah keras*. Candlenuts are similar to macadamia nuts, but are not the same. They are used in many Indonesian and Malaysian recipes, always crushed or ground before being mixed with other ingredients and blended to a paste. Raw macadamia nuts are a satisfactory substitute. Another alternative is ground almonds or blanched almonds. Don't eat candlenuts raw – they are mildly toxic until cooked.

carambola *belimbing manis*. In English, this is also called starfruit; the fruit has five sharply angled ridges, so that a slice of it looks like a five-pointed star. Usually sold fresh.

cardamom *kapulaga*.

cashew apple *jambu mete* ['mé-té]. This is not, in fact, a fruit; it is the swollen stem or pedicel, at the lower end of which the cashew nut develops.

cashew nut *kacang mete* ['ka-tchang 'mé-té].

cassava *ubi kayu*; in Java: *ketela* or *singkong* (*singkong*, a word taken from Chinese, is also used for *bengkuang*, or yam bean). Cassava is widely grown in Indonesia for its starchy roots; cassava flour is sold in most Asian food shops.

cengkeh ['tchéng-kéh] *Syzygium aromatica*, cloves.

cerme ['tchér-mé] *Cicca acida*, a small tree, the unripe fruits of which, about the size of grapes, are used as souring agents in cooked dishes.

chili peppers *cabe, cabai*. Today, these are grown and consumed in such huge quantities all over Southeast Asia that it is hard to imagine the region without them – yet they were brought by Europeans from Central and South America a mere 500 years ago. Children start eating food with chilies at any age from five years onward, and by the age of twelve are almost always addicted to them – "addicted" may not be too strong a word, as part of the pleasure they give is that their heat, sensed on special receptors in the soft parts of the mouth, stimulates production of endorphins, chemicals in the brain that soothe and give pleasure. Cooks will usually tell you that hotness is a secondary consideration; what they are after is flavor, and different varieties of chili have different flavors.

Red and green chilies are not different varieties; green ones are picked at an earlier stage of ripeness, and therefore tend to be hotter than red ones, although this is not an absolute rule. Likewise, smaller chilies tend to be hotter than large ones; *cabe rawit*, also known as bird chilies or bird's-eye chilies, are usually very hot. The hottest part is always the placental tissue holding the seeds; if these are removed, the placenta goes with them and the chili is somewhat milder. When handling chilies, don't rub your eyes or touch any sensitive part of yourself; a tiny trace of the active agent, capsaicin, can cause quite a lot of discomfort. It is, however, completely harmless, and the pain goes eventually – bathing the affected part (especially your eyes) in cold water reduces discomfort, although it does not dissolve the capsaicin. If you get a mouthful of unbearably hot chili, drinking cold water or beer is not much help; eating cold boiled rice is more soothing. It may also help if you reflect that chilies are vitamin-rich and very good for you.

chili flakes coarsely crushed dried red chilies, sold in packets or small jars, widely available from ethnic grocers or supermarkets.

Chinese cabbage There are so many species and varieties of Brassicas that it is hard to know which is which. In this book, "Chinese cabbage" means the variety, almost cylindrical in shape, with tightly wrapped, whitish leaves. It is sometimes called celery cabbage.

cinnamon *kayu manis*.

cloves *cengkeh* ['tchéng-kéh].

coconut *kelapa*; see pp. 112–17.

coriander *ketumbar* [kǝ'toom-bar]. Indonesians as a rule do not like coriander leaves or roots. For them, coriander, or *ketumbar*, means the seeds.

crisp-fried shallots *bawang goreng*. These are coarsely chopped shallot flakes, fried in cooking oil until browned and crisp, and very tasty. If you have

a Chinese supermarket within reach, you may well be able to buy them ready-made in large clear plastic jars at extremely moderate prices. These are just as good as any made at home, and as long as you keep the lid of the jar tightly screwed they will keep for months. Commercially produced *bawang goreng* are often made of onions, and are so labeled; they taste the same.

cumin *jinten* ['djin-tǝn].

daun a leaf. A great many species of leaves, wild and cultivated, are used in Indonesian cooking, including the following mentioned in the book:

jeruk purut *Citrus hystrix*; kaffir lime leaf.

pandan *Pandanus odorus*. The young leaves of this species of pandanus, pandan or screwpine are used by cooks in many parts of South and Southeast Asia to add a distinctive aromatic flavor and in some cases a delicate green color. In Indonesia, you buy *daun pandan* in the market in small square packets, the leaves having been chopped into lengths of about 2 inches. In the West, you can buy them in Asian shops, packed in plastic bags containing a few long leaves, so that you can, after washing them, cut them to the length you need, or freeze them until needed. Crushed or chopped into small pieces, they can be mixed with a little water and blended; the green juice is then used as natural green coloring (see recipe for *klepon* on pp. 33–4). Do not confuse this *Pandanus odorus* with other species of pandanus, of which, botanists will tell you, there are many hundreds, most of them tough-looking plants, with long, broad fibrous leaves armed with spines, prickles, hooks, and other weapons. Their principal use is in making mats, brushes, ropes, and so on.

salam *Syzygium polyanthum*, the salam tree. Its leaves are used similarly to bay leaves.

dried shrimp *ebi*. These tiny shrimp, shelled, dried and usually roasted, are sold in packets in many Asian food shops, but are surprisingly expensive. They are strong-tasting and salty, so use in moderation. Soak in hot water for 10 minutes before use, drain, then chop or put in a blender or crush using a mortar and pestle.

duku *Lansium domesticum*. A small buff-colored fruit, easily skinned, containing several pleasant-tasting white segments, one or more of which encloses a seed. Sometimes obtainable in Asian shops, where it is also known as *langsat*.

durian *Durio zibethinus*. See pp. 93–4 for recipe for durian ice cream.

ebi dried shrimp.

eggplant *terung* (also *terong*). These are grown all over Southeast Asia in various shapes, sizes, and colors. The familiar purple eggplant, big and glossy, has good texture, but can lack flavor. The smallest eggplant that we usually find in Indian stores, is the baby purple eggplant. Indian and Thai shops often sell apple eggplants – these are cultivars of *Solanum melongena*, which come in different shapes, typically globular or egg-shaped. They also come in different colors: purple, bright yellow, white, or shades of green ranging from light to intense, and often with whites and greens fading into each other. They are slightly bigger than a golf ball. *Terung gelatik* is the pea eggplant, green, rather hard, and quite bitter.

emping ['∂mp-ing] These can sometimes be found in Asian or Asian food shops. They look something like pale potato chips, and they must be fried shortly before they are eaten; they are rewardingly crunchy and have a pleasant nutty flavor, being made from the kernels or stones of the fruit of a large tree known by the Latin name of *Gnetum gnemon*. The Javanese call it *melinjo* or *belinjo*. *Emping* are delicious by themselves as nibbles, and are often scattered over dishes such as *gado-gado* (see pp. 61–4).

fiddlehead *paku*, or *pakis*. Both Indonesian words refer to a multitude of edible very young ferns. The only reliable substitute I can occasionally find for *paku* is North American fiddleheads, sold in glass jars.

flour *tepung* [t∂'poong] is flour; *tepung terigu* [t∂'rigu] is wheat flour; *tepung beras* [b∂'ras] rice flour; *tepung jagung* corn (i.e. maize) flour.

fried *goreng*.

galangal In Indonesian and Malaysian, this pinkish rhizome is known as *laos*, or *lengkuas*. Fresh galangal is quite easily available, especially in Thai shops. It has a bitter taste and is not as hot as ginger; it is hard to the touch, and a large piece is tough enough to damage the blades of a food processor. Peel a slice of fresh galangal and cut it into small dice before putting in a blender. alternatively, put a 1 inch piece of galangal in your cooking, e.g. *rendang* (pp. 180–1). Always take it out before serving – if someone bites on it, it can break a tooth.

garlic *bawang putih*.

ginger *jahe* ['dja-hé]. This is plain old-fashioned ginger, the English and Latin names of which both derive from the Sanskrit *singabera*. Ginger has been cultivated all around the Indian Ocean and South China Sea for many centuries. Recipes in the book call for ginger to be peeled, then chopped or grated; or just roughly chopped to be blended to a paste with other ingredients.

goreng bawang *See* crisp-fried shallots.

guava *jambu batu*, or *jambu klutuk*. These come in white or pink. Fresh ripe guavas (usually white) are often available in Indian shops or Chinese supermarkets. Canned guavas (usually pink) are easier to find and are satisfactory for making ice cream.

gula jawa *gula melaka*, *gula kelapa*; palm sugar, or jaggery. Indonesian palm sugar is made from the sap of coconut palms. It comes in a cake form, and

needs to be chopped or grated before use. Muscovado and demerara sugar make acceptable substitutes if necessary.

gurami *Osphronemos* spp., *Trichogaster* spp., *Helostoma temmincki*; in English, often spelled "gourami." The name is given to several species of large freshwater fish, often raised in tanks or ponds; all are good food fish.

ikan fish.

> **ikan asin** Dried and salted fish, still a major source of protein for all Southeast Asians. Large dried salted fish are available in many Chinese supermarkets. Salt cod (bacalao) is a good alternative. Both kinds, dried and salted fish imported from the East, and salt cod, need to be soaked for an hour or so before cooking.
>
> **ikan bilis** Very small *ikan teri*, dried and salted – the names are often treated as interchangeable. Packets of *ikan bilis* can be bought in most Chinese food shops, with or without heads; it is better to remove the heads before cooking.
>
> **ikan teri** *Stolephorus* spp. and similar: anchovy or whitebait. See previous entry.

jackfruit *nangka*. These large (often very large) fruit, looking like green rough-skinned cushions, can be bought whole in some Indian shops. Ripe jackfruit are eaten raw, as fruit. For cooking, the best are small green ones, weighing about 1 pound. All jackfruit produce a sticky juice which is very difficult to remove from skin or clothes. Canned green jackfruit can be bought in many food shops and is much easier to use.

jagung *Zea mays*, maize; see recipe for *jagung bakar* on pp. 144–5.

jahe ['dja-hé] *Zingiber officinale*, ginger.

jambu A catch-all name for a wide variety of fruits, more or less plum-like and mostly of the genus *Syzygium* (formerly *Eugenia*). Most are green-skinned, becoming darker and turning to red, purple or black as they ripen. They are juicy, astringent, and usually rather sour. *Jambu* by itself usually refers to the *jambolan*, or Java plum (*Syzygium cumini*).

jambu air *Syzygium aqueum*, water apple, said to be good for relieving thirst.

jambu batu, jambu klutuk *Psidium guajava*, guava.

jambu merah *Syzygium malaccense*, sometimes called Malay apple.

jambu mete *Anacardium occidentale*, the so-called "cashew apple."

jengkol The seeds of a large forest tree, *Pithecellobium jiringa*, which are eaten, raw or cooked, with sambal as a vegetable; in Sumatra, they are often made into *rendang*. They can be bought from Thai food shops. WARNING: uncooked jengkol, consumed in quantity, can cause kidney damage. It is safer to boil them at least twice, with a change of water, before making them into *rendang*, where long cooking will render them harmless. Even then, eat in moderation.

jeruk *Citrus* spp.; general word for citrus fruits.

jeruk Bali *Citrus maxima*, pomelo.

jeruk manis *Citrus sinensis*, orange.

jeruk nipis *Citrus aurantifolia*, lime.

jeruk purut *Citrus hystrix*, kaffir lime.

jinten ['djin-tðn] *Cuminum cyminum*, cumin.

jinten manis *Pimpinella anisum*, anise.

kacang generally, bean or nut.

kacang buncis *Phaseolus vulgaris*, kidney bean or French bean.

kacang hijau *Phaseolus aureus*, mung bean or green gram.

kacang kedele *Glycine max*, soy bean.

kacang mete *Anacardium occidentale*, cashew nut.

kacang panjang *Vigna sinensis var. sesquipedalis*; yard-long beans.

kacang tanah *Arachis hypogaea*, peanuts.

kaffir lime, kaffir lime leaf *daun jeruk purut*. The peel and the juice of the fruit are used for cooking, but it is only the leaves that are called for in most of the recipes here. The fruit produces very little juice, and is mainly used in freshly made sambal, instead of ordinary lime juice. The grated rind can be used instead of the leaves if the latter are not available. The leaves are easily available in Thai shops, and can be recognized by their figure-eight shape. They give much more fragrance than any other citrus leaves. Make sure to wash them thoroughly first, before putting them in your cooking. Although they are edible and have a refreshing taste, they are rather tough even after being cooked for a long time. Therefore, when using whole leaves, discard before serving.

kalamansi *Citrus mitis*. Calamondin: a small citrus fruit, indigenous to the Philippines. It has a taste between lime and orange. Sour, very refreshing as a cold drink, and an excellent souring agent; not usually available in Europe.

kangkung *Ipomoea aquatica*, water spinach.

kapulaga *Elettaria cardamomum, Amomum* spp., cardamom. Several species are sold, and give roughly similar flavors.

kayu manis *Cinnamomum zeylanicum*, cinnamon. *C. cassia* and other related species, often sold as cinnamon, taste nearly the same.

kecap ['ke-tjap]: soy sauce. Authentic Indonesian *kecap* is sometimes not easily found. Javanese-style soy sauce made in the Netherlands is available in two kinds: *kecap asin* (light and salty) and *kecap manis* (dark, sweet, and salty). Chinese supermarkets have a wide range of soy sauces. Japanese soy sauces are easily available, but are often labeled only in Japanese. For general use, I use Kikkoman, or at least a sauce that has "naturally brewed" on the label.

All soy sauce should be used in moderation, but "clear" or "light" sauce should be used sparingly: it is strong-tasting and very salty. Do not add more salt without tasting the food first. Also, clear or light soy sauce does not color food cooked with it, but dark sauce will make your cooking browner, which may make it look less appetizing. Peanut sauce (for satay) should be dark, so I use Indonesian *kecap manis* when making it. Peanut butter does not make good satay sauce, as it is pale and bland-tasting.

kedondong *Spondias cytherea*. This tropical fruit is about the size and shape of a large duck egg. As far as I know it is not yet available in the West. Its skin is green, and you peel it like an apple. The flesh is firm and in the center there is a single spiny seed. *Kedondong* can be eaten raw, but is too sour for many people. In Indonesia, I used it a lot as a souring agent in my cooking, instead of tamarind water or sour green mango. The leaf, *daun kedondong*, is used the same way.

kelapa *Cocos nucifera*, coconut: *see* pp.112–17.

kemangi *Ocimum basilicum*; *O. gratissimum*, basil. *See also* selasih.

kemiri *Aleurites moluccana*, candlenut.

kenari *Canarium commune*. This is a tall shade tree and is often grown along the sides of country roads, especially in eastern Indonesia. It produces nuts with rather oily kernels that look and taste like almonds, and *kenari*, almonds and *kemiri* (candlenuts) can all be used as alternatives to each other in cooking. *See* recipes for *kohu kohu* (p.158) and *boboto* (p.201).

kencur [kðn-'tjoor] *Kaempferia galanga*, lesser galangal.

ketumbar [kð-'toom-bar] *Coriandrum sativum*, coriander.

krupuk udang. Shrimp crackers. *Krupuk* (also spelled *kerupuk*) are commercially made and can be bought in many Asian food shops throughout the world. The shrimp crackers that are easiest to find are Chinese; these are small and do not expand much when fried. Real Indonesian *krupuk udang* are flat, pale, roughly oblong, and must be deep-fried, for a few seconds each, in canola or peanut oil in a wok. They must be absolutely dry before frying starts; on a hot, sunny day, you can spread them out to sun-dry for a couple of hours, otherwise spread them loosely in a warm cupboard. Fry one at a time. As each *krupuk* hits the hot oil, tiny air bubbles expand and the whole thing zooms to two or three times its original size and may also become lightly browned – but not much. It may also start to curl up a little during the short time it remains flexible; keep it as flat as possible by pressing gently with a large spoon. As soon as it seems to have fully expanded – 5 or 6 seconds usually – take it out and lay it on paper towels to dry.

kunyit *Curcuma domestica*, turmeric.

lalab Raw vegetables, crudités. *Lalab* is mentioned in this book because it is served at almost any rice-based meal as an additional accompaniment to fish, meat, or poultry dishes.

langsat See *duku*.

laos *Languas galanga*, galangal.

lemang sticky rice cooked in coconut milk, in bamboo segments. In West Sumatra, it is traditionally eaten with *rendang*, as an everyday meal and also on special occasions such as the two-day celebration at the end of Ramadan.

lemongrass *sereh*. So familiar now in the West and so widely obtainable that it hardly needs any introduction. For most dishes, cut the stem across into two or three pieces and wash; one piece is usually sufficient. Remember to remove it before serving. For curries, soups, and salad dressings, the outer leaves are stripped off (they can still be used in cooking, as above); only the inner tender part is used, chopped into rounds like spring onion and blended into a curry paste. For soups and salad dressings, you just use these thin slices raw.

lengkuas *Languas galanga*, galangal.

lesser galangal *kencur* [kən-'tjoor], the strongly aromatic rhizome of a herb that grows in many tropical countries.

lontong compressed rice (*see* p.132).

mace See *nutmeg*.

maize *jagung*.

makan, makanan food; a meal.

    makan kecil "small food"– snacks; nibbles.

mangga *Mangifera indica*, mango.

manggis *Garcinia mangostana*, mangosteen.

mango *mangga*. This is one of the best-known tropical fruits, cultivated in India for thousands of years. More than 40 varieties are now grown in Asia. Green or unripe mango can be used as an alternative souring agent. These are easily found in Thai and Indian stores. The Thai variety is usually larger than the Indian, which is mainly used for chutneys. For my recipes, I would use Thai green mangoes. Their sourness is checked by a pleasant slight sweetness. As a souring agent in general cooking, Indian green mango is also a very good choice.

mangosteen *manggis*.

milkfish *bandeng*.

mung beans *kacang hijau*.

nangka *Artocarpus heterophyllus*, jackfruit.

nenas *Ananas comosus*, pineapple.

nut *kacang*. See also bean.

nutmeg *pala*.

onion *bawang merah*.

orange *jeruk manis*.

pakis, paku fiddlehead. There are several edible species, including bracken (*Pteridum aquilinum*), which is found in most parts of the world. What we cooked in Indonesia was probably *pucuk paku*, shoots of vegetable fern, or *Athyrium esculentum*. I have occasionally been able to buy jars of a North American fern, I think *Matteuccia struthiopteri*, or ostrich fern.

pala *Myristica fragrans*, nutmeg.

pandan *Pandanus odorus*, pandanus.

papaya *Carica papaya*.

paria *Momordica charantia*, bitter cucumber.

parsley *seledri* [sə'ledri]. NB: (1) this is flat-leaf parsley; "English" curly-leaf parsley does not usually grow in the tropics; (2) *seledri* also means a kind of thin-stemmed celery. *Seledri* may be sold in the West as Asian celery or Asian parsley.

peanuts *kacang tanah*. or peanuts, are popular all over Southeast Asia; they are cheap, filling, and nutritious, and taste good. They are available just about everywhere in ethnic grocery shops and supermarkets, in their shells or ready-shelled. Their thin outer skins range in color from pink to almost red, or, if they have been blanched and dried, an off-white color. Peanut sauce tastes and looks much better if you use pink or reddish nuts. Dry-fry first for 6–8 minutes, stirring continuously, or deep-fry in hot oil for 4 minutes. Drain on paper towels and leave to cool, before grinding finely..

petai *Parkia speciosa*, "stink beans": see recipe using this on pp.224–5. These can be bought in many Thai food shops, shelled and peeled, packed in brine and sealed in plastic. They may be labelled "*peteh asin*." Once opened, the beans can be kept in the refrigerator for about 48 hours at most. It is unfair to call them stink beans, but they do have quite a strong smell, somewhat like garlic. In Indonesia, we would buy them in the long, slender pods in which they grow.

pineapple *nenas*.

pisang *Musa* spp.; banana.

plantain *pisang raja*.

pomelo *jeruk Bali*.

rambutan *Nephelium lappaceum*. The word *rambut* means "hair"; these plum-sized fruits have thick skins covered in short, quite soft, slightly hooked protrusions. The soft white flesh inside is delicious. They are available from Thai shops in the UK when in season.

rice cooking water This is a natural thickening agent used in Indonesian cooking. As a rule, flour or corn flour is not used to thicken our sauces. If we want the sauce to be thick, we reduce it by cooking it longer. This is not often necessary if the food is cooked in coconut milk because coconut milk will become thicker as it cooks, leaving its oil on top and a thick creamy sediment at the bottom. Rice cooking water is obtained when cooking rice in a saucepan; as the rice boils, the thicker "cooking water" stays on top, waiting to be absorbed by the rice. Take out a spoonful or two of this water if you need it to thicken any sauce. If you are cooking *lontong* (compressed rice), you will have plenty of rice cooking water after the *lontong* has been cooking for 1¼–1½ hours. Reserve whatever quantity of this cooking water you need. It can be safely refrigerated for up to 48 hours before use.

sago *sagu; Metroxylon sagus*. A staple food of low-rainfall areas in eastern Indonesia, this starchy substance is produced in large amounts in the trunk of sago palms before the trees flower.

salam leaf *daun salam*. Its leaves contain an aromatic volatile oil which gives a subtle flavor to certain dishes if a single leaf is placed in the pan during cooking. The dried leaves can be bought in *Indische winkels* (small Indonesian food shops) in the Netherlands. In Indonesia, the salam leaf plays something like the same role as the curry leaf in India. The latter, however, comes from a quite different tree, *Murraya koenigii*. Curry leaves are available, dried and fresh, in Indian shops.

sambal ulek Commonly spelled "sambal oelek" in English, *sambal ulek* is made by crushing chopped fresh red chilies with a little salt, using a mortar and pestle. It is available ready-made from Asian food stores and supermarkets.

seledri, sledri *Apium graveolens*; celery, flat-leaf parsley.

sereh *Cymbopogon citratus*, lemongrass.

shallots, crisp-fried *See* crisp-fried shallots.

shrimp paste This is sold in hard blocks, or individually wrapped slices, usually labeled *terasi/trassie, balachan* or *blachen*. It is the Indonesian/Malaysian equivalent of fish sauce. It is extremely strong-smelling and salty. Use very sparingly. In many recipes in this book, I specify ½ teaspoon or a teaspoon of crumbled *terasi*. You can crumble *terasi* only after a piece of it has been either fried in a little oil or dry-fried in a small frying pan; alternatively, cut the whole block of *terasi* into small pieces, wrap in a double thickness of foil, and roast in the oven at 300°F (150°C) for 8–10 minutes. Raw *terasi* is a sticky and elastic substance, and difficult to crush with a pestle; it would stick to every blade of your food processor. After frying or roasting, *terasi* becomes soft and can be crumbled for easy measuring with a teaspoon. It will last almost for ever if kept in an airtight container, which will also keep the strong smell confined.

soy bean *kacang kedele* ['ka-tchang kə-də-'lé].

soy sauce *See* kecap.

starfruit *belimbing manis*. Also known in English as carambola.

sweet potato *ubi jalar*.

tamarind *See* pp.118–19.

"tamarind slices" *See* asam gelugur.

tempe tempeh. *See* pp.120–4.

terasi *See* shrimp paste.

terung *Solanum melongena*; eggplant.

   terung gelatik pea eggplant.

tofu *tahu* in Indonesian: beancurd, a soy bean product, or a thick curd made from soy "milk". Very nutritious, but bland in taste and texture; delicious when cooked with flavors that it readily absorbs. There are Chinese and Japanese styles of tofu. They are sold fresh, in small blocks immersed in water. These can be refrigerated for about three days, with a change of water each day. In Japanese shops and most Chinese supermarkets, long-life tofu, both firm and silken, are available, packed and sealed in cartons. Firm long-life tofu is a reasonably good alternative to fresh tofu. In Chinese supermarkets, fried tofu is also available, with a slightly different version available in Japanese shops. Fried tofu pieces are usually destined to be stuffed with mixtures of vegetables and shrimp, to give its blandness a more interesting taste. In this book, suggestions and recipes are for fresh tofu.

turmeric *kunyit*. Red and white varieties of turmeric are available in Thai and Chinese supermarkets. This rhizome has been in popular use for a very long time all over Southeast Asia. As with galangal and ginger root, turmeric needs to be peeled, then chopped, and added to other ingredients to be blended to a paste. If you can't get fresh red turmeric, use ground turmeric instead – ½–1 teaspoon is all you need for a curry paste if you are cooking for four.

ubi jalar *Ipomoea batatas*, sweet potato.

ubi kayu *Manihot utilissima*, cassava.

warung A small, very informal, public eating house. It usually has at least semi-permanent premises, but these may range from a simple bamboo shelter to a modest timber or even brick-built space with a small separate kitchen. Most *warung* owners stick to a very limited range of dishes, but in cooking these may be very expert. The *warung* effectively bridges the gap between street food and the smaller *rumah makan*, which literally means "eating house." Prices are kept low, by tourist standards; though a *warung* may attract tourists, its real clientele is made up of local residents and workers.

water spinach *kangkung*.

wonton A Chinese speciality usually eaten in a thin, highly flavored soup. Individual wontons are casings made of thin pastry, about 2 inches on a side, filled with a savory spiced mix of ground meat or flaked fish, or shrimp with cut-up vegetables and spices. Wonton skins can be bought in packets in Chinese and other Asian food shops almost anywhere.

yam bean *bengkuang*. This also known in English by its Mexican name, *jicama*: a climbing plant, the purple, sweet-pea-like flowers of which give way to long green seed-pods. When young, these can be eaten like beans. (The mature seeds are toxic.) The plant is chiefly cultivated for its starchy, heart-shaped root, which is peeled, cut up, or grated, and used in *rujak* (spicy fruit salad). It is usually eaten raw, and is good in salads; I suggest tart, crisp apple as an alternative.

yogurt Unsweetened Greek-style yogurt makes a very good alternative to coconut milk, especially in curries and similar dishes.

BIBLIOGRAPHY

Burkill, I.H., *A Dictionary of the Economic Products of the Malay Peninsula*: Crown Agents, London, 1935; reprinted by Crown Agents on behalf of the Governments of Malaysia and Singapore, 1966.

Davidson, A.E., *Seafood of Southeast Asia*: Federal Publications (S) Pte Ltd, Singapore, 1977; Macmillan London Ltd 1978; 2nd edn: Prospect Books, Totnes, 200?; Ten Speed Press, Berkeley, California, 2004.

Davidson, A.E., *The Oxford Companion to Food*: Oxford University Press, Oxford and New York, 1999; 2nd edn: Oxford University Press, Oxford and New York, 2006.

Herklots, G.A.C., *Vegetables in Southeast Asia*: George Allen & Unwin, London, 1972.

McFadden, Christine, and Michael Michaud, *Cool Green Leaves and Red Hot Peppers*: Adams Media Corporation, Cincinatti, 1999.

Morton, Julia F., *Fruits of Warm Climates*: Florida Fair Books, Florida, 1987.

Owen, Sri, *Indonesian Food and Cookery*: 2nd edn, Prospect Books, Totnes, 1984.

Owen, Sri, *The Rice Book*: Transworld, London, 1993; St Martin's Press, New York, 1994; Frances Lincoln, London, 2003.

Owen, Sri, *Indonesian Regional Food and Cooking*: Doubleday, London and Sydney, 1994; Frances Lincoln, London, 1999.

Owen, Sri, *Noodles: The New Way*: Quadrille, London, 2000.

Owen, Sri, *New Wave Asian*: Quadrille, London, 2002; Whitecap, Canada, 2002.

Rahman, Fadly, *Rijsttafel: Perkembangan Budaya Makan di Pulau Jawa (1870-1942)*: Universitas Padjadjaran, Indonesia, 2006.

Various authors, *Mustikarasa: Buku Masakan Indonesia*: Department of Agriculture, Jakarta, 1967.

FURTHER READING

Fischer, Louis, *The Story of Indonesia*: Harper & Bros., New York, 1959.

Geertz, Clifford, *The Religion of Java*: University of Chicago Press, Chicago and London, 1960.

Mulder, Niels, *Inside Indonesian Society: Cultural Change in Java*: The Pepin Press, Amsterdam and Kuala Lumpur, 1996.

Ricklefs, M.C., *A History of Modern Indonesia since c. 1200*: 3rd edn, Palgrave, Basingstoke, 2001.

Wallace, Alfred Russel, *The Malay Archipelago*: Macmillan & Company, London, 1869; reprinted OUP Singapore, 1989.

INDEX

Names and page numbers of recipes are shown in *italics*; page numbers of illustrations are shown in **bold**. Recipe names have capital initial letters.

PHOTOGRAPHIC CREDITS

All photography by Gus Filgate, except those credited below

2 Beren Patterson / Alamy

8 Damon Coulter / Alamy

15 Mally Kant-Achilles, c. 1960; by kind permission of Dr Herdin Achilles

16 Damon Coulter / Alamy

23 IML Image Group Ltd / Alamy

27 www.murnis.com

36 Thomas Cockrem / Alamy

39 Fadly Rahman

40 JTB Photo Communications, Inc. / Alamy

42 Wolfgang Kaehler / Corbis

43 Justin Guariglia / Corbis

65 Glen Allison / Alamy

67 Jurnasyanto Sukarno / epa / Corbis

68 Luca Tettoni / Corbis

79(b) Fadly Rahman

82 Roger Ressmeyer / Corbis

83 Albrecht G. Schaefer / Corbis

85 Mathew Lodge / Alamy

106 Jon Arnold Images Ltd / Alamy

127 James Green / Robert Harding World Imagery / Corbis

161(l and r) Achmad Wirono

201(l) blickwinkel / Alamy

222 J Marshall – Tribaleye Images / Alamy

225 Stuart Westmorland / Corbis

236 Jonathan Copeland, www.murnis.com

238 Peter Netley / Alamy

239 Peter Horree / Alamy

242 Jonathan Copeland, www.murnis.com

256 KIMIMASA MAYAMA / Reuters / Corbis

258 Owen Franken / Corbis

261 Patrick Ward / Corbis

262 Roger Ressmeyer / Corbis

265 Lindsay Hebberd / Corbis

10, 11, 12, 26, 35, 41, 46, 47, 48, 50, 71, 77, 79(t), 93, 122, 126, 128, 144, 145, 147, 161(l and r), 168, 197, 201(r), 204, 207, 209, 234(t and b), 254, 255 Sri and Roger Owen

ACKNOWLEDGMENTS

This is a cookbook, but also a personal testament. I want to record here the names of people near to me who at each stage of my life have given me their knowledge, love, friendship, and support.

First, my own family. In my birthplace in Sumatra, I owe most to my father's mother, who I knew only as Inyiek, "Grandmother." She loved to cook, as did her son, my father. My mother was born in West Java, and spent her life teaching mathematics and raising six daughters. My sisters have unfailingly answered my queries about every aspect of Indonesian food.

I must mention lifelong friends from my high school and university days: in Java, Sri Mangkarawati (Tjitjik), Retno and Sukarno Hadian, Achmad Wirono, and Soeatminah; in Bali, Anak Agung Gede Rai, and Ni Wayan Murni, founder and owner of Warung Murni in Ubud. Other friends who have helped me are William Wongso in Jakarta, Jonathan Copeland in Ubud, and Fadly Rahman in Bogor. These also sent me their photographs to be used in this book.

In Britain, Dr. John Dransfield and his Indonesian wife, Dr. Sujatmi Dransfield, Ika Whitehead, and Philip Iddison have solved problems regarding Indonesian ingredients. When I came to England in 1964, I was with my quite-new husband Roger. He remains a constant presence in all my books. Our sons and daughters-in-law – Irwan and Liz, Daniel and Eva – are excellent cooks and lovers of good food and wine, and supportive in all my writing and cooking.

Italy plays a large part in this book, as it has in my career, and I must mention friends in the Veneto and Piemonte. In the Veneto: Gianluca Bisol and his family, winemakers whose Prosecco di Valdobbiadene is among the region's finest; and Giovanni Oliva and Elisa de Conto, formerly colleagues in the Bisol sales team. In the west among the Langhe hills: the Ceretto family, and their tireless office manager, secretary, and personal assistant, Bruna Manzone. These are wonderful people and I love their wine.

Coming to practicalities: I must mention my agents, John McLaughlin and Charlotte Bruton, at Campbell Thompson & McLaughlin Ltd, patient and resourceful as ever. Emily Preece-Morrison and Anna Cheifetz have nursed the book through its many stages to publication. My thanks also to commisioning editor Kate Oldfield, copy editor Siobhan O'Connor, and two enthusiastic members of the marketing team, Laura Brudenell and Komal Patel. Food photography is the work of Jane Suthering and her assistant, Faenia Moore, who cooked dishes for the camera, and Gus Filgate, who, with his assistant, Jonathan, photographed them. Other location shots that are not from agencies were taken by Roger or myself.

Finally, I owe recognition to the doctors, consultants, nurses, pharmacists, and medical technicians who, in the near-forty years since I had my first small heart attack, have kept me upright and on the rails. Special appreciation goes to my GP, Dr. Jane Allen, and to Marjan Jahangiri, Professor of Cardiac Surgery at St George's Hospital Medical School. Miss Jahangiri, with her brilliant team at St. Anthony's Hospital in Cheam and at St. George's, performed on me a quadruple heart bypass in October 2007, so I was able to finish this book.

BIOGRAPHY

SRI OWEN was born in Sumatra and spent her early life there and in Java, during years of foreign occupation and Indonesia's struggle for independence. As a student at the nation's oldest university, she was a sportswoman, broadcaster and writer, and enthusiastic follower of traditional Javanese theater. After graduating in English Language and Literature, she became a junior lecturer, interpreter, librarian, and secretary to two professors, then married an English colleague. In due course they came to London, where she made a long and successful career with the BBC Indonesian Service. A keen cook, hostess, and lover of good food, she found her arrival in Europe had coincided with an upsurge of interest in Southeast Asian cuisines. Her own cooking met with the approval of an ever-widening circle of dinner guests, and her first Indonesian cookbook was published by Faber in 1976. It has been followed by more than a dozen others, including *The Rice Book*, *Indonesian Regional Food and Cookery*, and *New Wave Asian*. She has won several awards, including the André Simon Memorial Award in 1993. For some years she ran her own Indonesian delicatessen in Wimbledon. She has traveled, taught, and lectured in many countries, and today describes herself as a freelance writer, traveling cooking teacher, and researcher into Southeast Asian food and its history. With her husband Roger she is currently working on *The Oxford Companion to Southeast Asian Food*.

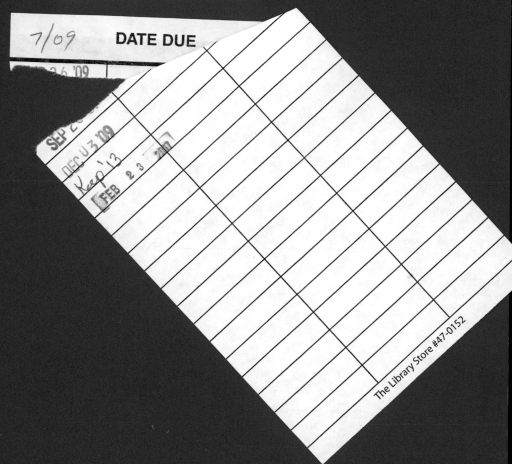